THE PRAYER-MEETING,

AND

ITS HISTORY,

AS IDENTIFIED WITH

THE LIFE AND POWER OF GODLINESS,

AND

THE REVIVAL OF RELIGION.

"Then they that feared the Lord spake often one to another."—MATT. iii. 16.
" And they continued steadfastly in the Apostle's doctrine and fellowship, and in breaking of bread, *and in prayers*."—ACTS ii. 42.

PITTSBURGH:
UNITED PRESBYTERIAN BOARD OF PUBLICATION.
1870.

Entered according to Act of Congress, in the year 1870, by the UNITED PRESBYTERIAN BOARD OF PUBLICATION, in the Clerk's Office of the District Court of the United States, in and for the Western District of Pennsylvania.

S. A. GEORGE & CO.,
STEREOTYPERS AND PRINTERS,
PHILADELPHIA.

TO

THE STUDENTS OF THEOLOGY,

LICENTIATES,

AND

YOUNG MEN IN TRAINING FOR THE GOSPEL MINISTRY

IN THE

UNITED PRESBYTERIAN CHURCH,

THIS VOLUME IS MOST AFFECTIONATELY

INSCRIBED BY THE AUTHOR,

J. B. JOHNSTON.

ST. CLAIRSVILLE, OHIO, July 1, 1870.

Gift
J H Russell
5-29-33

CONTENTS.

PART I.—THE PRAYER-MEETING.

CHAPTER III.

FROM CHRIST TO THE REFORMATION.

CHAPTER IV.

FROM THE REFORMATION TO THE REVOLUTION, 1688.

CHAPTER V.

FROM THE CLOSE OF THE SEVENTEENTH CENTURY TILL THE GENERAL DECLINE OF RELIGION, TOWARDS THE CLOSE OF THE EIGHTEENTH.

CHAPTER VI.

FROM THE PERIOD OF GENERAL DECLINE, TOWARDS THE CLOSE OF THE LAST CENTURY, TILL NEAR THE MIDDLE OF THE PRESENT.

CHAPTER X.

THE PRAYER-MEETING AMONG THE CHURCHES.

CHAPTER XI.

REVIVALS AND PRAYER-MEETINGS IN SCOTLAND, WALES, ENGLAND, FRANCE, AND GERMANY.

CHAPTER XII.

REMARKABLE PRAYER-MEETING AND REVIVAL INCIDENTS.

CHAPTER XIII.

PRAYER-MEETING INCIDENTS AND NARRATIVES, CONTINUED.

CHAPTER XIV.

PRAYER-MEETING IN CONNECTION WITH MISSIONS, FOREIGN, HOME, CITY, AND COLPORTAGE OPERATIONS.

CHAPTER XV.

REVIVAL PRAYER-MEETINGS AND UNION CONVENTIONS.

CHAPTER XVI.

CHURCH CREEDS AND THE PRAYER-MEETING.

THE PRAYER-MEETING.

PART I.

INTRODUCTION.

THE subject of the following pages is divided into *Two Parts*. The *First Part—The Prayer-meeting*—is the principal, and is that Part for which the other was written.

The *Prayer-meeting*, viewed as a subject of vital interest, has engaged the attention of the writer for more than the third of a century, though never, till very recently—indeed within the present year—with even the remotest idea of presenting to the Christian public his views through the press. And even now the force of circumstances in Divine Providence, rather than any desire to appear as an author, has induced him to submit his views to the public eye.

The merits of the theme—the almost entire want of any standard work on the subject, so far as known—the importance of some settled scriptural views and practise in relation to this precious institution of divine worship—the religious sentiment and feeling of the age, and the tendency of the evangelical Churches to harmonize in views and practise here, all seem to invite to reflection and conscientious investigation. Few, if any, in these churches entirely ignore the Prayer-meeting; yet many can give very little "reason of the hope that is in them," in regard to its claims. Very loose, vague, crude views—perhaps no well matured views at all—are entertained by too many.

Christians too often assemble themselves together in the

Prayer-meeting only because the multitude move that way, and under excitement are carried along, without considering whether there is any Divine warrant for this way of worshipping God. Or, if it be deemed an ordinance of divinely instituted worship, it is not seriously considered for what end appointed, or how, or when, or by whom to be observed.

The question whether this is an ordinance of religious worship, appointed by the Head of the Church to be observed by all Churches and Christians, as other acknowledged ordinances of worship; or, whether being simply *sui generis*, it comes under no Scripture recognition, as all other ordinances of religious worship divinely appointed, but not being forbidden, may be observed as other indifferent things; or, may be ignored altogether, has, perhaps, received from Christians, generally, very little consideration.

It is not strange if the Prayer-meeting, as viewed and practised in many of our Churches, should fail to bring forth the blessed fruits that should be produced by a believing and faithful observance of it as an ordinance of Divine authority, encouraged by precious promises on which worshippers can take hold, and from which they can draw the grace designed to be communicated through this channel. If the worshipper cannot answer the question—Who hath required this at your hand? how can he in faith wait on God, and with confidence ask his blessing on the service of the worshipper? But if he have an intelligent assurance that Christ is in the Prayer-meeting, by the record of his name in his appointed Institution, and by the promised presence of his Spirit and his grace, with what confidence then, and comfort too, can he come to the place " where two or three are gathered together," *because* of his appointment, and the promise of his presence there!

In presenting this humble treatise, upon a very grave

and important subject, the writer is well aware that his topic is very far from being exhausted. Perhaps, in regard to every part of the subject, little has been presented beyond what is merely suggestive. And if even this much shall be found true, and some other and abler pen shall be called out to do higher justice to the subject, he will rejoice. Or, should it call the attention of praying people to a prayerful consideration of its importance, and stimulate to efforts and measures for bringing out to duty, in this matter, many who, though they otherwise profess and practise the duties of religion, yet either neglect the Prayer-meeting entirely, or give it a very limited share of their concern, we shall feel more than amply rewarded.

As the day approaches when the promises and predictions, relating to the last times, shall be fulfilled—promises and predictions of the most exciting interest, on which the faith of God's people has so long waited, and for which their prayers have so long ascended, the motives and call to concerted prayer become stronger, louder and more distinct.

As the signs of the times indicate still more and more distinctly that the glorious period must be at hand, when the gospel will be preached to every nation, kindred and people on earth—and as vast fields for missionary enterprise are opening to the benevolent, as never before, so should the Church hear and regard the command of the Saviour concerning united prayer—"Pray *ye*, therefore, the Lord of the harvest, that he would send forth laborers into his harvest." Just now, the unusual demand for laborers, the discouraging paucity of their numbers, and the extraordinary enlargement of the fields, white for the harvest, call for new interest in the Saviour's command, and new earnestness in the Prayer-meeting.

As there are now earnest yearnings for union of the divided members of Christ's body; and as the signs of the dawn of that happy day, when the watchmen shall see eye to eye, begin to appear more distinctly; so, as when "the sound of a going in the tops of the mulberry trees" was heard, now should the people of God bestir themselves in frequent and earnest concerted prayer.

There is some earnest concern—we hope general—among Christians, on the subject of the revival of religion. Many are mourning over the low state of religion in their own hearts, and in the Church; the time is nearing when the day of the Lord, in the power of revival, shall be great as the day of Jezreel, the first fruits of which were given in the Pentecostal baptism of the infant Christian church. These were the first fruits of the "refreshing times from the presence of the Lord." As he has promised, "I will pour water upon him that is thirsty, and floods upon the dry ground; I will pour my Spirit upon the seed of the Church, and my blessing upon her offspring; and they shall spring up as among the grass, as willows by the water courses;" so, is there a loud call for earnest and concerted prayer for the fulfilment of these promises concerning the gift of the Spirit in revival.

As prayer—especially *concerted prayer*—is placed in an inseparable connection with the fulfilment of all the promises made by a covenant God, in regard to all those glorious events now so earnestly looked for; so, *concerted prayer* must be employed by the Church before she can enjoy the blessings and the glory of the times of the coming of her Lord. And if the Spirit of prayer is the power of the Church by which she takes hold of the hand that moves the world, then is she now called to gird on her strength. "Awake, awake; put on thy strength, O Zion; put on thy beautiful garments, O Jerusalem; shake thyself from the dust; arise, and sit down, O Jerusalem; loose thself from the bands of thy neck, O captive daughter of Zion."

CHAPTER I.

THE PRAYER-MEETING IS A DIVINE ORDINANCE OF RELIGIOUS WORSHIP, INSTITUTED BY CHRIST IN THE WORD.

1. *The prayer-meeting is founded in man's moral social nature.*

MAN is a moral, or, a religious being. He has a moral sense. He has a conscience—a sense of right and wrong—and of accountability to God, his Creator. As a religious being, he is also social. The law of his nature inclines him to worship; and the religious, social principle, inclines him to seek the communion of kindred spirits. "And doth not even nature itself teach you?" "It is not good for man to be alone." "For when the Gentiles, which have not the law, do by nature the things of the law, these, having not the law, are a law unto themselves."

There are Divine ordinances founded in *law natural*, acknowledged to be such by all Bible believers, though not found in specific terms, or direct commands of institution, in the Word. All Christians recognize civil government to be an ordinance of God—founded in the law of nature—existing without the Bible, and among nations where revelation has never gone. We prove it to be a Divine ordinance from the Bible, just as we prove all other Divine ordinances of its class. We prove it, substantially, as we do the prayer-meeting, with all the difference in weight, and clearness of evidence, in favor of the latter. The Bible recognizes its existence. It defines its privileges. It regulates its duties, its obligations, upon rulers and ruled; and so establishes it to be a Divine ordinance. "Let every soul be subject to the higher powers," is the recognition of the existence of such higher powers—not the mandate, in express terms, instituting the ordinance of civil government. "Whosoever resisteth the power, resisteth the *ordinance of God,*" is the language of direction in regard to the duties of obedience to an institution, in terms denominating a Divine ordinance "the ordinance of God." The testimony of the Bible as clearly establishes the truth of the "divine ordinance" of civil government, as the "divine ordinance" of the gospel ministry. But the one, being founded in law moral *natural,* needs not *positive* terms of institution. The other, being founded in law moral *positive,* must, of necessity, have *express* positive enactment to prove it to be a divine ordinance.

Men prompted by the dictates of nature only, would, and do, pray to God. Men would naturally, as all nations do, form civil government without "any passage of Scripture prescribing" anything in regard to its institution. But the gospel ministry, and the sacraments of the church, can have no existence, nor would men without revelation naturally resort to them—nor would they have validity—without *express positive* institution in the word. Let this suffice to make clear the distinction involved in the proposition, that "the prayer-meeting is a divine ordinance, founded in man's social nature."

One of the most precious privileges enjoyed by saints, this side the perfect felicity of the state of glory above, in the presence of God, in the company of angels and fellowship of the redeemed, is the communion of saints.

"To saints on earth, to the excellent, where my delights all placed."

Grace sanctifies the religious social principle of our nature, and places in very striking contrast the state of our race without the sanctifying power of grace. Here, sinners are "living in malice and envy, hateful, and hating one another." How intense must the sufferings of the damned be, when thrust down together in hell, forced to associate together where the social bond is—not love binding in one, but hate—under the penal decree of inflexible justice, holding, in the presence of the hated and hateful, only to enhance the misery eternal! With the universal creed of the universal church, the Christian heart beats responsive, "I believe in the communion of saints." The Christian feels the power of truth and grace constraining to love Christ and his fellowship. And this same love of Christ constrains to love the brethren. A pre-eminent design, in calling out from the world, of organizing a visible Church out of those called into a holy fellowship, and of the ministrations of the gospel, in all its precious institutions, is to prepare for and induct into the enjoyments of the communion of saints here on earth, and ultimately in heaven. The social nature, sanctified by grace, demands the society of kindred spirits sanctified by the same grace.

By the communion of saints, believers—the members of one holy family, partakers of the common salvation, and of the same blessed hope—have a mutual interest in matters of the highest importance. They are separated from the rest of the world, and incorporated into one spiritual body. Marked with the same seal, and distinguished by the same badge of a holy profession, they are called to like solemn duties, are inclined to engage in similar services, are exposed to encounter like fears, dangers, and common enemies. They have joys and privileges in common; they live to the same high end; they cherish the like expectations; and are animated by the same blessed hopes of the one blessed inheritance. Hence result the mutual offices of a sacred brotherhood. A warm interest and complacency in saints, are results of regenerating grace, and its certain evidence. Here is the prominent characteristic of all who belong to the household of faith —"We know that we have passed from death unto life, because we love the brethren." "Every one that loveth him that begat, loveth him also that is begotten of him."

The whole doctrine of the communion of saints is founded on man's social religious nature, which prompts to seek enjoyment from sources congenial to that social nature. Spiritual life, restored through gospel means, bases its operations here upon, and acts through the social nature of the moral being—quickening its aspirations, and leading its instincts, under all the pressures of life, to seek that companionship where kindred sympathies commingle. In all our burdens, in all our afflictions, here, as in the tender bosom of the Elder Brother, is a feeling of our infirmities in the heart of every brother—a bearing half the burthen, and nerving to sustain the other. "If one member suffer, all the members suffer with it." All who have the spirit of adoption, feel with the apostle that, "We being many, are one bread and one body, for we are all partakers of that one bread."

From the very nature of the fellowship of saints, and from the inward cravings of the renewed nature after its congenial enjoyment, there seems to be a dictate of reason and nature requiring some distinct ordinance of religious social worship, in which saints, as nowhere else, can specially and fully enjoy its blessed and heavenly privileges. The prayer-meeting answers to this demand of the spiritual brotherhood, with more exclusiveness and direct fitness than any other ordinance of religious worship. Secret and invisible communion with God, is not enough to satisfy all the demands of the social religious nature, sanctified by grace to love saints, and love the fellowship of saints. Nor, in addition, is it enough to enjoy inward affection for brethren in Christ, and secret and invisible communion with loved objects, with whom we can seldom hold visible and intimate communion, where hearts together may burn, and mutually reciprocate the enkindling glow of affection kindled in each by Christ's love. Nor will occasional interviews with kindred spirits and loved ones, in public ordinances, where there cannot be free and generous interchange of Christian sentiment and affection, satisfy this desire. While all the ordinances of religious worship have their general uses and ends—while all edify the body, building up in holy faith and comfort, preparing saints for the heavenly communion, still, each has its special end and use, and without each in its place the divine system of institutions of grace would be incomplete. As there is a beautiful symmetry in the body—the church organic—so in the complete system of divine ordinances, appointed to nourish and beautify this spiritual body. "From whom the whole, fitly joined together, and compacted by that which every joint supplieth, according to the effectual working in the measure of every part, maketh increase of the body, unto the edifying of itself in love."

To the prayer-meeting the instincts of nature would lead even the heathen—and much more, these natural impulses of the renewed nature, when brought under the influences of evangelical religion, the attractions of ecclesiastical organization, and the Christian brotherhood; and, above all, the constraining power of divine grace and love of Christ. Thus, Jonah's mariners, when tempest-tossed, in straits and at their wits end, cried unto their gods: and not only so, but they sent Jonah to prayer to his God. And ultimately, all, in united prayer-meeting, called on Jehovah. "So the shipmaster came to him, and said unto him, What meanest thou, O sleeper? Arise, call upon thy God, if so be that God will think upon *us*, that *we* perish not." And not satisfied, in their distress, with the proxy prayers of the Prophet, they unitedly engaged with intense earnestness in prayer to Jonah's God—"Wherefore *they* cried unto the Lord, and said, WE beseech thee, O Lord, WE beseech thee, let us not perish—lay not upon us innocent blood." And these united prayers were approved, and heard, and answered, and entered on the record for our learning. Many, and significant too, are such instructive words. Many such have an interesting place in the devotional songs of social praise—records of instruction to the end of the world.

"In trouble then *they* cried on God, He *them* from straits did save."
"In grief *they* cry to God; He saves *them* from *their* miseries."
"Then *they* to God in trouble cry, who *them* from straits sets free."

The heathen Ninevites, moved by the religious social principle, when the circumstances called into exercise that *natural law* of our religious nature, resorted for relief to fasting and *social prayer*. "So the people of Nineveh believed God, and proclaimed a fast—let man and beast be covered with sackcloth, and *cry* mightily unto God." The united prayers of these children of nature were heard, and judgments arrested. Social prayer is a dictate of natural religion. God has entered his approval upon the record for our learning. Let us take heed lest "The men of Nineveh shall rise in judgment with this generation, and shall condemn it." Social prayer is a dictate of nature. And yet "we have a more sure word of prophecy."

2. *The prayer-meeting formed a part of the divinely-appointed worship of the patriarchal and Abrahamic dispensations.*

Sacrifices were offered by our first parents, by Abel, by Noah, and by Abraham. They were not confined to this form of worship alone. Prayer was among the very first forms of religious worship known and practiced by our fallen race. The history of the operations of saving grace would be substantially the same in the first converts and in all after-conversions by the same divine spirit—the same in Adam, in Abel, in Enos, in Noah, and in Abraham, and all their cotemporaries, as in Saul of Tarsus, who gave evidence of a gracious change by his new life of prayer. "Behold, he prayeth!" That was the final evidence of Christian character. So, the truly pious were men of prayer in all ages. Men began early to call upon the name of the Lord. Enos, the second from Adam, and the sons of God in his generation, seem to have practiced social prayer. "*Men* called on God." Men, moved by grace, would then, as now, find enjoyment in social prayer, and would, consequently, be led by its power to practice it as now. So Abraham, moved by the same faith that moves to social prayer now, "planted a grove in Beersheba, and called there upon the name of the Lord, the everlasting God." Gen. xxi. 33. This worship of the grove, or in "the *High-places*," was practiced during the whole patriarchal period. Afterwards, to guard against the confounding of the worship of the grove and of the altar, God charged Moses, in the giving of the law, to preserve both these ordinances of worship pure and distinct. "Thou shalt not plant thee a grove of any trees near unto the altar of the Lord thy God, which thou shalt make thee." Deut. xvi. 21. It was in later periods of Hebrew history that, in violation of this law, God's worship was corrupted by erecting altars under every green tree, and in the groves, and on the high-places, there offering sacrifices, as in the days of Ahab, and other wicked kings.

This persistent violation of law, in the corrupting of divinely-appointed worship, was at length arrested by the captivities of the ten tribes and of Judah. After the return, idolatry never again became the prevailing sin of the Jews; nor have we any account of the worship of the altar being blended with the social worship of the Proseucha among the groves or on the high-places.

To the Proseucha, or place for prayer, and not to the synagogue, the Psalmist seems to refer in Ps. lxxiv. 8, where it is said "they burnt up all the synagogues of God within the land." The Proseucha, as a place of worship, was well known among the Hebrews from the days of Abraham. The synagogue, which was confined to cities and towns, did not obtain till after the captivity; and then grew out of the circumstances of the times, the necessity for the more general reading and knowledge of the law, the ignorance of which was prevalent before and during the captivity. To correct this, Ezra instituted the synagogue for the reading and expounding of the law.

We are by no means singular in our views of the Proseucha and synagogue worship. That this may be seen, and the reader have the subject more fully before him, we shall quote from some authors of standard reputation. Prideaux, in his *Connections*, says, vol. i, pp. 307–309:

"Those who think synagogues to have been before the Babylonish captivity, allege for it what is said in the seventy-fourth Psalm, verse 8: 'They have burnt up all the synagogues of God in the land.' But, in the original, the words are—[*col moadhe el*]—'all the assemblies of God;' by which, I acknowledge, must be understood the places where the people did assemble to worship God. But this doth not infer that those places were synagogues; and there are none of the ancient versions, except that of Aquila, that so render this passage. The chief place where the Israelites assembled for the worship of God, was the temple at Jerusalem—and, before that was built, the tabernacle; and the open court, before the altar, was that part in both of them where the people assembled to offer up their prayers to God. But those that lived at a distance from the tabernacle, while that was in being, and afterward from the temple, when that was built, not being at all times able to resort thither, they built courts like those in which they prayed at the tabernacle and at the temple, therein to offer up their prayers unto God, which in after times we find called by the name Proseuchæ. Some of the Latin poets (Juv. Sat. 3) make mention of them by this name; and into one of them our Saviour is said to have gone to pray, and to have continued therein a whole night. (Luke, vi. 12: 'And he continued all night in a Proseucha of God.') And in another of them, St. Paul taught the people of Philipi. (Acts xvi. 13, 16, what we render in our English version by the word *prayer*, is in the original a *proseucha*, a place of prayer.)

"And, besides these proseuchæ, there were other places in which the Israelites, before the captivity, frequently assembled, upon the account of religion; for they often resorted to the cities of the Levites, to be taught the ritual and other ceremonies of Mosaical law, and to the schools of the prophets for all other instructions relating to the things of God; and to these last, it is plain from Scripture, that they usually resorted on the Sabbaths and New Moons; and what end could there be of this resort, but for instruction in their duties to God? And therefore these places also, as well as the proseuchæ, were Moadhe Al—*i. e.*, places of assembling on account of religion—and consequently of all these may the Psalmist be understood to speak in the places above mentioned. Whether this Psalm, as well as the seventy-ninth, was written by David, or by that Asaph who lived in the time of the Babylonish captivity (to which it is plain they both relate), or by some other after it, as is most probable, I shall not here examine. All that is proper for me here to take notice of is, that nothing which is in either of these Psalms can prove, that there were any such things as synagogues, wherein the Scriptures were read, or public prayers offered up unto God, till after the Babylonish captivity.

"And if it be examined into, how it came to pass that the Jews were so prone to idolatry before the Babylonish captivity, and so strongly and cautiously, even to superstition, fixed against it after that captivity, the true reason hereof will appear to be, that they had the law and the prophets every week constantly read unto them after that captivity, which they had not before. For before that captivity, they having no synagogues for *public* worship or *public* instruction, nor any place to resort to for either, unless the temple at Jerusalem, or the cities of the Levites, or to the prophets, when God was pleased to send such among them, for want hereof great ignorance grew among the people—God was little known among them, and his laws in a manner wholly forgotten; and therefore, as occasions offered, they were easily drawn into all the superstitions and idolatrous usages of the neighboring nations that lived round about them. Till at length, for the punishment hereof, God gave them up to a dismal destruction in the Babylonish captivity. But after that captivity, and the return of the Jews from it, synagogues being erected among them in every city, to which they constantly resorted for *public worship*, and where every week they had the law from the first; and after that, from the time of Antiochus's persecution, the prophets also read unto them—and were, by *sermons* and exhortations, then delivered at least every Sabbath day, instructed in their duty, and excited to the obedience of it. This kept them in a thorough knowledge of God and his laws. And the threats which they found in the prophets, against the breakers of them, after these also came to be read among them, deterred them from transgressing against them. So that the law of Moses was never more strictly observed by them, than from the time of Ezra (when synagogues first came into use among them,) to the time of our Saviour; and they would have been unblameable herein, had they not overdone it by adding corrupt traditions of their own devising, whereby at length (as our Saviour chargeth them,) they made the law itself of none effect. And as, by this method, the Jewish religion was preserved in the times mentioned, so was it also, by the same, that the Christian religion was so successfully propagated in the first ages of the church, and hath ever since been preserved among us. For as the Jews had their synagogues, in which the law and the prophets were read unto them every Sabbath, so the Christians had their churches, in which, from the beginning, all the doctrines and duties of their religion were every Lord's Day taught, inculcated, and explained unto them. And by God's blessing upon this method chiefly was it, that this holy religion still bore up against all oppressions, and, notwithstanding the ten persecutions, and all other *artifices* and *methods* of cruelty and oppression which hell and heathenism could devise to suppress it, grew up and increased under them—which Julian, the apostate, was so sensible of, that, when he put all his wits to work to find out new methods for the restoring of the heathen impiety, he could not think of any more effectual for this purpose than to employ his philosophers to preach it up every week to the people, in the same manner as the ministers of the gospel did the Christian religion."

Calmet, under the word "*Synagogue*," observes, p. 871:

"*Synagogue*, a word which primarily signifies an assembly, but like the word *church*, came at length to be applied to places in which any assemblies, especially those for the worship of God, met, or were convened. From the silence of the Old Testament with reference to these places of worship, most commentators and writers on Biblical antiquities are of opinion that they were not in use till after the Babylonish captivity. Prior to that time, the Jews seem to have held their *social meetings* for religious worship in the open air, or in the houses of the prophets. (See 2 Kings iv. 23.) Synagogues could only be erected in these places when ten men of age, learning, piety, and easy circumstances, could be found to attend to the service which was enjoined in them. Large towns had several synagogues; and soon after their captivity, their utility became so obvious, that they were scattered over the land, and became the parish churches of the Jewish nation.

"The stated office-bearers in every synagogue were ten, though in rank they were but six. Their names and duties are given by Lightfoot, to whom the reader is referred. But we must notice the *Archisynagogos*, or Ruler of the Synagogues, who regulated all its concerns, and granted permission to *preach*.

"The service of the synagogue was as follows:—The people being seated, the minister, or angel of the church, ascended the pulpit and offered up the public prayers; the people rising from their seats, and standing in a posture of deep devotion. The next thing was the repetition of their phylacteries; after which came the reading of the law and the prophets. After the return from the captivity an interpreter was employed in reading the law and the prophets, (see Neh. viii. 2–10) who interpreted them into the Syro-Chaldaic dialect, which was then spoken by the people. The last part of the service was the expounding of the Scriptures, and preaching from them to the people. This was done either by one of the officers, or by some distinguished person who happened to be present. The reader will recollect one memorable occasion, on which our Saviour availed himself of the opportunity thus afforded to address his countrymen, (Luke iv. 20) and there are several other instances recorded of himself and of his disciples teaching in the synagogues. The whole service was concluded with a short prayer or benediction."

Horne, in his "Introduction to the Study of the Bible," treating of "*The High-Places, The Proseucha or Oratories,*" Vol. II., pp. 101, 102, says:

"*Besides* the Tabernacle, which has been described in a former section, frequent mention is made, in the Old Testament, of places of worship, called *High-Places,* which were in use both before and after the building of the Temple.

"From the preceding facts and remarks, however, we are not to conclude that the prohibition relating to *High-Places* and *groves,* which extended chiefly to the more solemn acts of sacrificing there, did, on any account, extend to the prohibiting of other acts of devotion, particularly *prayer,* in any other place beside the Temple, the high places and groves of the heathen, (which were ordered to be razed) only excepted. For we learn from the sacred writings, that prayers are always acceptable to God, in every place, when performed with that true and sincere devotion of heart which alone gives life and vigor to our religious addresses. And therefore it was that in many places in Judea, both before and after the Babylonian captivity, we find mention made in the Jewish and other histories of places built purposely for prayer, and resorted to only for that end, called *Proseucha* or *Oratories.* It appears that in heathen countries they were erected in sequestered retreats, commonly on the banks of rivers, or on the sea shore. The Proseucha or Oratory at Philippi, where the Lord opened the heart of Lydia, was by the river side, (Acts xvi.) Josephus has preserved the decree of the city of Halicarnassus, permitting the Jews to erect oratories, part of which is in these following terms: 'We ordain, that the Jews who are willing, both man and woman, do observe the Sabbaths, and perform sacred rites according to the Jewish law, and build *proseucha by the sea side, according to the custom of their country,* and if any man, whether magistrate or private person, give them any hindrance or disturbance, he shall pay a fine to the city.'

"Calmet, Drs. Prideaux and Hammond, and others have distinguished between these two sorts of buildings, and have shown that though they were *nearly* the same, and were sometimes compounded by Philo and Josephus, yet that there was a real difference between them—the synagogues being in cities, while the proseuchæ were without the walls, in sequestered spots, and usually erected on the banks of rivers," etc.

Brown, of Haddington, in his Dictionary of the Bible, says:

"*Synagogue,* the place where the Jews met for their *public worship on ordinary occasions, as we do in our churches.* As most of the Jews from the beginning of their settlement attended the tabernacle or temple only at the three solemn feasts, it is probable they had a kind of synagogue, or schools, or proseucha, or prayer places, in one of which last our Saviour prayed all night. Luke vi. 12. These differed from synagogues, as in them every one prayed for himself. They were in retired places, as by river sides, (Acts xvi.) and were uncovered, like groves; whereas, synagogues were in elevated places, were covered with a roof, and one prayed as the mouth of the rest. Perhaps it was the proseucha that were the '*mohede*' (synagogues) or meeting places, burnt up by the Chaldeans." Psalms lxxiv. 8.

To the Proseucha, and not synagogue, there seems, very evidently, to be reference in Luke vi. 12, where it is said, "Jesus went out into a mountain to pray, and continued all night *in prayer*"—"*en te proseucha tou Theou.*" "*In a proseucha of God*"—a *place* of prayer. So in Acts xvi. 13, it is "*proseucha,*" a *place* "where prayer was wont to be made"—out of the city, by the river side, where the women resorted.

From these references it may be seen that the prayer-meeting had a distinct place among the institutions of divine worship, from the earliest history of the church down through the patriarchal dispensation, to the institution of the synagogue, and ever after, as distinct from that form of worship, answering to our ordinary public worship of the Sabbath in the ministration of the word by the ordained ministry.

3. *The prayer-meeting formed a part of the divinely appointed worship during the whole period of the Levitical economy, distinct from Tabernacle or Temple, and from the synagogue worship.*

In the giving of the law by Moses, the Hebrews received their written constitutions, both as a church and as a nation. Many provisions in both constitutions were original, peculiar to that dispensation, and radical, designed to introduce radical change in the state of society, civil and ecclesiastical. The patriarchal state was abolished. A national organism was formed, and a more complete ecclesiastical organization was effected. Many of the precious institutions with which that people were favored were first given them in the wilderness, and incorporated in their new constitutions and laws. On the other hand, many of the provisions of the ecclesiastical and civil constitutions then given were modifications, or regulations merely, of institutions already existing under the patriarchal dispensation—institutions carried over from the one into the other, so that by the change of dispensation, or revolution of the form of polity, no blessing or privilege was either lost or even abridged. Circumcision, the Sabbath, social worship, etc., were all preserved intact, and incorporated with the new order of things, and now regulated by written statute law. Here we find the place of the social prayer-meeting recognized and regulated by the constitutional law of the last form of the Old Testament dispensation.

Abraham had planted his grove in Beersheba, and there enjoyed the private social conference with brethren, and communion with God in social prayer. Isaac, Jacob, and other faithful patriarchs long preserved their Proseucha distinct from the sacrificial altar. The Divine testimony assures us that the father of the faithful commanded the obedience of his children and household after him. The worship of the grove was not unknown to Moses. To preserve for the new dispensation the ordinances of the grove and the altar intact, and to guard against confounding the worship peculiar to each, God charged Moses to incorporate a prohibitory statute with the Levitical code: "Thou shalt not plant thee a grove of any trees near unto the altar of the Lord thy God, which thou shalt make thee." Deut. xvi. 21. In later periods of the history of the Hebrews, in violation of this law, God's worship was corrupted by erecting altars under every green tree, and in the groves, and on the high-places. There, in the days of Ahab and other wicked kings, they offered sacrifices. This persistent violation of law, in the corruption of divinely appointed worship, was at length arrested by the captivity of Israel and Judah. After the return, idolatry never again became the prevailing sin of the Jews; nor have we any account of the worship of the altar being blended with the social worship of the proseucha among the groves, or on high-places.

Two sources and forms of instruction, in addition to the law of Moses, will furnish us some pleasing and conclusive evidence of the existence of the prayer-meeting during the whole period of the typical economy. From the time of Moses to near the close of the Old Testament canon, the Book of Psalms was being composed and compiled. These Psalms are full of evidence bearing upon our subject. And the prophets speak a language confirming the devotional allusions of the Psalter. We select but a few of the many Psalms from which we might draw argument.

First, the *Thirty-fourth:* This Psalm, as will be seen from its title, and from First Samuel, the twenty-first chapter, from the tenth verse forward, was penned by David when banished far from the enjoyment of the sanctuary and public worship. In his flight from Saul he had the company of some good men. These, in his solitude, he called around him, and in the language of the third verse, invites to social worship thus, "Extol the Lord *with me;* let *us* exalt his name *together*." Many of the Psalms, like this one, were composed and sung amid the forests, and mountains, and caves of the south of Judah, by David and his fugitive companions, in their lonely prayer-meetings. Passing the 42d, the 63d, and many others penned under similar circumstances, and first sung in the prayer-meeting, we notice the *Sixty-sixth.* Here is the familiar language of prayer-meeting conference, verse *sixteenth*, "All that fear

God, come, hear, I'll tell what he did for my soul." Could ever such language have been used by a man, by a *heart* unused to the social prayer-meeting? Could it have been understood by any religious people to whom the prayer-meeting was unknown? Just here, in the prayer-meeting, is the appropriate—*the perfectly appropriate* and *appointed*—place for carrying out the *spirit* and *letter* of this heart-warming conference among kindred spirits.

Again, in the One hundred and eleventh Psalm, first verse, we have, in terms, clear testimony to the social and private worship of the fellowship meeting. The Psalmist engages to worship God, using these significant words, "I will praise the Lord with my whole heart, *in the assembly of the upright, and in the congregation.*" Two assemblies are here specified. The one composed of select and distinguished characters, *the upright ones.* The other is here distinguished from the assembly of the upright by every rule of interpretation, from the meaning of the words as well as from their connection. "The *congregation*" here means the great assembly of the people, of all classes, the unjust and the upright—the mingled masses of the people assembled together for public worship. "The assembly of the *upright,*" is the *private* meeting of such select ones for private social worship. The word "*assembly*" here, in the original, means *secret*—shut in, within doors—a *secret assembly.* Corresponding to this idea, we have the familiar expression, "The doors being shut," used where the application is made positively to the prayer-meeting. Jno. xx. 19. "When the *doors were shut.*" And verse 26, "And after eight days, again his disciples *were within.*" "Then came Jesus, the *doors being shut.*" The coincidence is remarkable. Christ's prayer-meetings with his disciples and the pious women, were held in the upper rooms, "the doors being shut." So, here, the Psalmist engages to worship

God in the private social meeting, with select ones—the *upright*, and of kindred spirit—for prayer, and to praise Him.

The internal evidence of the One hundred and thirty-seventh Psalm bears, at least, suggestive testimony to the prayer-meeting. The pious among the captives, in their solitude and in their sorrow, sat down by the river's side, the place of the proseucha of their fathers, where prayer was wont to be made. There they remembered Zion. Bitter and tearful remembrance! There they conferred of Jerusalem and her desolations. There was the prayer-meeting, for there they prayed, "Remember, O Lord." There, amid the defection and afflictions of the times, a few of those "who feared the Lord, and thought upon his name, spake one to another," in retired privacy, and engaged in devotional services appropriate to the prayer-meeting.

We might multiply references to the Psalms. This specimen must suffice. The argument from this devotional book may be thus stated: The Psalms are a book of praises prepared for the church of God in all ages as a manual of worship. Whatever form of worship they suggest—as individual, family, social, or public—either from the history of the penmen, or the complexion of their subject matter, that suggested form, and the adaptation of the matter of the Psalm to such form of worship would intimate three things. *First*, that the penman was familiar with that form of worship for which he was called to prepare devotional songs. *Second*, that the people, for whose worship devotional praises were prepared, were familiar with and practised that form of worship. And, *Third*, that the form of worship recognized in this manual of praise, in everything not local, not typical, not abolished, has the sanction of the Head of the Church, and is an institution moral, unalterable, and for the church in all ages. Such is the prayer-meeting; and such is its recognition in the book of the church's praises.

The prophets speak in regard to social prayer in a way confirmatory of the teachings of the Psalms in their devotional allusions. Daniel acknowledges the neglect of prayer as a reason of the evils of the captivity and other chastisements. "As it is written in the law of Moses, all this evil is come upon us; yet made *we* not *our prayer* before the Lord our God, that we might turn from our iniquity, and understand thy truth. Therefore, hath the Lord watched upon the evil, and brought it upon us." Dan. ix. 13, 14. Jeremiah predicts social prayer as a means of revival and reform in connection with the return from the captivity. "Then shall *ye* call upon me, and *ye* shall go and pray unto me, and I will hearken unto you. And *ye* shall seek me and find me, when *ye* shall search for me with all your heart. And I will be found of you, saith the Lord; and I will turn away your captivity." Jer. xxix. 12–14. This had its fulfilment in the prayer-meeting held by the river Ahava on the return of the captives. Ezra viii. 21–23. The principle of the prayer-meeting is referred to in Song vi. 1, "Whither is thy beloved turned aside? that we may seek him with thee." And in Mal. iii. 16, we have the application in social conference and prayers of the pious, in a time of great decline. "Then they that feared the Lord spake often one to another, and the Lord hearkened and heard, and a book of remembrance was written before him for them that feared the Lord, and that thought upon his name." That Malachi refers to the prayer-meeting, observed by the few pious Jews of those times, is suggested by the following points prominent in the passage: *First.* "They spake often *one to another.*" Here is conference, reciprocal and mutual, inapplicable to any kind of public, or temple official service. It was inapplicable to family worship, never spoken of as a conference meeting where there is speaking one to another. It can be applied to social conference, as in the prayer-meeting, where alone reciprocal conference, admonition, and exhortation, are admissible. *Secondly.* There was evidently prayer, for the Lord hearkened and heard it—heard and answered prayer, of which the language and circumstances are suggestive. *Thirdly.* The Lord unequivocally marked these meetings and their observance with Divine approbation. To such conference meeting the Psalmist invites the fearers of the Lord. "Come and hear, all ye that fear God, and I will declare what he hath done for my soul."

From these references, it may be seen that social prayer-meetings had a distinct place among the institutions of divine worship, from the earliest history of the church down through the successive dispensations till the apostles' times.

In subsequent references to the passages already noticed from the Old Testament, and in other connections, the argument deduced will gather strength as we proceed.

4. *The practice of Christ and his apostles makes clear the divine appointment of the prayer-meeting.*

Much of Christ's life is for the example of every Christian—much of it for the example of the ministers of religion. He often sought retirement alone. He, with his disciples, often retired from the multitudes for conference and prayer. After preaching the gospel of the kingdom, and feeding the multitudes, it was *his manner* to retire with his disciples, the better to instruct them, for prayer and for the exposition of his parables and sermons. "As he was alone praying, his disciples were with him." Luke ix. 18. "And when they were alone, he expounded all things to his disciples." Mark iv. 34. Such advantages no men ever enjoyed as these disciples, in private special conferences for the expounding of his public instructions delivered to the multitudes in parables, often dark and not understood by the disciples themselves.

If Christ, as a public Teacher, practised social prayer while he was with his disciples, and thus exemplified the prayer-meeting; and, especially, if, in this connection, he taught them so to pray, the authority for the prayer-meeting is established. It is, therefore, worthy of special notice, that when Christ taught his disciples the duty of secret prayer, he so particularly uses the singular, " But *thou*, when *thou* prayest, enter into *thy* closet; and when *thou* hast shut *thy* door, pray to *thy* Father which is *in secret;* and *thy* Father which seeth *in secret* shall reward *thee* openly." Matt. vi. 6. Here we have, beyond doubt, plain and express warrant for secret prayer. The very *terms* dissipate all shadow of doubt here. Then, immediately following, and in juxtaposition, yet clearly distinct, and as a new subject of exhortation, he changes the terms accordingly. Now he turns to social prayer, and with characteristic precision, says: " *But* when *ye* pray, after this manner, therefore, pray *ye: 'Our* Father—Give *us.'*" Matt. vi. 7–11. As the principle of secret prayer, its divine institution, and imperative obligation, are clearly stated here, so the *principle* of social prayer, its divine institution and imperative obligation as a *divine ordinance*, are as clearly taught.

The closing incidents in the life and history of Christ and his disciples, as recorded in the evangelists, are certainly very suggestive, as confirmatory of the truth in regard to their social and religious life during the period of Christ's public ministry. They formed a religious community—a social organism—a church fellowship. They, together and exclusively, sat down around the sacramental table. And they, certainly, often prayed together. Their habit was to resort often to the Mount of Olives for conference and prayer. This was well known to Judas Iscariot. Though he had deserted Jesus, and left the fellowship of the other disciples at the passover and first communion-supper, he knew where to find them an hour after. Luke records thus: "And he came out, and went, *as he was wont,* to the Mount of Olives, and his disciples also followed him." John also records: "When Jesus had spoken these words, he went forth *with his disciples* over the brook Cedron, where was a garden, into the which he entered, *and his disciples.* And Judas also, which betrayed him, knew the place; for Jesus oftentimes resorted thither *with his disciples.*" Hallowed grove! Blessed group in that *High Place!* What grove since Abraham's in Beersheba so redolent with heaven-inspired prayer, as that on Olivet's side and in Gethsemane's Garden!

Now, the question arises, and is justly deserving of an answer, For what did Christ and his disciples, so often and so regularly, as to form a custom wont to be observed, resort alone, and in the night, to that grove of thick, shady Olives, if not for prayer and conference? They did hold prayer-meeting there. They did confer there of heavenly and sacred things. Beyond the appropriate exercises of a prayer-meeting what did they there? What *but these* filled up the dark and sombre hours? This conclusion is strengthened by the practice of the disciples from the time of Christ's death, and forward, so long as habits formed under the power of his life and society would retain their influence upon the minds and habits of his followers. So, on the evening of the *First* day of the week, the evening of the day of Christ's resurrection, the evening of the *First* Christian Sabbath, and about the evening hour of the Mount Olivet prayer-meeting, the disciples grouped together—not in the Temple, not in the synagogue—but *in a private room.* And *for what?* Happily, we are, in subsequent historic record, informed, "Then the same day at evening, being the first day of the week, when *the doors were shut,* where the disciples were assembled for fear of the Jews, came Jesus and stood in the midst, and saith unto them, Peace be unto you." Jno. xx. 19. Then, again, on the evening of the second eighth day—just as before—not at the hour of the temple service, nor time of the synagogue worship, but in the evening, and time of the prayer-meeting. "And after eight days again his disciples were within, and Thomas with them; then came Jesus, *the doors being shut,* and stood in the midst, and said, Peace be unto you." Jno. xx. 26. What a coincidence here in circumstances, suggesting the same train of thought as in the One hundred and eleventh Psalm! "*The doors being shut!*" "In the *secret* assembly of the upright." As the church of the fathers had their well-known *private assemblies* for the select social worship of select upright ones, as distinct from temple and synagogue service, so here, Christ and his disciples, week after week—and oftener, for it was but the third night after the Mount Olivet prayer-meeting, till the evening of the *First* day of the week prayer-meeting, in the upper room, *the doors being shut*—held their private social meetings for prayer and conference. And we are assured that they continued in these evening prayer-meeting observances during the succeeding five or six weeks, till after Christ's ascension, and till the day of Pentecost. The record confirms this truth. After the disciples had stood gazing from Mount Olivet upon their ascending Lord, they, according to their custom, returned to Jerusalem, to their upper room prayer-meeting. Hear the record: "Then returned they unto Jerusalem from the Mount called Olivet, and when they were come in, *they went up into an upper room* where *abode* both Peter and James. These *all continued* with one accord *in prayer and supplication,* with the women, and Mary, the mother of Jesus, and with his brethren."

Here we may notice, as the key to the argument establishing the *divine right* of the prayer-meeting, *First,* the meetings held *continuously* for "prayer and supplication with the women," were not in the temple or in the synagogue, or in any other place where public worship was ever held; but in a room, in an *upper room* of a private dwelling, where Peter and others *abode.* We have here the appropriate *place* for the prayer-meeting. *Secondly,* this meeting was pursuant to well known former meetings of like kind, forming series of meetings held by Christ and his disciples, one of which was the Garden meeting; and among them were these evening meetings, on the evenings of the first day of the week, "the *doors being shut.*" *Thirdly,* the *specified object* and *exercises* of these meetings settle their character and establish the prayer-meeting as a *divine ordinance* of religious worship. "These all *continued* with one accord in *prayer* and *supplication.* These views are the more confirmed by the following: "And they *continued steadfastly* in the apostles' doctrine and fellowship, and in breaking of bread, *and in prayers.*" Acts ii. 42.

On the day of Pentecost the disciples were together, according to their custom, for prayer and conference, waiting the fulfilment of the promise of the Father concerning the outpouring of the Holy Spirit. They were still continuing in prayer and supplication with the women, "in the house where they were sitting," whether in an upper room or a lower, we are not here informed. Nor is it said whether the doors were shut; for details of this morning meeting are not given. But while in the house, perhaps at the beginning of the services of their prayer-meeting—certainly before the third hour, or nine o'clock, the Spirit descended upon the apostles with a sound as of a mighty rushing wind, and in cloven tongues, like as of fire. This miraculous outpouring of the Spirit upon a prayer-meeting, unitedly by concert pleading that thing promised, produced that commotion which attracted the multitudes without, which were then gathered at Jerusalem ; and soon the masses were congregated around in a confused, promiscuous crowd, amazed at the supernatural displays, eliciting the severe criticism of those not anticipating an answer to the promise on which the apostles were waiting.

This prayer-meeting, so distinguished by the fulfilment of the promise of the outpouring of the Holy Spirit, and converted into an extraordinary mass-meeting of awakened, earnest sinners, and unawakened, ignorant mockers, called out the first great apostolic sermon, brought Peter to his feet, and opened his mouth in giving utterance to that powerful, impromptu discourse, crowned with the first fruits of the apostolic gospel harvest—the conversion and baptism of three thousand souls.

The mind instinctively follows those thousands, the new converts of that memorable day, so summarily inducted into the new faith, and new fellowship of the apostles. A very interesting inquiry is suggested here. Were they reliable converts? Could they, indeed, be steadfast in the faith and practice of those praying men, and followers of the man of prayer, who taught his disciples how to pray? We are not left to conjecture here. We have a very distinct and decisive answer: "They continued steadfastly in the apostles' *doctrine.*" They heard the word, received, believed, and practised the gospel as preached by the apostles. "They continued steadfastly in the apostles' *fellowship.*" "They were added to the church." They, being called, came out from the world, entered the communion of the church, just recently organized, and continued to observe faithfully the conditions of that fellowship, here called "the breaking of bread." Nor were these all. "They *continued steadfastly in prayers.*" This last is distinct from the other conditions of fellowship in the apostolic church, as settling apostolic, Christian practice. If apostles' doctrine have a divine authority; if apostles' fellowship or communion of saints have a divine appointment; if the breaking of bread or the Lord's Supper be a divine ordinance, then how can prayers, as practised by Christ and his apostles, or the prayer-meeting be otherwise than a *divine ordinance* of religious worship? How, since placed in the same category with ordinances unquestionably divine?

Besides faithfully fulfilling all the other conditions of the new organic communion, these new converts observed their meetings for prayer, as certainly and as faithfully as they observed the preaching of the word or the communion of the Supper, and as Christ with his disciples did, and as the apostles certainly did in their upper rooms, "the doors being shut," with the women, in the evenings when temple and synagogue services were closed, or at the morning dawn before public services were opened. Instant in season and out of season were the apostles and the first Christians in their prayer-meetings, till defection in doctrine, and spiritual decline in vital godliness crept in among them, when the manner of some was to forsake the assembling of themselves together in the prayer-meetings.

In confirmation of these conclusions we have examples of prayer-meetings unequivocal, and clearly establishing the early practice of the Christian church. On that night, in which Peter lay in chains in prison between two Roman soldiers, "Prayer was made without ceasing of the church unto God for him." Acts xii. 5. By miracle his chains fell off, and the prison doors opened; and he walked at large through the streets of the city while its inhabitants were wrapped in slumbers and security, except the anxious little bands grouped together in different houses, in different parts of the city, holding prayer-meetings. Their eyes, like Peter's, now opened, knew no sleeping. Mary's house was, at that hour of the night, a house of prayer, "where many were gathered together praying." Acts xii. 12. Thither Peter went, and with some difficulty gained admittance among the astonished brethren and sisters assembled for their humble and earnest night prayer-meeting. Not content with visiting that one surprised prayer-meeting, he sends messengers to James and other brethren, in another place, and in like manner engaged—for the whole church, now numbering many thousands, was engaged in prayers that night—and then himself sets out for still another place, doubtless where was another group, of the many thousands, of wakeful, praying Christians, whose hearts were in unison with the little praying circle in Mary's house. These apostolic Christians knew the prayer-meeting.

There are some prominent and important points here. *First.* "The church," the whole church, or the church generally, were engaged, by an understood arrangement, in prayer on the same evening. *Secondly.* They were all collected in small groups in different places, and in the *private houses* of the members of the church. *Thirdly.* They met at night, the ordinary time for week-day prayer-meeting, when all could conveniently meet in neighboring contiguous houses, and when unoccupied with the labors of the day. *Fourthly.* Though they met in many places, and though there must have been at that time in the church tens of thousands of members, they were all united, by concert, in one special object of prayer. "But prayer was made without ceasing of the church unto God for him."

When Paul and Silas were at Philippi, as recorded in Acts xvi., they went out of the city, on the Sabbath, by a river side, "where prayer was wont to be made, or where was a Proseucha, a *place* of prayer." There they prayed, and conferred with the praying women who resorted thither. While in that city, abiding for some time, Lydia was converted. After her conversion, she brought Paul and Silas home to her house, and entertained them there. And while abiding there, their custom was to attend the prayer-meeting. "And it came to pass as we went to *prayer*"—not to family worship—for, "a certain damsel possessed of a spirit of divination *met us*"—on the way to the prayer-meeting. "The same *followed* Paul and *us*"—"and this did she many days." These things must have occurred on the way to the prayer-meeting, from day to day, which was held at the Proseucha, by the river side, where pious women resorted.

Soon the prayer-meeting by the river side, as also the public ministrations of the apostle and his companions, were interrupted. They were cast into an inner cell of an old Roman prison, and their feet made fast in the stocks. But even there they *would* have their prayer-meeting, and they *had one*. "And at midnight Paul and Silas prayed, and sang praises unto God"—not secret prayer and praise, but social and audible; for "the prisoners heard them." And the ear that hears prayer, united prayer by two or three, heard the song and prayer of this live prayer-meeting. "And suddenly there was a great earthquake, so that the foundations of the prison were shaken." The jailor was converted. Paul and Silas were set free. The brethren were comforted. The gospel triumphed. Christ approves the prayer-meeting.

5. *In the Epistles the prayer-meeting is enjoined by apostolical authority.*

As the Epistles give the last, so they furnish the clearest light in regard to the order and the worship of the Christian church. If the Epistles enjoin the prayer-meeting; if they enforce attendance, and reprove non-attendance; if they give directions for the exercises and duties of the meeting, then its divine warrant is established. Paul, in exhorting the Hebrews to a faithful maintenance of their profession, and to a practice becoming the gospel, uses these words, (Heb. x. 23–25) "Let us hold fast the profession of our faith without wavering; for he is faithful that promised; and let us consider one another to provoke unto love and good works: not forsaking the assembling of ourselves together, as the manner of some is; but *exhorting one another.*" Here the reference cannot be to family worship; for families are together, and the gathering together by assembling must, more naturally, be applied to the coming together of the members of different families into some assembly formed for the occasion, either as an assembly for public worship, or for some private purpose. Nor can the reference be to a meeting for public worship, as the preaching of the word, or the administration of the sacraments; because in such assemblies there cannot be, consistently, a reciprocal exhortation. Here the authorized ministry officially exhorts; but never submits to formal exhortation—one exhorting, then another, in turn. But the reference must be to some meeting in which the right of exhorting, and the duty of receiving exhortation are reciprocal. And since there is no ordinance in the church but the prayer-meeting to which this will apply, and in which it can naturally be carried out, it must have its application there. Here the members *can*, and of right *should* speak one to another. Here the exhortation is not confined to the ordained ministry, who alone speak to hearers in the public assembly, and who there wait not to be exhorted in turn by all whom they exhort, or who may think proper, or feel disposed to exhort others. The Epistles recognize some meeting in the church where reciprocal rights and privileges are enjoyed. They recognize family worship, social private worship, and public worship. In the family the worship is conducted by the head, and then parental admonition should never be made a part of the worship, but administered as a distinct family ordinance; as much so as the administration of the rod of discipline, and to which branch it properly belongs. It is true, that in the family the father is prophet, priest, and king; and so it still preserves some of the venerable foot prints of the patriarchal dispensation. But it is also true that the functions of these offices are distinct even in household administrations. As a prophet the parent trains in the nurture of the Lord; as a priest he offers morning and evening sacrifices; and as king he administers discipline. In the public worship the ordained ministry teaches exclusively; and here exhortation belongs to teaching, not ruling power. No unofficial member of the church can claim any more authority to exhort in the public congregation than woman prohibited from public teaching. This privilege of reciprocal exhortation is, therefore, applicable to the prayer-meeting, and so designed by the apostle. With these views understood, it will not be difficult to apply the teaching of the Epistles

Two passages more from the Epistles, of similar import, will suffice for this part of the Scripture testimony to the divine institution of the prayer-meeting. We shall consider them together. "Speaking to yourselves in psalms, and hymns, and spiritual songs, singing and making melody in your heart to the Lord." Eph. v. 19. "Teaching and admonishing one another in psalms, and hymns, and spiritual songs, singing with grace in your hearts to the Lord." Col. iii. 16.

These beautiful texts, hackneyed in partisan controversy, perverted from their true meaning and proper application, can hardly be quoted without exciting prejudice, or calling up pre-conceived opinions. What, then, do they mean? What is their obvious teaching? What duties do they inculcate? To a mind unabused by controversy, the language, the terms, their connection, their use, their affirmations, their meaning, indeed, all seem very obvious. Then, what do they say? What command? To what direct? Whom do they address? In what relations do they recognize those addressed? Do they address individuals as such merely, or do they recognize social relations and social duties? Now, let us mark what they do say, and what they do not. They *expressly* inculcate *speaking, teaching, admonition, singing, thanksgiving, heart-melody.* They *impliedly* inculcate acquaintance with the Scriptures —the word of Christ. Other things may be inculcated impliedly. Some things they do *not* enjoin, either expressly or impliedly. They do *not* enjoin *writing, composing, making,* except in the heart, nothing out of it. If these texts require *writing* or composing the compositions named, they require an absurdity; if not, an impossibility. Outside of the Bible, no man can tell what these distinctions mean, nor can any man tell what these compositions mean, nor can any man apply them. We know these distinctions and the respective compositions are in the Bible, for the Bible says so, and that is about all we know. But how to make the *one,* or the *other,* or the *third,* and exhibit their distinctions, is a work about as much within human skill as for a blind painter to fill an order for *high, deep,* and *broad* colored paintings! To the blind the one would be indistinguishable from the other. So here, the poets are blind. And as blind are all interpreters who blindly wring from these passages authority for hymn-*making*. These beautiful portions of Christ's word do inculcate plain Christian duties, do give plain directions how to perform them, and do plainly indicate their application to persons and their contemplated relations.

The proper questions arising, in order safely to apply, and not misapply, are these: To what duties are we here exhorted? and how apply the exhortation?

The duties inculcated are expressed; we need not repeat them. The application of these exhortations is the main thing before us now. The text and context clearly suggest relative social duties—duties Christians owe to *one another reciprocally*. These exhortations cannot all apply to an individual, because the reciprocity of the term "one another," can find no place in the field, by the way, or in the closet with a lone individual. They cannot all apply to family worship, or family training, or discipline, because the reciprocal, the mutual, the equal application of the obligations, cannot find place here. A family may all sing together; but teach, admonish, speak to *one another*, must necessarily fail in reciprocal application. In public worship, and in gospel ministrations, the free and reciprocal application can find no place. Where then? In what relations? To what ordinance can all that is here enjoined find an easy and natural application and exemplification? In the prayer-meeting only. Here any one may speak to others. For, "they that feared the Lord spake often *one to another*." And may say, "Come, and hear, all ye that fear God, and I will declare." Here, any one may sing, as well as any other. Here any one may teach as well as any other—"teaching one another." Here any one may admonish—"admonishing one another." Here all may give thanks together. Here all may make melody in their hearts tegether. Everything here is plain. Everything here finds an easy application in the prayer-meeting. To all Christians "not forsaking the assembling of themselves together, as the manner of some is, but *exhorting one another*," in the prayer-meeting assembly, every word of exhortation here is plain, naturally pointing to this ordinance for its full and appropriate application. To all Christians, free from partisan obliquity, and having no sectarian object to gain, tempting to the invention of interpretation forced and unnatural, these precious texts will furnish "sincere milk," nourishing to babes, in the prayer-meeting, where "brethren dwell together in unity."

In another connection we shall have farther use for these plain portions of the word of Christ.

6. *The prayer-meeting is encouraged and sanctioned by Bible promise.*

The promises encouraging and sanctioning the prayer-meeting are of two kinds. There are general promises sanctioning prayer simply—all kinds of prayer, and without reference to any particular form or kind, and equally available and applicable to all. There are also special promises made in specific terms for the encouragement of social prayer, and to the prayer-meeting.

Promises made to warrant prayer, in general, are all promises encouraging social prayer, since social religion and social worship are equally authorized with personal and individual. Then all such promises as these—and they are very numerous and full—encourage and sanction the prayer-meeting, "Ask, and ye shall receive;" "Seek, and ye shall find;" "Knock, and it shall be opened;" "Whatsoever ye ask believing, ye shall receive." "Whatsoever ye ask in my name, that will I do."

Still other and various forms of promise encourage to

social prayer, in common. God is revealed as the Hearer of prayer—as having a throne of grace from which he hears and answers prayer. He has opened a way of access to the mercy-seat. There is One appointed as a Mediator and Intercessor, in whose name all are authorized to pray. Another Intercessor, the Spirit, is sent to intercede within and inspire the heart with desires and groanings that will be acceptable to the Hearer of prayer. God has appointed prayer as his way of dispensing, and our way of obtaining all promised good. There are general commands enforcing all kinds of prayer, and all these imply encouraging promise. All these, and many other general forms of promise, encourage and sanction social prayer equally with all the other forms of prayer recognized in the word. There are also special promises expressly sanctioning social prayer and the prayer-meeting, just as there are special promises sanctioning *secret* prayer, and of equal force, authorizing it as an ordinance of religious worship.

If there are *special* promises made to any number of persons, two or more, encouraging them to agree to meet together and pray together; if *special* promises of Christ's presence are made to such meeting as approved by Him, and that such prayers made there shall be heard and answered, then the prayer-meeting is authorized by the Head of the church as a *divine ordinance.*

Christ told his disciples, "That if two of you shall agree on earth, as touching anything that they shall ask, it shall be done for them of my Father which is in heaven." Matt. xviii. 19. This promise will warrant any two Christians to confer together touching any proper subject of prayer, to agree to go together jointly to a place of prayer, and there together pray for that thing, assured that our Father in heaven will do for them as they shall thus ask. Then, farther, the promise takes a specific form, and is directed to the *place*—the *meeting* where the prayer of two is offered to God. "There am I in the midst of them." Christ is present *where* two meet together, by agreement, to pray. Still clearer is the application of the promise to the divinely appointed ordinance of the social prayer-meeting—to *any* meeting for prayer, of any Christian people desiring to worship God in spirit and in truth. "For where two or three are gathered together *in my name*, there am I in the midst of them." But the meeting in Christ's name is a meeting bearing the stamp of his authority. His *Name* written thereon marks the Institution as his, and is the evidence of his appointment, and the divinity of the ordinance; for any other way not appointed in his word, and so *not in his name*, must fail to secure his promised presence. His presence is secured where his name is recorded, not elsewhere. The divine warrant for the voluntary prayer-meeting, formed by consent and agreement of two or more Christians, is here as clearly stated as in the form of promise any warrant, or divine appointment, can have a statement. The prayer-meeting, thus having the impress of Christ's name, has the advantage of a reduplication of general promise, and so, in terms, applied to the prayer-meeting as of unquestioned divine appointment. To this end, the following promise of general character may here be specifically applied: "In all places where I record my name, I will come unto thee, and I will bless thee." Ex. xx. 24. This record of Christ's name, and pledge of his presence and blessing, establishes finally the truth of the doctrine—"the prayer-meeting is a divine ordinance of religious worship, instituted by Christ in his word."

CHAPTER II.

THE EXERCISES OF THE PRAYER-MEETING.

1. *Prayer.*

THIS is the *principal* exercise, from which the Institution and the meeting receive the distinctive name. Around this the other exercises cluster as appendages, some of which may not be so essential that circumstances might not warrant their omission. But we can hardly conceive of an assembly convened for the worship of God in which it would be proper to omit prayer. In all our ways God should be acknowledged; and prayer seems to be the appropriate, if not the only, way of acknowledging him, as required in his word, and in observing the ordinances of his appointment. In nearly every reference already made, in endeavoring to establish the divine warrant for this ordinance of worship, prayer is expressly noticed as the essential element in the exercises of this meeting. In many of them, it is probable, there was nothing but prayer and conference; as in the case of Jonah and the mariners, Christ and his disciples at night in the garden, and the impromptu prayer-meeting of Paul and the elders of the church at Ephesus at their parting farewell.

In regard to this exercise, the Scriptures seem to give prominence to *concerted* prayer. And to this we ask particular attention: *First,* Because of the intrinsic importance of this much neglected, if not entirely overlooked, *duty* and very precious *privilege*—concert in prayer. And, *Secondly,* Because here we are furnished with strong and satisfactory evidence of the divine appointment of the prayer-meeting; for, it is hard to conceive of concerted prayer as separable from two or more together praying for the same thing by previous agreement. But this is the prayer-meeting. "If two of you shall agree as touching anything that they shall ask, it shall be done for them of my Father which is in heaven." In this connection we have reference to the prayer-meeting, where the concerted prayer is understood to be made—"For where two or three are gathered together in my name, there am I in the midst of them." Matt. xviii. 19, 20. This gives warrant and encouragement for agreement, in every meeting for prayer, upon some matter of petition which, for the time, shall be the special object of joint supplication. And here seems to be one of the special channels through which God sends down special blessings. What a stimulant here to both prayer and faith! There is a *power* in conferring and covenanting, on the part of kindred spirits, to come before God, and plead together some special promise—an *incentive power* to awaken in the hearts of God's people a soul-warming exercise of grace.

If *concerted* social prayer—united prayer for some specific object, made the matter of voluntary covenant, agreed upon by two or more—be warranted as a divinely appointed way of worship, it is then a Christian duty, and privilege as well, on which hang consequences involving the spiritual interests of the soul, and the vital interests of the cause of religion. This being so, if it be neglected by the church, and Christians overlook it, great loss must consequently be experienced. In so vital a matter, interfering with a channel which God has opened, and through which he conveys richest blessings, this loss will be, and as we think is, felt in the low state of religion evidently prevailing everywhere throughout all the departments of the church. And then, is not the omission of this ordinance, of duty so important, and of privilege so precious, an evidence that the measure of the Holy Spirit's influences in us is indeed very limited? Is it not evident that, before we shall enjoy special refreshings from God, in enlarged measure, we must have respect to his way of sending promised blessings? Perhaps one reason why prayer-meetings are so often so lifeless is, that Christians attend them without an object—without a reflection—and so return as they go. But when some matter of deep interest presses upon the mind, and some ardent desire lifts up the awakened powers of the soul, and Christians come together with hearts all filled and upraised with that same desire, what fervency must inspire their prayers!

If the subject of conference, agreed upon for the meeting, should at the same time, by agreement, be made the subject of special prayer, how much more earnestness might be elicited in the prayer-meeting than is ordinarily enjoyed, when all minds and all desires are dissipated, when unity and unison are wanting, and when, consequently, Christian sympathies and Christian graces are not awakened, as the claims of the prayer-meeting demand. For example: if revival of religion were agreed upon as the subject of conference, and exchange of thought for the meeting, and at the same time, by previous agreement, made the subject of united prayer—could this subject be earnestly discussed, and made the subject of earnest prayer, and earnest Christian hearts not be warmed? Two disciples, after their conference with the Saviour, said—"Did not our heart burn within us while he talked with us?" And in this state of warm-heartedness, were they not in happy frame for prayer, and for a successful prayer-meeting? They returned to Jerusalem, found the eleven; and there all gathered together, renewed the conference, and, doubtless, held a prayer-meeting, in the upper room where Jesus was found, "in their midst, the doors being shut," and their hearts were all made to burn.

Here we may inquire, Can special objects of prayer—objects of deep interest and importance—be long so wanting in any earnest praying circle, that they cannot unite their prayers on anything? Here may be the clew to that dreadful evil, formality in prayer—that same set of phrases—the repetition of the same forms as if stereotyped, and for use on all occasions, in family prayer, in the social prayer-meeting, and everywhere else. Such were not the prayers of the united hearts in those concerted prayer-meetings, for concerted prayer held simultaneously in the city of Jerusalem on that night when Peter lay in chains in the prison kept by four quaternions of soldiers. No; "For prayer"—concerted prayer—"was made without ceasing of the church unto God for him." These were not stereotyped prayers; but the earnest outbursting of hearts by covenant united in pouring out, as one desire, their united desires for the release of a brother beloved in prison. Concerted prayer is the leading—the all-controlling exercise of the social prayer-meeting.

Examples illustrating and enforcing concerted prayer are numerous. Down through the line of the history of the prayer-meeting its way-marks are so conspicuous that he that runneth may read, and the way-faring need not err. Esther called together her praying friends for concerted prayer, and the captive nation was saved. Daniel, in his extremity, called together his three friends, laid before them a very grave subject of united prayer; they met and prayed for the desired mercy.—Their united prayer was heard and answered, and Nebuchadnezzar's decree of indiscriminate slaughter averted, and Daniel and his friends saved. Ezra called for concerted prayer; the concert was held; the right way sought; the concert was successful, and a right way was opened for the safe return of the pilgrim captives to the city of their fathers. Examples might be multiplied, and discussion here extended. The reader is referred to the history.

2. *Conference* is an important part of the social exercises of the prayer-meeting.

Next to prayer it is, perhaps, the most important. It is often by Christians, who understand and prize its value, called the "Conference Meeting." After the "Meeting for prayer and conference." And this accords with the Scripture view as often distinctly presented, referring to conference as the exercise to which prominence is given. It is very natural to conceive of concerted prayer as calling out conference, in a prayer-meeting, upon the subject of that concerted prayer. The one seems necessarily to require the other. All seasonable meetings among men, especially religious meetings, seem to demand speaking as a leading part of the exercises. The social principle in man, the attractions of the communion of saints, the love of brethren, the sympathies of the Christian's sanctified nature —all seem to demand exchange of thought, and sentiment, and feeling, as essential to the enkindling of the exercises of the graces of the soul. Hearts burn while talking together. Such is the law of Christian life; and for the higher enjoyment of this gracious life, imparted by the Spirit of God, is the prayer-meeting appointed, and conference as its principal soul-stirring exercise. David called on the fearers of the Lord to come and hear him relate what God had done for his soul. Ps. lxvi. 16. This seems very explicitly to refer to the exercises of the social meetings of the pious for conference on the subject of experimental religion. The principles involved here are these: David felt the pious impulses of his soul prompting him to give expression to his feelings, and impart to others the secret of his happy experience. He had learned, by experience, that in declaring what God had done for his soul, much of his religious social enjoyment was found. For the exquisite pleasure of communing with kindred spirits, he called on them to hear while he would impart his joys to those who could rejoice with the rejoicing. And here, too, he found a wide field opened for doing good to others, and for advancing his Master's cause. The pleasure of doing good, and the obligation binding thereto, here sweetly meet and mingle together.

Malachi refers to well known religious social meetings for conference, when he states expressly that "the fearers of the Lord spake often one to another, and the Lord heard." In those dark times, when religion was very low, everything cold and Laodicean like, the few fearers of the Lord were attracted together, that they might enjoy the heart-warming power of religious conference, just as in the cold the fire draws the shivering around it to receive and enjoy its warmth. Here is the burning fire of hearts whose heat is increased by gathering the scattered brands together, adding brand to brand, till hearts are made to burn together with intensified fervor. Thus by Christian conference, according to a fixed law of the kingdom of grace, love, and every Christian grace, receive, in the prayer-meeting, renewed life and power.

Paul, writing to the Hebrews, refers to conference in their religious social meetings as a custom with which they were familiar; and one practised by Christ and his disciples while he was with them, by the apostles long after his Ascension, and by the early Christians everywhere. Desertions appearing among them, he urges the faithful to their duty—"not forsaking the assembling of themselves together, as the manner of some is, but exhorting one another." Conference here receives the divine sanction as a leading exercise in the social prayer-meetings, and as the appropriate means of preserving and strengthening what faithfulness still remained among the few in the midst of the general forsaking of the conference meeting.

In the Epistles to the Ephesians and the Colossians, exhorting Christians to speak to one another, to teach and admonish one another, the apostle urges this very exercise in their social religious meetings. And more, he gives very specific instruction in regard to one of the very important modes of conducting this conference—by the use of "psalms, and hymns, and spiritual songs." What plainer or more natural construction can be put upon these words than that, in the prayer-meeting, a portion of a psalm may be taken as the basis of remarks. Not only singing psalms in the prayer-meeting—for that, too, is specified in addition—but speaking by or through the psalm or hymn, and instructing one another by exchanging views in regard to the doctrinal meaning, to the duties inculcated, and the lessons of Christian experience taught in the psalm. Every Christian having the undoubted right to judge of the meaning, and to explain the Scriptures for himself, he has the right of imparting to his brethren in the prayer-meeting the benefit of his interpretation, and so communicating any instruction or comfort to others he may have drawn from them for himself. This can in no way intrench upon the prerogatives of the church or the ministry. It is no more than exercising the rights of the noble Bereans, who searched the Scriptures for themselves, and communicated the results of their research for the benefit of others.

Conference as a divinely appointed exercise of the prayer-meeting, as also its advantages, will be found more fully illustrated in the *fourth* chapter, and in the history of the subsequent pages.

3. *Singing praise.* The Psalmist formally engaged to sing praise in the divinely appointed worship of God in the private assemblies of the upright, as well as in the great typical gatherings of the people on the great anniversaries of the Temple service, or the ordinary gatherings for the worship of the weekly Sabbath. Ps. cxi. 1. The priests and the Levites appointed to keep watch by night in the temple, according to their divisions and their courses—one course for each of the three Jewish watches of the night—were not assigned their places to pass the hours in idleness, nor even in silence. But each course, in turn, was appointed to observe religious services, each during the hours of its watch. In these night devotions of the official ministers of the sanctuary was held a ministerial prayer-meeting, in which praises were sung. Ps. cxxxiv.

"Behold, bless ye the Lord, all ye that his attendants are,
Even you that in God's temple be, and praise him nightly there.
Your hands within God's holy place lift up, and praise his name,
From Zion's hill the Lord thee bless, that heaven and earth did frame."

Paul and Silas, on that eventful night in which they lay in the old Roman prison of Philippi, and their feet fast in the stocks, held that memorable prayer-meeting, whose songs waked the prisoners—for when they had prayed they changed the service, "and *sang praises unto God.*" Praise is comely in the prayer-meeting.

There is, in the Epistles, authority of a more positive kind, for the exercise of praise in the prayer-meeting. Referring to the social meeting, Eph. v. 19–21, he says, by command—"Speaking to yourselves in psalms and hymns and spiritual songs, singing and making melody in your heart to the Lord; giving thanks always for all things unto God—submitting yourselves one to another."

And still more plainly by authority, Col. iii. 16, "Let the word of Christ dwell in you richly in all wisdom; teaching and admonishing one another in psalms and hymns and spiritual songs, *singing* with grace in your hearts to the Lord."

Analogy confirms the use of praise in the prayer-meeting. Praise is employed in the worship of the family. It is used in the public worship of God in the sanctuary, and should, therefore, and for the same reasons, be employed in the prayer-meeting. If God is to be worshipped at all, or ever, by singing praise, and if the prayer-meeting is an ordinance of religious worship, then God's praises are to be sung in the prayer-meeting.

4. *The Scriptures should be read, ordinarily, as an exercise, in the prayer-meeting.*

Here authority must rest upon inference, and general principles, rather than express Scripture statements. So must reading the Scriptures in family worship, and in public worship, rest upon this class of proof. Reading the word being an effectual means of salvation, it should dwell richly in every one. It should be the subject of search, and study, and meditation alway—by day and by night—in the house and by the way. Deut. vi. 6–9.

CHAPTER III.

THE ADVANTAGES OF THE PRAYER-MEETING.

THE prayer-meeting is not, in its principal, or special design—like the preaching of the word—a converting ordinance. It may be admitted, as a general principle, applicable to all ordinances, that each has some specific end for which it was appointed by the Head of the church; and yet each has many other important uses. As the Sacrament of the Supper had the commemoration of Christ's death for the end of its appointment, and yet has its various and important uses, as the conversion of sinners and the edification of saints in the broadest sense; as the preaching of the word is the special means of converting sinners, and yet has its general use in common with all other means of grace; as church government, discipline, censures, have all their special ends, and yet their general uses, and in many respects their common ends, to build up in comfort and holiness through faith unto salvation, so the prayer-meeting has its special end of appointment.

As secret prayer is specially designed for the personal and spiritual benefit of the individual, and as family worship is specially appointed for the benefit of the family, so the prayer-meeting is instituted specially for the edification of the church in her membership, or the circle agreeing to meet statedly, or occasionally, for social prayer. Its fellowship is Christian, not ecclesiastical fellowship. Any society, or social circle, may voluntarily associate for prayer, and make its own terms of fellowship, while not infringing the laws of the church. A class of young men might form a circle for prayer and mutual advantage, and make their society exclusive. There may be reasons why a class of youth, not professors of religion, yet sensible of its importance, might form a prayer-meeting for the special purpose of aiding one another in earnest seeking after Christ and the salvation of their souls. All the ends of these supposed organizations would have their corresponding advantages, special and consistent with the general designs of the prayer-meeting.

The advantages of the prayer-meeting are secured by the general promises made to prayer, and by the special promises made to the prayer-meeting. Any number—two or three—agreeing, and pursuant to that agreement, meeting, and together praying, have the promise of acceptance and answer. There are guarantees here of special kind specially encouraging to social concerted prayer.

2. *The prayer-meeting is a special means of developing and cultivating Christian graces, and of promoting individual and social edification.*

"As in water face answereth to face, so the heart of man to man." "Iron sharpeneth iron; so a man sharpeneth the countenance of his friend." Nowhere have these maxims a happier application than in the prayer-meeting. Iron is sharpened by friction, not contact simply. The file may be thrown into the same promiscuous heap with the axe, the mattock, the goad, and these remain dull and useless still. Christians may be thrown into the company of Christians, and neither receive from the other spiritual advantage in either quickening, or holiness or comfort; because their communications may lack spiritual savor. Their communications may be of evil, and so tend mutually to corrupt good manners. But let their conversation be as it becometh the gospel of Christ—let it be of heaven and godliness, and both will feel the sharpening influences of Christian graces glowing by the power of attrition with Christian graces. In the prayer-meeting, as nowhere else, are Christian graces thus brought together with powerful reactionary and reflective forces. Here love enkindles love—hearts burn while talking of Jesus by the way: for Jesus will be there with them, though to eye unseen it may be. Here faith is strengthened by the testimony so simply and so sweetly brought to each other's hearts mutually by exchange of views and feelings. Here hope is confirmed by mutual review of the ground of each other's hope. Here experience is enlarged by mutual exchange of Christian experience, each saying to other, "Come, hear, I will declare what the Lord hath done for my soul." So, here, doubts are removed as doubts seldom are in any other way. As the conversation of the Saviour with the woman of Samaria caused her to say, "Come, see a man that told me all that ever I did," so may the Christian disciple often have cause to say of the prayer-meeting conference, that here, as in a mirror, he sees his own heart in the unbaring of a brother's heart, in the freedom of conference, as he never saw himself before. O, how mutually comforting to exercised Christians, the comparing of Christian experience! How often have Christians been kept from falling by the influence of the company and conversation of live Christians, exerted through the prayer-meeting! "Two are better than one—For if they fall, the one will lift up his fellow; but woe to him that is alone when he falleth; for he hath not another to help him up."

The prayer-meeting is an instructive and successful school for correcting faults, and supplying defects in Christian character. Here diffidence, which so often destroys Christian usefulness, may be gently corrected by a kind training that can be enjoyed nowhere else so happily. Silently, gradually, and yet thoroughly, can men, comparatively useless in the church, be trained to eminent usefulness, and even leadership in every good work. So, in regard to many other faults and delinquencies; a brother can be taken by the hand, and lifted up, and led along, in company, in the right way. If lacking in public spirit, here are influences inciting to liberality. A lover of the prayer-meeting will be a man of social feelings and of a public spirit. A liberal man, devising liberal things, he will be a working man.

Here, too, the Christian will find a good school for the correction of errors in Christian experience. It has often been remarked, that Christians differ very little in their prayers, however much they may differ in their creeds. If the prayers of saints are more reliable, because of greater freedom from errors, than their professions, then their prayers will be a better glass in which to see our mistakes in our experience. Christians pray as they feel; and in prayer they feel themselves in the presence of God, the Hearer of prayer, and the Searcher of hearts. And here, where experience is interchanged in unguarded simplicity before God, the humble Christian will find much to chasten and perfect his experience.

We have suggested social edification as among the fruits of intelligent and conscientious observance of the prayer-meeting. Reason, experience, history, and Bible testimony, concur in establishing this truth. Unity in the faith, harmony in efforts, and organic strength are promoted and cherished in the prayer-meeting. The early Christians "continued steadfastly in the Apostle's doctrine and fellowship, and in breaking of bread, and"—just so long as, and because they continued—"in prayers." When they began to "forsake the assembling of themselves together," in their conference meetings, for prayer and for exhorting one another, then wavering in the profession of their faith began to appear among them. Then, too, that blessed, fraternal "provoking of one another to love and good works" began to disappear, and lose its power to stimulate and bind together brethren in unity of heart and effort. Differences in opinion, and fierce religious controversy, or, Laodicean deadness and cold apathy, will prevail in the same communion among brethren, usually, in the absence of the practice and power of the prayer-meeting, and in the absence of revival of religion, where the prayer-meeting is always a commanding power. The spirit of prayer, and the love and practice of the prayer-meeting, will so give organic strength to the church as to make her terrible as an army with banners. The period of the organic strength of the Apostolic church was the period of her continuing steadfastly in prayers, not forsaking the assembling of themselves together in their prayer-meeting conferences. The period of the organic power of the Reformed churches was the period of their revived prayer-meetings. The periods of all the revivals and re-unions of Reformed churches were the periods of revived prayer-meetings. These things the History of the prayer-meeting and of revivals fully attest. We dismiss the subject here even before well opening it, by referring the reader to the entire historic part of this work. The church has preserved unity in faith; she has preserved harmony in effort; she has preserved organic power whenever and so long as she cherished and preserved alive the spirit and practice of the prayer-meeting.

3. *The prayer-meeting may be received as a test of the state of religion.*

This may be applied to the religious state of the whole visible church, and to all the evangelical departments of the household of faith; it may be applied to any particular congregation as the test of its spiritual condition; and it may determine much of the spiritual state of the individual.

Secret prayer is, to the individual himself, an appropriate test of his own personal religion. Family worship is a very proper test of family religion, and of the piety of the individual members of the family. Prayer is the breathing of the soul born of the spirit, and is the evidence of spiritual life, whether breathed in the closet, or at the family altar. A graceless man will be a prayerless man. Every subject of grace will breathe prayer, and so, in some form, by breathing, give evidence of spiritual life, and change of character. The report, "Behold, he prayeth," satisfied the trembling Christian disciples that Paul was a Christian and harmless. As secret prayer is to the individual in this respect, and as family prayer is to the family, so is the prayer-meeting to the church, or circle forming a prayer-meeting, "the church in the house."

As the existence of personal religion, and the degree of its power, in the individual may be determined by the fact, and fervor, and constancy of secret prayer, so the state of religion in any congregation may be determined by the fact of prayer-meetings, their constancy, and the spirit by which they are sustained. As the fact of family worship, its earnestness, regularity, and moulding influence upon all the members of the household is the satisfactory evidence of family religion, so of the prayer-meeting—because, secret prayer and family religion sustain the same relations to the individual and the family that the prayer-meeting does to the church.

As prayer-meetings decline in a congregation, so will religion decline—or, so religion is declined, rather; for as the one revives, so will the other. As prayer-meetings fail in a congregation, so will the ministrations of the pastor become unfruitful, the preaching of the word fail to convert sinners and promote holiness in the professors of religion. Here, by the concerted prayer of the godly, in the prayer-meeting pre-eminently, are the hands of the ministry stayed up while wielding the sword of the Spirit, ordering the battles of the Lord. Like Moses' hands, stayed by Aaron and Hur—they two in concert—fit type of concerted prayer, two or three together, make the hands strong. It has been often said—and truly—that the prayer-meeting is the pulse of the church. The history of revival, whether of the individual, or of the church, is an extended series of illustration of this truth. Every converted sinner is a soul revived to prayer. Every saint restored from backsliding, is a soul returned to the life and power of prayer. Every congregation enjoying an outpouring of the Spirit, is a congregation revived and alive to the prayer-meeting. So echoes the history of revival of religion. Three thousand souls on the day of the pentecostal revival—all converted—all revived, and all, every one of them, cried out, What must we do? So the Jailor, "Sirs, what must I do to be saved?" So Paul, when converted, began the life of prayer with this earnest cry—"Lord, what wilt thou have me to do?" When saints have fallen into sin, then, with speech refrained, and silenced tongue, they are straitened in confession, and thanksgiving, and supplication. To live in sin is to quench the spirit of prayer. To receive pardon and peace and an unction from the Spirit in revival, is to restore to the love of prayer, the love of the fellowship of saints, and the prayer-meeting. Reader, do you love to be there?

Here, too, we must leave this subject, and refer to the history of the prayer-meeting for fuller illustration.

4. *The prayer-meeting is an ordinance designed specially for the revival of religion.*

Every prayer implies this; for, in every prayer, we ask grace, an answer to which will bring revival. This every Christian needs daily; and for this we need prayer always

Without prayer religion in the soul would die, as without respiration temporal death would ensue. Prayer is the breath of the soul. "Hide not thine ear at my breathing, at my cry," said the prophet, when speaking of prayer.

The history of revivals presents an unbroken series of facts illustrating the truth that the revival of religion and the prayer-meeting are inseparable. The prayer-meeting has always been employed as a means of revival; and has always followed as a fruit of revival.

During the forty days that Christ was on earth after his resurrection, he spent much time with his disciples in the prayer-meeting. In the last one he told them to "tarry at Jerusalem till they should be endued with power from on high." This we know they did, "waiting for the promise of the Father." And the manner of their waiting the fulfilment of the great promise we have in statement as distinct: "Then returned they unto Jerusalem from the Mount called Olivet, and when they were come in, they went up into an upper room; these all continued with one accord in prayer and supplication with the women. And when the day of Pentecost was fully come, they were all with one accord in one place. And suddenly there came a sound from heaven, as of a rushing mighty wind." Thus ushering early on the morning of the day of Pentecost that first great revival, at a prayer-meeting, in answer to concerted prayer, the *first fruit* of the last great Millennial revival, which shall be great as the day of Jezreel for its showers of the outpouring of the Holy Spirit.

So, down through the centuries till our own times, the history of all true revivals is the same repeated rehearsal of the prayer-meeting. The disciples and their new converts continued steadfastly in prayer as the cause of religion grew and spread. With the decline of prayer and the prayer-meeting, "the forsaking of the assembling" of professed Christians for conference and mutual admonishing of " one another," the dark ages advanced upon the church, and the power of religion passed away.

When the light of the Reformation began to dawn upon Western Europe, and the Isles of our covenant fathers, the prayer-meeting began to revive, and with its revival true religion revived. Luther and his contemporaries were men of prayer, and often met together for social prayer. Calvin and Zwingle were men of prayer, and mingled often with kindred spirits in social prayer. John Knox—the North Star of the Reformation, the champion of the prayer-meeting—moulded his Scotland and his Scottish Church with its forming power in the very incipiency of his organization. The Melvilles, too, with Henderson and Rutherford, and Cameron and Renwick, and of later times, M'Cheyne—all men of prayer, all revivalists, and most of them sharers in revival. But we are trenching upon history. To that department we must again refer the reader. Only here, some facts of our own times, now passing into history, and briefly. The times of 1858 were times of conventions, and prayer-meetings, and revivals, of which a United Church has been, for these eleven years past, the historic witness, as also to the truth that the prayer-meeting is a means of revival of religion. In any local revival for these twelve years past, in any of our congregations, in every instance the revival of the prayer-meeting has been the revival of religion, and the revival of religion has been the revival of the prayer-meeting. These angels of blessing God has joined together inseparably; to enjoy the one is to enjoy the other.

5. *The prayer-meeting is a means of promoting unity in the Church.*

Whenever unity obtains in the church, there is a revived state of religion. "Behold how good and how pleasant it is for brethren to dwell together in unity." Like the unction from the Holy One; like the dews from heaven; there the Lord commands the blessing—the blessing of everlasting life. Here is the life-power of religion. The prayer-meeting in a congregation brings Christian brethren often together. Here more intimate acquaintance is formed. As true Christians know each other better, so will they love each other more. As they love each other more, they will feel their interests the more closely identified, and the bonds that bind in one strengthened. Like one loving family bound together by the identity of interest, and the bond of affection; like one body, one member suffering, all the members suffer with it. Here they cultivate harmony in affection, so in judgment, mind and faith, and so live and walk together in blessed unity, preparing more and more for that perfectly blessed harmony when all shall come together in one with Christ.

Experience and the divine testimony concur in confirming the truth that the prayer-meeting is the ordinary and efficient means of promoting union of divided churches. While discussions from pulpit and press, and argument in all proper ways may aid in bringing discordant churches to see eye to eye, yet all these without prayer will not only fail, but will, very likely, occasion parties differing to diverge from truth and unity more and more. Prayer must be employed to secure the spirit and love of unity. Controversy without the spirit of prayer will tend to foster prejudice and party spirit, perhaps strife and discord, and the confirming of party issues and party lines more and more.

A spirit of prayer and a love for Christian conference will bring Christians together face to face in the prayer-meeting and religious convention, from which positions Christian brethren will understand each other better than from any other stand-point. And as Christian brethren understand each other better, they will love each other more. And as they understand and love each other more, so will they desire the more to dwell together in unity. But to secure these is the desideratum. Their spirit is from God and of his grace, we are assured; yet united prayer is the means of securing this love of the brethren, this unity of mind and of judgment, and mutual desire to enjoy fellowship in the bonds of peace. Such we have seen and known in times past. Christians and Christian churches long alienated, and Christian feeling imbittered by controversy, have been sweetly subdued under the spirit of unity; but only through the power of prayer and Christian conference. These have a power—not a mere sensational power, without reason, sense, or truth—a power like the morning cloud; but the power of a divinely ordained instrumentality, taking hold of the heart, and deepened by the Holy Spirit, the Author of the spirit of prayer and unity.

It was the spirit of unity, induced by united prayer and conference of sweet remembrance, that brought together in one united church fragments long alienated by distance and controversy. For many long years that union hung quivering in the balances, putting to severest test the strongest faith. Sometimes the friends of the union almost despaired of success, or again were called to hope against hope, till the period of prayer-meetings and conventions came, bringing brethren together face to face, in the spirit of prayer and love. Then, as by the direction of the finger of God, the union was happily consummated, to the joy of its friends, and to the practical illustration of the advantages of the prayer-meeting in promoting union of churches, and dispensing in a united church the spirit of unity, and strengthening the bonds of peace. As this united church was brought forth under the influence of the prayer-meeting, and as she still thrives under, and largely enjoys its power, may she long cherish its hallowed and uniting influences, and practice the assembling together of kindred spirits for prayer and conference.

While we would not predict, but reason from analogy, from the history and experience of the past, and from the direct teaching of the word of God, we would say, we have little hope of successful union of the divided churches, in the future, till we see earnest prayer-meetings and religious conventions for conference on the subject of ecclesiastical union. And that this happy future may soon come, let all in their respective circles cherish the spirit of concerted prayer, and sustain the social prayer-meeting.

If unity of faith, confidence, brotherly love and harmony, in operations, be maintained in the church and in our congregations, the prayer-meeting, in its true spirit, as designed by the Head of the Church in appointing the ordinance, must be observed. Not the prayer-meeting as appended to some form of official pastoral administration—not the prayer-meeting in name, and the pastoral week evening lecture in fact—not the prayer-meeting of a few, and these of pious women mainly; but the apostolical meeting in the private upper rooms, the doors being shut, the prayer-meeting of the people, for the people, by the people, and in such way as will bring—not one-tenth of the church membership only—but the whole to the assembling of themselves together, in primitive manner and spirit. *Here* it is that unity has its birth-place; *here* it is cradled; *here* it is trained; *here* it becomes a three-fold cord; *here is* the centre of the unity of the church; *for here* is the soil—the genial soil beside the waters—where unity strikes deeply its roots, and whence it draws its life-power to bind together in comely brotherhood.

6. *The prayer-meeting is the normal school of the church for training young men for public usefulness.*

A ruling elder should be not only a man of piety, but to be efficient and useful, fitted for all the duties of his office, he should be qualified to conduct prayer-meetings, and lead in their exercises intelligently and dispassionately, with grace and solemnity. He should be qualified for visiting the sick, and to meet all the varied duties of such visits. Here is call for a ripe, Bible-trained mind—need for one who can with readiness speak to the dying from the word of God. Here is need for calmness, ease, and fulness of unction in prayer. The prayer-meeting opens for the young men of the church just the school required for training the material for an efficient eldership. Here young men should be called to lead in prayer. And to prepare for this part of the normal school exercises, let young men be early called to lead in family worship, and in the young men's prayer-meeting. If young men pray in secret; if they are called, in their father's absence, to lead in the worship of the family, thus they can pass up from primary to higher normal training, and become efficient members of the prayer-meeting. Thus trained, the young men of the church may be qualified for leading in prayer in any public meeting, or religious convention, or ecclesiastical assembly; as also at the sick bed for the edification and comfort of the sick and dying. Had we such an eldership, then everywhere might the sick be encouraged to carry out the injunction, as authoritatively binding on them and on the ruling elder as on the pastor: "Is any sick among you? let him call for the elders of the church; and let them pray over him, anointing him with oil in the name of the Lord." James v. 14. Can we expect our eldership to have, and to impart such unction around the sick bed without training?

It is a manifest evil, observed by all discerning men, and lamented by good men, that the ruling eldership exerts so little influence in the church, and that in church courts particularly it approximates so nearly to a *sinecure*. The inquiry is often made, "Why is it so?" And why—since Presbyterianism boasts its parity of power among the lay and clerical elders—have we generally such small minorities of the lay class in our church courts? And why in these is almost everything managed by the teaching elders while the other class sits in such passive muteness? While these things ought not to be so, and while several reasons may be assigned, yet here lies the principal difficulty: Our elders are not trained in the prayer-meetings as they should be, by leading in their exercises, especially in prayer and in the free and full discussion of the topics of religious conference. Were they trained in the exercises of "speaking often one to another," and to presiding in the prayer-meeting, and leading in all its exercises, they would, without question, be better qualified for understanding their responsibilities, and for filling their places in church courts.

Here let me say to ministerial brethren to whom it may apply, shut down upon your Wednesday evening prayer-meeting lectures, or, what will be far better, continue them as your own ministerial meetings, and, in addition, open district prayer-meetings in every convenient quarter of your charges, so that on many evenings of the week, and in many places all over your congregations, you may have apostolical fellowship meetings that will bring out every family, every young man, and every elder to the meeting, and open the way to every one to take part in the exercises. This normal school arrangement will bring out all the latent power and talent of the church, and put it under training for usefulness, and, indeed, for work in the field at once. "Standing idle all the day," just now, when there is so much work to be done, is the terrible bane of the church, in all her departments. It is a part of the ministerial work to bring out every member of the church to his place, point out and assign to him his work, and so see to it that no one under his charge is permitted to expose himself to the challenge of the Master of the vineyard, "Why stand *here* all the day idle?" In this way all our church courts may be well supplied with a controlling and safe ruling eldership.

New measures, innovations upon the established doctrines and order of the church, putting in peril her unity and peace, are seldom introduced by the lay eldership. Were our church always fully represented by a well-trained eldership, disposed to act independently upon their own judgments, unbiased by clerical influence, winds of doctrines, and popular novelties, subverting the truth and obliterating "the footsteps of the flock," and the ways of our fathers, would not so easily mar the unity and retard the prosperity of the church. Much of the purity, spirituality, unity and success of the church must depend upon a well-trained lay eldership. And the school for their efficient and practical training is the prayer-meeting.

Thorough training here will qualify for work in any department of the great field assigned to the church by the Master of the vineyard. What young man—or old even—is fit to superintend the Sabbath school who has never enjoyed training in the prayer-meeting? And here we might raise a very proper, timely, and important inquiry, Why is the Sabbath school, with its system of operations, so lamentably superficial and ineffectual in the solid and reliable training of the children and youth of the church? Why are they so painfully unequal, in their religious attainments, to the advanced privileges and opportunities of the age? Is it the miserably light and chaffy reading matter of the Sabbath school library? This may have its part in inducing this evil. But after all the reasons are summed up, here lies the burden of the crushing trouble—the light and chaffy attainments of Sabbath school teachers, who need themselves to be taught first principles. Take a young man who has been trained from childhood in an old Cameronian prayer-meeting, accustomed there to hear weekly discussions of every kind of subjects connected with Sabbath school teaching, who has, in addition, been, for seven years, an active member of a young men's prayer-meeting; other things being equal, such young man will be found better qualified for Sabbath school teaching than one-half of our theological students, who are strangers to such training, but have just filled their seminary curriculum. Three years' connection with a live prayer-meeting, leading in its exercises, taking interest and part in the discussion of the subjects of its conference, will accomplish more in training for practical usefulness in the Sabbath school, than three years listening to lectures in a theological seminary. If thorough indoctrinating in fundamental and distinctive truth; if stores of Bible knowledge and aptness in communicating, are of importance in fitting for usefulness in the church, then is the *scriptural* prayer-meeting important as a school where such training can be acquired.

The ministry for the times and for the rising generation, is an object of deep solicitude, and justly, to all godly men in the church. Like Eli, when Ark, and Israel, and all were in jeopardy in the high places of the field; so now, in the perilous times that are upon us, their hearts, trembling for the Ark, are turned with concern to those to whom its keeping will soon be committed. While the ordinary theological training is theoretically the main thing in preparing for the ministry, yet there is a practical training, important in its place, and without which no candidate for settlement should ever be deemed qualified, and which should be made a matter of serious inquiry by every congregation in making out a call for a pastor. The importance of this practical training to which we refer, we are happy to say, seems to be duly appreciated in our Christian colleges, and in our theological seminaries. In these, students, with the concurrence and encouragement of faculties, are formed into prayer-meetings, and here receive a large amount of practical training for future work. But this is all based upon principle—the importance of prayer-meeting training. Here is a good stand-point, from which a congregation can consider the qualifications of a candidate for a pastoral charge, perhaps better than the Presbytery before which he may display the flowers of rhetoric and the charms of eloquence, by which too many light minds are carried away. That young man, no matter how brilliant his talents, no matter how extensive his literary and theological acquirements, if he have neither experience in the prayer-meeting, nor taste for its exercises, is unfit for the pastorate, and unworthy the suffrage of any pious congregation. Candidates for the ministry cannot too soon be brought under the influence of this precious normal school training. Parents dedicating sons to the ministry, pastors and sessions having oversight of these children of the 'church, should co-operate in leading them forward early in life to take leading part in the prayer-meeting exercises. Here the first and best "inclinations" are given toward that higher grade of practical qualification for the pastoral work.

7. *The prayer-meeting is the rallying point where the power of faith in the church concentrates, and takes hold on the arm that moves the world.*

Here the mighty in faith and prayer, who, as princes, have power with God, combine, agree, and ask God, who, in answer to prayer, according to his word, performs wonders for his church. "I say unto you, that if two of you shall agree on earth as touching anything that they shall ask, it shall be done for them of my Father which is in heaven. For where two or three are gathered together in my name, there am I in the midst of them." Matt. xviii. 19, 20. The prayer-meeting has made earth to quake, prison doors to open, shackles to fall from prisoners, and jailors to tremble. It brought down the promise of the Father, in the gift of the Holy Spirit, in the pentecostal baptism of an infant church, followed by the conversion of thousands. It has brought down all the judgments predicted in God's word, that have in all the past scourged our sin-cursed world. It has secured the fulfilment of all the promises of the eternal covenant, and brought down all the blessings of that covenant ever enjoyed by God's covenant people in all past ages. It is the channel through which all will come till the present economy of the church and government of the world shall close. Could we trace the chain of causes and effects in the government of the Mediator, over the world and in the church, and in the progress of the gospel in the salvation of sinners, we should then be able to have some clearer comprehension of the importance of this part of the divine plan for the accomplishment of the divine purposes. Everything God has done for his church; everything he is doing; everything he will yet do in the fulfilment of his promises for her, and in the execution of judgments predicted—all are in answer to prayer—eminently in answer to concerted prayer in the prayer-meeting. What an engine of power!—moving that Power which moves mountains, subdues kingdoms, stops the mouths of lions, quenches the violence of fire, puts to flight the armies of the aliens! The history of the prayer-meeting is itself a series of illustrations of the power of concerted prayer, and of the advantages of the prayer-meeting, as a *divine ordinance*, appointed as an instrumentality employed for the accomplishment of the divine purposes.

8. *The prayer-meeting largely compensates for the lack of a regular gospel ministry.*

Many of the Psalms give us the key to the practical application of the principle, and furnish an illustration of the advantages of this ordinance under the circumstances here stated. The Psalmist would not supplant the Tabernacle or Temple service by waiting on the private worship of social prayer. He well understood the principle underlying the statement that God delighted more in the gates of Zion than in the dwellings of Jacob. When he had access to the public worship represented by the "gates of Zion," he went with the multitude that kept the solemn, holy days. But when under different circumstances, he pursued a different course. In all his banishments, and in all his desert wanderings, on the mountains or in the caves, when deprived of the regular ministrations of the sanctuary, administered according to God's appointment, he resorted to the fellowship meeting with kindred spirits, where he could say very familiarly—"Come, hear, I will declare what God hath done for my soul." When beyond the Jordan, on silent Sabbaths, he repaired to the Hill next precious to Zion, to which only he had access—the "Mizor," or, little hill—to the prayer-meeting, and there worshipped his God.

The psalms penned in the wilderness of Judah, during the flight from Saul's persecution, indicate the circumstances and the use to which first applied in the lonely prayer-meetings of the mountains and the caves. There the Psalmist and his wandering companions felt largely compensated for their lack of access to the Ark, around which clustered the affections of every pious Hebrew.

The captives in Babylon found the only proximate compensation for the lost privilege of their Temple worship in their resorting to the river side for prayer, praise and conference.

The disciples of Christ were, after his death, for a time destitute of the regular administration of divinely appointed public worship. The typical service of the Temple was abolished. The time for entering upon the official work to which they had been called had not yet come. They were commanded to stay at Jerusalem till the promise of the Father should be fulfilled, and they endued with power from on high. Till then they could not enter upon their public ministry. During this destitution of public ordinances, they, on successive Sabbaths, each eighth day, met together with the women—in their upper rooms—the doors being shut, where they enjoyed the compensatory prayer-meeting till the day of pentecost.

The persecuted Christians, true, indeed, to the example of all the persecuted before them from the beginning, wandered in deserts, and in mountains, and in dens, and in caves of the earth, making them vocal with their prayers and praises in their prayer-meetings. This practice held together the Waldenses for ages. It formed the rallying point of the Bohemian churches, and the faithful Huguenots in their trials. It was the refuge of our Scottish ancestors when "the killing time" blocked up the way to the sanctuary, and silenced the voices of their beloved Shepherds.

The Cameronians in Scotland, after twenty-eight years of terrible persecution, and during eighteen years of destitution of a single minister on whose ministrations they could wait, found their societies the common bond that preserved their ecclesiastical organization from a complete disintegration. And to this day their adherents, good and true to the spirit of their fathers, in all the countries where they are scattered, are preserved in compact organization, by the observance of the prayer-meeting, always and everywhere, Sabbath day and week day. Without this compensating ordinance, preserved in its integrity, that people would have been scattered to the four winds, and must have become extinct generations ago.

John Wesley organized his followers distinctly on the principle of the prayer-meeting's compensatory place in the absence of the gospel ministry. The discipline under which they were trained, required their assembling together in their Societies every Lord's day, with or without the regular ministrations of the word by their ordained ministry. Here lies the secret of the wonderful early and compact growth of that church, and its wonderful success in securing a firm foothold wherever its people have settled, and wherever its missionaries have gone.

So, in the new settlements of the wide West, embryo churches have grown up and stood out against surrounding trials that put weak organizations to test, just in proportion as they acted upon this scriptural and common sense principle. The prayer-meeting largely compensates for the lack of a regular gospel ministry.

CHAPTER IV.

PRINCIPLES AND RULES FOR THE GOVERNMENT OF THE PRAYER-MEETING.

HERE we may distinguish the ordinary prayer-meeting, from the voluntary, or independent. One forms a constituent and elementary part of every well organized congregation. The other is outside of any ecclesiastical relation or control. The ordinary prayer-meeting is under the supervision of pastoral care and the control of ecclesiastical rule.

A congregation without a prayer-meeting is essentially defective in its organization, and so must be limited in its efficiency. Every congregation is expected to have its prayer-meetings, and consequently the prayer-meeting, as a divine ordinance, is common to all the congregations of the church, and the common privilege of all the membership. It may be subjected to standing rules, common to all the social meetings of all the congregations of the whole church, just as the public worship of all the congregations may be subjected to the same general principles and rules of directory for the sake of order and uniformity.

Besides this, the institution of social prayer contemplates all the exigencies of Christian social life, and all events of providence that may pass over the church, and over Christian communities, suggesting a call, and opening a door for social prayer, in the application of the divine rule, "pray always." Circumstances must determine much, as also Christian prudence, in conducting all kinds of independent meetings.

Rules of directory for worship must be founded on principles contained in the word of God, the only rule of faith and worship. The church may apply Bible principles to matters relating to worship, but never usurp prerogative of giving rule, or law, to the free conscience of the moral agent accountable to God, and under a law to Him by which the creature must be judged. Rules here should be nothing more than deductions from principles, and so arranged as to be easily applied in the observance of an ordinance of worship. The principles of the Bible are often very general, and their application very natural and easy. Nature itself will often teach and supply what may seem to be wanting in a general principle, as, "Let everything be done decently and in order." The law of the prayer-meeting is positive. It is a divine ordinance. The forms, or order, that may be preserved in the observance of this institution of worship, is the matter to which rules are to be applied.

For the ordinary prayer-meeting of the congregation, the following Rules may be observed:

1. In every congregation, whose numbers and locality will justify, there should be several social prayer-meetings organized. And to this end the families should be divided into districts, or quarters, and, if convenient, under the care of some particular ruling elder residing in the district. Every family and every member should know to what society, or prayer-meeting, each belongs, and where each should be recognized and be expected to attend. Every society should know its own members, and every member should recognize his privileges and his obligations.

Still farther—upon the same principle, and for similar reasons, in every case, in small organized congregations, in mission stations, or wherever a few families, or a few individuals, members of the church, are so located together that they can conveniently meet together, they should do so weekly, or more or less frequently, according to circumstances. The end in all cases being the same, and the principle the same, namely: that every family and every member of the church may enjoy the advantages of the prayer-meeting.

The principle here stated, and the rule suggested, have advantages over all other arrangements for the prayer-meeting. Because,

First, they harmonize more with the spirit and design of the institution as taught in the word of God. They correspond better with the practice of Christ and his disciples, and of the early Christians who continued steadfastly in the Apostles' doctrine, fellowship and *prayers*. Here we have the nearest resemblance to the prayer-meeting in the upper room with the women, in the evening, and the doors being shut. Here we have really, in the true sense, "the church in the house"—the assembly—"*ecclesia*"—gathered from several households into one private room, or dwelling, where Christians can "speak one to another"—can "admonish one another"—can "exhort one another," as in no other form of meeting.

Secondly, the prayer-meeting, according to the principle and rule suggested, is less liable to the serious defects of the meeting held in the church, professing to be for the whole congregation, and conducted by the pastor. To this kind of meeting we do not here object on principle—only as on the assumption that such a meeting is *the prayer-meeting*. It is really neither the prayer-meeting nor public worship. It is rather a blending of both. We object to this meeting when it usurps the place of the prayer-meeting of the Bible, and cuts the people off from its privileges. Comparatively few ever pretend, or dare pretend, to take part in the conference—to "speak," or "admonish," or "exhort one another." Comparatively few of the members, and sometimes even of the elders, lead in such meeting. Comparatively few take any active part, but ordinarily sit, mute spectators, as in the public worship conducted ministerially by the pastor. And still a greater defect obtains here—comparatively few of the members of the congregation give a regular attendance to the prayer-meeting at all. Unless under some spasmodic excitement, it is the exception, not the rule, that a full meeting of all the families, and all the members, old and young, of the congregation can be secured.

Now, what are the facts in regard to principles here, and the forms, the rules and directories for applying them? In congregations where the Scriptural form of the prayer-meeting is observed, where they are carefully and judiciously divided into prayer-meeting districts, we know the result, the average attendance on the prayer-meetings, is nearly equal to the Sabbath day attendance of *members* on public worship. On the other hand, congregations—and particularly large city congregations, whose members are from three to eight hundred—not so districted, but enjoying the Wednesday evening lecture, or meeting, in the basement, conducted by the pastor, fail here, lamentably fail. See, over there, that large congregation of *six hundred* communing members—*fifty persons* meet with the pastor on Wednesday evening. *Forty* of these are women. None of *these*, of course, are expected to lead, or pray, or speak here. Of the *ten* males, *five* may, perhaps, when called on by the pastor, lead in prayer. This is no fancy picture. We know it is not universal, and may not be general in its application. Still, this state of things is too common. It should never be; it need never be in any congregation. On what principle will *one-twelfth* only of the members of a congregation enjoy the privilege of the prayer-meeting?—and only about one out of twenty-five of the whole congregation worshipping on the Sabbath? On no principle, or principles, but these—the Scriptural prayer-meeting is ignored. Then, consequently, the state of religion is low, and the prayer-meeting is a name merely. There is not power to make it a vitality. Should not the Lord's people be trained to something better? Should they not be brought to taste something better, since our kind Master has, in his word, prepared something better? His prayer-meeting is for all, and all should enjoy it.

One aim—from principle—should be ever before a congregation in organizing and in conducting a prayer-meeting: That system which will bring the greatest number—and that number most—under all the influences of all the advantages of the prayer-meeting.

2. In cities, and wherever congregations are sufficiently compact, meetings should be held in the evening. They should, also, be held weekly; and, so far as can be conveniently arranged, go from house to house. To secure, as much as possible, the visits of pastor and elders, the several meetings should be held on different evenings of the week.

There are several obvious reasons suggesting the propriety of some such arrangements, beside the presence of the pastor and some of the eldership occasionally. Many of the business and laboring classes, from their engagements, find it difficult to secure leisure so as to attend without distraction at any other time than evening. Some are aged or infirm. Some may be indolent. Women and children may not at all times be able to leave home. These evening alternations will bring the prayer-meeting into most of the houses, and will tend, as a stimulant, to bring many weak ones out, who would otherwise very seldom, if ever, attend a prayer-meeting. Such arrangements will open the way for every member to take a proper part in the exercises and duties of the meeting; will remove occasion for excuse for absence from every one disposed to frame excuses; will open the way to the eldership for personal and more intimate acquaintance with every family and every member of the congregation; and, through the eldership, will make the way much easier to the pastor to form a personal acquaintance with his whole flock, and, especially, will make the way easier to every sick bed, to the heart of the sick and dying, and to every anxiously-inquiring sinner. Here, too, is the pastoral high-way to the acquaintance and the affections of every youth and child of the church. Many young and weak members can be induced not only to attend prayer-meetings, but to lead in prayer, and to speak on subjects of conference, and in this way called out to early training for usefulness in the church.

These arrangements, with many other subordinate details that may grow out of them, will in no way interfere with monthly prayer-meetings for the whole congregation, conducted by the pastor, and to give opportunity for sessional consultations. Nor need they interfere with the Sabbath evening lecture, or prayer-meeting, or any other form of religious service for Sabbath or week-day.

These evening prayer-meetings should be visited by the pastor as often as possible, and frequently by the elders. Here they can find the most convenient and happy way of forming acquaintance with a class in greatest need of attention, the extremely diffident, who need to be taken by the hand and led forward in Christian duty and in Christian work. There can be no better stand-point from which the pastor may inspect the condition and wants of his charge than in such prayer-meeting.

Every member of the church, male and female, old and

young, should conscientiously study and practice constancy and punctuality—that is, to be always there, and always there on time. If Christians understand and believe the Scripture teaching and the Scripture obligation in relation to this institution, they must feel the importance of its faithful observance. If Christians were rightly indoctrinated and trained here, how could they, as in many congregations they do, by hundreds, neglect the prayer-meeting altogether? Every member should be present at the hour of opening the meeting, and the exercises should be commenced promptly at the time appointed.

There is a good faith—a compliance with express or implied engagements, which as a band holds together every reasonable society. If this lose its power, disintegration, partial or complete, will be the result. Confidence will be weakened, and the ends of organization frustrated. Without sufficient cause no member should be absent from the prayer-meeting, or late in attendance. In case of continued absence, absentees should be visited kindly by a committee of one or two members appointed by the society, or by the ruling elder. This need in no way interfere with visits from either pastor, or elder, or any other member. If it be understood that absence is an evidence of sickness or some other providential intervention, then this would furnish a proper occasion for a voluntary visit, not likely to be offensive; for any person will receive with friendly feeling a paternal call of inquiry in relation to health and welfare. This rule, practised in kindness, would operate as a powerful stimulant to faithfulness in duty. Besides its good influences in many other respects, it will, at the same time, operate as a system by which all sickness and affliction and need of members may be known by elders and pastor.

4. In conducting the exercises members should, as near

as can be conveniently, preside in rotation. At the hour of meeting, the member whose turn it is to preside for the evening, should promptly take the chair, call the meeting to order, open its exercises by singing a portion of a psalm, reading a portion of Scripture, and with prayer by himself or some other person at his instance. Then, after singing and prayer alternately for a short time, the chairman calling on members to lead in prayer, as near as possible in rotation, the subject of conference agreed upon at the former meeting should be called up, and all the members in the order of their sitting called on to speak. After some twenty or thirty minutes being spent in conference of an intimate, simple, and affectionate Christian character, the meeting should agree upon the next place of meeting, if not otherwise understood, and upon the subject of the subsequent evening's conference, and promptly close by singing a short portion of a psalm. The whole time spent in the prayer-meeting should not, ordinarily, exceed an hour, or an hour and a half.

The importance of rotation, ordinarily, among all the members in presiding and in all the exercises, should not be overlooked. If the weak and diffident are habitually excused or passed by unnoticed, their diffidence and other infirmities will be confirmed, and consequently their usefulness permanently impaired. The prayer-meeting is one of the departments of Christ's school for training disciples for his work. There, in the secluded meeting of a few Christian friends, in the private house of neighbor and brother, the most diffident may be induced to break over that diffidence, and venture upon a course of practical training in company with others equally distrustful of themselves, and so, one encouraging another, and at the same time bearing one another's burdens, all are encouraged and trained together. Here, in the private room, the doors being shut, almost any weak brother who has ever bowed the knee in family worship, can bow in the same manner and lead in prayer with comparatively little embarrassment. The frightening embarrassments thrown around the public prayer-meeting held in the church deter many from standing up there, exposed to gaze, and leading in prayer, if called by the pastor. And more; this terror of exposure keeps many from the prayer-meeting altogether.

Many minds, by nature gifted for usefulness, are lost to the church, because by themselves buried in their own diffidence, and by their brethren overlooked and never called out in proper place for bringing into activity latent and inert mental and spiritual endowments. And let it be remembered—the Head of the church needs every gift and grace he has bestowed on every member of his body; and every one of these he has given to be developed, trained, and used. Few church members feel willing to lead in prayer, in the church, before a large congregation, and before the pastor in the desk; and fewer still, in such circumstances, can summon up courage to speak dispassionately and intelligently on any subject of conference, however simple or common-place it may be. Yet such diffident persons can be induced to bow the knee and lead in prayer at the fire-side of a friend, and in the company of a few familiar brethren; and in the same social Christian circle will venture to express their feelings and views on subjects of religion, to the edification and comfort of all. These things once ventured, and for a little while practised, the most diffident may be relied on for more public duties, and for more enlarged usefulness.

5. In regard to the exercise of *Conference* in the prayer-meeting, something more in detail may be noted in this connection. Perhaps in no other department or feature

of this precious institution is there so much and so extensive failure. Many congregations, which think they really have such a thing as a prayer-meeting, have no such thing as conference in it, and know nothing really about such a thing at all. They have hired a preacher, and they expect him to do all the religious talking for them. And if they ever go to prayer-meeting, it is to hear him talk. And hence, alas! there are so many men in the churches who can make political speeches without any particular embarrassment, who would tremble and hesitate to speak a word in a prayer-meeting on a plain religious subject, or to exchange a thought on experimental godliness for the edification of godly people. Is there nothing wrong in this state of things? And is there no remedy for these crushing evils? To meet just such a case, and just such a state of religion as these things indicate, has Christ appointed the prayer-meeting, and the conference exercise for the prayer-meeting. To meet this state of things it is appointed that professors of religion should "speak often one to another"—"exhort" and "admonish one another," "not forsaking the assembling of themselves together" for this very conference purpose. Then, to aid in securing profitable conference in every meeting, some rules may be of advantage. As,

First. The subject of conference should be agreed upon in the meeting previous to that in which it is discussed.

Secondly. Opportunity, and inducement, should be offered to every person present to speak to the subject of conference.

Thirdly. Experimental and practical questions should be carefully selected for discussion, ordinarily, if not exclusively—and controversy avoided.

Fourthly. If a text of Scripture be proposed, it will, ordinarily, be better to present a question or topic raised from it, and speak to the question proposed, rather than to the text directly. As, for example, Hosea xi. 7, "*My people are bent to backsliding.*" From this text this question might be proposed to the meeting for discussion:—*What are the signs of backsliding from God?*

This question having been before the members of the Society during the week, as a subject of reflection and prayer, could not each one have something to say, or some answer to give to the question that would aid every other member in striving against backsliding? One member might think of this sign: Beginning to dally with temptation. A second might think of this: Beginning to feel indifferent about the evil of sin. Another might think of a different answer: Less relish for spiritual things. A fourth might have his mind turned to this, as an answer: Increased difficulty in duty. Thus, in answer to the same question, involving serious experience, each might think and feel differently, and yet all rightly; each feeling his own answer to represent his own experience, would give something to profit all.

Beside the ordinary week evening prayer-meeting, held weekly in the several quarters of the congregation, meetings should be held monthly, or oftener, in the church. Here any fit person may preside, or the pastor, or an elder; and the ordinary rules observed. This may be a mass meeting, in which the whole congregation may participate. Or, it may be a meeting of the pastor, the elders, and delegates from the several weekly district meetings, especially, if the membership of the congregation be widely scattered.

The monthly general meeting of the congregation will give opportunity not only for prayer, but for the consideration of subjects relating to congregational interests—to the state of religion in the several district weekly prayer-meetings—to the cause of missions—to the general objects of benevolence, and to the awakening and cherishing of a deeper interest in the cause of Christ. Here, too, opportunity is given to each member of the congregation to form a personal acquaintance with all the members—to exchange experience and knowledge—to strengthen the bonds of unity, and encourage one another in every good work.

In large and compact congregations—and, indeed, in every congregation where circumstances will permit—the Session should have its prayer-meeting monthly, or oftener. Here the members will have opportunity for consultation and conference in relation to all matters concerning the welfare of the congregation, and matters coming under the official notice of the Session, whether of discipline, or any other matters in which pastor and elders have a joint concern. In these meetings opportunity will be offered to the elders to report from their different quarters the state of religion, and the condition of the several weekly prayer-meetings, as also anything that should require the cognizance of the Session, or the attention of the pastor. Through these, by the aid of a faithful and co-operating eldership, the pastor may always know the spiritual state of his flock, and the particular wants of every member, as also, of every opening from without for the extension of his labors and usefulness. A good Staff is sometimes of more importance than a good General-in-Chief. Indeed, without a good Staff, how much could the most skilled generalship avail? So, here, how important a discerning and faithful staff to secure ministerial success! Many fruitful fields and inviting openings for doing good are overlooked and lost to the pastor through the neglect of an eldership defective in systematic vigilance. Pastors are often charged with dereliction in duty while ignorant of the occasion of such reflections. And when a vigilant eldership brings to the notice of a pastor openings for doing good, that pastor must be wanting, indeed, who would suffer himself to fail in answering such calls. To meet all such contingencies in the administration of the affairs of a congregation, and to promote its peace and prosperity, such Sessional prayer-meeting is important.

In congregations, where numbers and other circumstances will warrant, there should be young men's prayer-meetings. Obvious considerations suggest the importance of such meetings. Young men unwilling and unfit to form prayer-meetings, will generally be found unfit for the membership and the privileges of the church. If it be a law of our Master's kingdom, that from the mouth of babes he perfects praise to the glory of his grace, then every young man in the church should be competent and willing to pray in company with his equals. Here young men of promise can be brought forward and trained for usefulness more successfully than in promiscuous meetings—much more certainly and happily than without the advantage of such associations. Here young men feel themselves among equals, and surrounded by those who can reciprocate sympathies. Here they can give utterance to their feelings and views with greater freedom from disabling fears from the presence of supposed superiors. And here the exchange of experience and sentiments will be more congenial, and the communion more of kindred spirits. Here young men can, with more liberty, discuss theological questions, benevolent enterprises, and schemes for mutual improvement. And here, beyond question, they can be trained and prepared for higher spheres of usefulness in every department of the church, and of society. By analogy, all young men's Lyceums, debating clubs, associations for literary and all other laudable organizations for mental or moral improvement, furnish strong, indeed, irrefutable argument for young men's prayer-meetings. For, if religion and religious improvement be more important than all these, then the prayer-meeting is expedient, and more important than they all.

Once more in this connection. We feel confident in affirming that it will tend greatly to promote the cause of religion, the spiritual health of a congregation, as well as the personal advantage in spiritual edification, and progress in the divine life of the persons concerned, to organize female prayer-meetings wherever a sufficient number of praying women can be conveniently gathered together for that purpose. Can any congregation deserve an organization, and be fit to sustain its efficiency, which has not in its membership as many praying women as could form a prayer-meeting? Churches encouraging and fostering the female prayer-meeting have pre-eminently the advantage of all other churches. The history of the past fully demonstrates this. John Wesley understood here two things: The spirit of religion and its power as taught in the word of God, and human nature. In his discipline, according to which he organized his societies, he drew largely upon his knowledge of the latter. Hence is sketched the plan of his female band societies for married and single women, each separately from men, and from each other. In the better days of his societies, women prayed much and frequently together. History furnishes abundant and cheering example of the importance and efficiency of female prayer-meetings.

The age is upon us when female influence is beginning to be appreciated as never before in the history of civilization and progress of the gospel. Foreign mission fields begin to resound with their earnest calls for woman to come over and help. As the spirit and power of Christianity pervade, so will woman's place and work be accorded to her. The propriety of an organized female missionary society, in every congregation where numbers justify, is conceded by, perhaps, every one. Then why not have the same material organized into a prayer-meeting? Would Christ be among them less? Would they have Christian gravity more or less? Would the bonds of sisterly affection be less strong or lasting? Would their influence upon their children for good be more or less? Would the whole generation of the seed of the church be affected for better, or for worse, by earnest female prayer-meetings in every congregation of the church? If our youth grow up in the house of God like the flourishing palm-tree, towering erect and strong, much must depend on the inclination given to the twig. And this is pre-eminently the work of pious mothers' hands.

The more praying force there is in any congregation, and the more that praying force is employed, other things being equal, the more effective power is there, the more work is done, the more growth is secured, the more prosperity is enjoyed. Then, the important practical question arises—How can that praying force be effectively called out and employed? Surely the church needs the use of all the grace that is in her. She has no surplus grace to spare, or to lie at rest and dormant—nothing to be buried in the earth—all to be put in good bank, returning her own with usury. Then, if three praying women can be found in any congregation to begin with, with those three begin the female prayer-meeting. That much is bearing interest. So much is well invested.

Thus far we have stated principles and rules for the ordinary prayer-meetings of congregations settled, or ripe for settlement, with memberships sufficient to maintain such full organizations. Small congregations, congregations greatly scattered—missionary stations, and small groups of families providentially cast together, wishing to form nuclei around which material may be gathered for the organization of congregations—these all, according to the peculiar circumstances of their several localities and surroundings, must more or less apply general principles and rules, varying and supplying as Christian prudence may dictate. Probationers and missionaries ministering in vacancies and mission stations, should perseveringly labor to secure the organization of Sabbath schools and prayer-meetings, so that every family and every member may enjoy them and give them regular attendance. If Sabbath schools and prayer-meetings were organized in all such places, and the people taught and encouraged to work in them and sustain them, so that on every Sabbath they sustain Sabbath school, and on every Sabbath day, without supply of the preaching of the word, they occupy the time of ordinary public service in prayer-meeting—these, together sustained, unite, and consolidate, and mature into vigorous growth many flourishing congregations that otherwise "*die e'er they be grown.*" One reason why so many of our vacancies and mission stations dwindle and fail, is simply because, when visited by their supplies, the probationer preaches his sermon on the Sabbath, receives his "*per diem,*" and is away: and the people are seldom, if ever, together for Sabbath school, or for the prayer-meeting, on week day or Sabbath, till another appointment of supply is to be fulfilled. If people professing a desire to build up congregations cannot be induced to sustain Sabbath schools and prayer-meetings, they had better disband, and Presbyteries had better send their supplies to labor where they can find material that can be permanently built into the church for beauty and for strength. Untempered and uncongenial material built—not into—

but only about the church, will be but lumber marring her unity and power. If well organized congregations, vigorous and growing, find from experience they can neither advance their growth nor even sustain themselves without these appliances perseveringly administered, much more will infant organizations fail of success without them. No congregation, great or small, will ever succeed without continuing steadfastly their assembling together every Sabbath day, and observing means divinely appointed for the building up of the church. Congregations are not like indigenous plants, or like Satan's tares, growing up to perfection without culture.

Our Home Missionary operations must be subjected to failure, more or less, without some radical change, not so much in principle as in the vigorous and systematic carrying out of well known and recognized truth. While the prayer-meeting is never to supplant, or interfere with public worship appointed in the word, yet when a brotherhood of disciples are grouped together, recognizing their organic fellowship and its conditions, they should feel themselves bound the more to observe the prayer-meeting in the absence of public worship, after the example of the disciples, in meeting during consecutive weeks for prayer, with the women, in their upper rooms, in the evenings of the eighth day. Just here the assembling of ourselves together has its greatest power: for just here its careful observance is most of all needed. Here it proves, as its institution indicates, the vital cord binding together, above all others, those of like spirit and faith. How, we may well challenge, can a group of Christians, of like profession, bound together in bonds of ecclesiastical organization to maintain all divine ordinances of worship, for a time destitute of ordinances, maintain their organization without either prayer-meeting or Sabbath school?

Still more, might we challenge, how can any congregation, especially one while forming and in the process of compacting, gather numbers and power while forsaking the assembling of themselves together? Who will be persuaded of their high claims upon the accession of those without, when the attractive power of their profession fails to gather themselves together in the maintenance of the institutions to which they have given their sacramental pledge? The man who believes not his own creed, will find it hard to persuade honest men to embrace it. And the man who fails to endeavor, even, to practice the duties of his profession, will find few to respect either himself or his creed. Next to the word and Sacraments stands the prayer-meeting as an instrumentality for building up the church both in holy faith and membership.

Condensing these general principles into specific rules, in reference to the Home Mission field, we notice the following:

1. In every vacant congregation, mission station, or group of church members, week-day prayer-meetings should be organized, and these should assemble weekly, or semi-monthly, or monthly, as circumstances may permit.

2. In connection with the Sabbath school, Sabbath day prayer-meeting should be held, occupying the hour of public worship when that is not supplied.

3. The prayer-meeting and Sabbath school should be so arranged that on every Sabbath all can participate in both, and so the church organization encouraged and strengthened.

4. It should be recognized as the imperative duty of all ministerial supplies, sent by Presbyteries or the Home Board, to aid, superintend, and encourage the prayer-meetings, both for the week-day and the Sabbath.

5. Presbyteries should exercise supervision and control over all these, holding congregations, missionaries, and supplies to account, as having higher pastoral charge over all vacancies, and ecclesiastical control over all their supplies.

HISTORY OF

THE PRAYER-MEETING.

PART II.

INTRODUCTION.

THE *Second Part* of this work—The *History of the Prayer-Meeting*—is designed to illustrate and confirm the truth and importance of the Prayer-meeting itself, and the view taken throughout this discussion.

If the true church from the beginning down through the ages, has observed this institution of religious worship as a *divine ordinance*, this historic fact, well established, must tend to confirm our faith in its divine authority, and in the importance of the faithful observance of the ordinance in spirit and in truth.

It is at all times the duty of the Christian and the church to observe carefully that wholesome direction of the prophet, "Thus saith the Lord, Stand ye in the ways, and see, and ask for the old paths, where is the good way, and walk therein, and ye shall find rest to your souls." Often, it may be, the Christian is in doubt in regard to what is the way to which the word of God really directs. In the midst of this doubt he may hesitate to go forward at all, but may be tempted to stand still, and remain inactive, halting between opinions where decision and promptness are demanded. Just here, that very word, which, through our weakness, seems to fail to shine directly upon our pathway, utters clearly its voice of instruction and direction, final, decisive and satisfactory: "If thou know not, O thou fairest among women, go thy way forth by the footsteps of the flock, and feed thy kids beside the shepherds' tents." The footsteps of the true church are marked distinctly by the prayer-meeting, all along, down the way of her past history.

God has had a covenant people, in all ages, distinct and separated from the world; and in nothing more distinguished than in the faithful observance of the worship of the true God, as required by himself. The footsteps of that covenant society may be traced from Enos to Malachi; from Jesus of Nazareth down through the ages to a scattered people, and holy, now in the close of the reign of antichrist—the people who worship God *in all the ways of his appointment.*

Christ and his disciples, instant in prayer, in their upper rooms, with the women, often at night, the doors being shut, left their testimony to the prayer-meeting. The primitive Christians, true to their allegiance to the Master whom they professed to follow, and whose footsteps they did promptly follow, "continued steadfastly in the apostles' doctrine and fellowship, and in breaking of bread, *and in prayers.*" In times of trial and persecution, which soon succeeded the apostolical period, "the church in the house," the church in the catacombs, the church in the "dens and caves of the earth," the church "of whom the world was not worthy," was found clustering around this precious ordinance, which holds the Master's presence.

For centuries that heroic band, in the wilderness, during the dark ages, walked through the fires of persecution; yet, like the bush burning and not burnt, that church lived by the soul-nourishing prayer-meeting—that church known and read of all. The Waldensian church stands to-day, and points back to her footsteps, extended over a thousand years, stained with blood, and marked by social prayer.

True to the footsteps of the Waldensian witnesses, the Huguenots, the churches of the Netherlands, the churches of the Covenants, National and Solemn League, were all formed with the prayer-meeting prominent in their organization. With this Knox laid Scotland's corner-stone. With this her martyrs built, and by this her faithful remnants lived and survived her "killing times." On this her faithful sons still thrive in every land where her children are dispersed, and where religion, true and vigorous, lives and grows.

The Prayer-meeting has its history. Its record will be found with that church whose footsteps are marked with blood. And, like the Ark of the Covenant, it has ever been found with those of whom the world was not worthy. History confirms the truth that wherever evangelical and vital religion flourish, there lives the earnest gatherings for social prayer. Wherever religion is revived, there the prayer-meeting is revived. Wherever religion declines, there the prayer-meeting dwindles, pines away and dies. Such are the confirmations of history.

Antichrist, with all the Sectaries which "deny the Lord that bought them," have, in their whole line of history, failed to preserve intact the prayer-meeting. Where and when have even Catholics, "good and true to holy mother," observed the prayer-meeting? Where and when have Arians, and their kindred spirits, preserved the earnest prayer-meeting? *Never!* NOWHERE!! unless under some unnatural spasmodic excitement; and then for only a brief season. The prayer-meeting has ever been cherished by evangelical and living churches only. History establishes this.

But this history has never been written. And we are led to believe no attempt really has ever been made to write it. Incidentally much that is valuable has been written. The History of Revivals, indeed the History of the Church even, could not well be written without incidentally writing more or less of the History of the Prayer-meeting. We have not written its history. We have not even pretended an approximation to such a history as would be worthy the title. We have not even attempted an outline of such a history. At most and best, we have only shown that it has a history. And we shall rejoice if we have succeeded in showing that such a history might be written—that it should be written—that the interests of true religion and of the true church demand the writing of such a history. The material is abundant; but it has never been collected or arranged. The labor adequate to such a collection alone would require as many years as the months we have spent in this work of mere incipiency—this mere gleaning from a few corners of the field. To find the material for a few of the closing chapters of such a history, and that history, too, confined to our own country, and to only fifteen years of the prayer-meetings of this land, would require the research of the files of all the leading journals which made a record of the revivals and religious conventions for some five or six years before and after 1857.

And in addition to all such research and compilation, the hidden life and practice of all the live evangelical churches, with the full detail of their church organizations, would have to be scanned and studied before such history could be even epitomized. Many histories of revivals have been written. Here more, perhaps, than anywhere else, we have collected history of prayer-meetings ; but incidentally only. If, by our feeble effort to write a brief essay on this interesting department of church history, we shall succeed in turning attention to its study, this will far more than reward us for our feeble attempt to do what we know we have but very imperfectly accomplished.

CHAPTER I.

HISTORY OF THE PRAYER-MEETING.

The Patriarchal Prayer-Meeting—Summary View from Adam to Moses.

THE History of the prayer-meeting is important from two considerations, especially. It confirms our faith in its *divine institution:* and illustrates the *Divine will* in regard to its *observance.*

If it has a divine warrant, and a place among divine ordinances of religious worship, then it will take hold upon the conscience, and impress a sense of obligation to observe it. Its observance will, at the same time, call out the exercise of faith in the promise of its Author. The Christian feels at home where Christ's name is recorded.

It has always formed the way-marks in the progress of religion, and the criterion by which its vitality has been tested. Its history establishes its relation to revivals of religion as inseparable. Wherever revivals have been enjoyed, the prayer-meeting has been the most prominent instrumentality employed in promoting them; and in retaining the spiritual vitality and activity imparted by them; and it has always followed, as a result of revivals, a blessed fruit. The prayer-meeting and the revival have always been so identified as to exhibit, in their influences and fruits, the relation of cause and effect reciprocal, each producing and reproducing the other. Many other minor considerations show the importance of the history of the prayer-meeting.

The fields from which we must glean our history here are the records of the inspired historian—the way-marks and foot-prints of the church in all her journey, from her first organization down to our own time—the history of religion and the history of revivals: for, the history of the church, the history of religion, the history of revivals--all record the prayer-meeting. The history of the one is the history of the other; sometimes the one, sometimes the other, occupying the foreground in the sketch.

It may be well to note carefully here, that this whole history is intimately connected with the history of evangelical and vital religion, whose progress always, and its very existence often, stands identified with the history of social prayer in this form. Like the history of everything else connected with the church, and forming a part of her history, and like the history of everything identified with the cause of Christ and his kingdom, in the field of the world, at first small as a grain of mustard-seed—true religion, surrounded and intermingled with prevailing false religions, the lines of the history of social prayer during the early ages must, of necessity, be very dimly drawn. Much must be left to induction and inference from facts known, and from parallel lines of history marked with more distinctness. Guided by known historic facts and first principles, which must have a place in dealing with history, as well as in all our reasonings and researches after truth, we shall be aided in forming satisfactory conclusions in regard to those periods in which the direct evidence upon this subject rises no higher than tne suggestive or probable.

Man, as a moral, religious, and social being, the *subject* of our history, will form a basis, or stand-point, from which our reasonings and inferences will shape their direction in reaching safe conclusions in regard to historic truths and their moral lessons in this investigation. Soon after the fall, intercourse was opened, through a Mediator, betwixt God and our first parents. God, the Mediator, talked with *them* in the garden: settled, in form, a talking *place* after their expulsion. The Cherubim, a symbol of Divine mercy and its administrations toward rebel and outcast man, was placed at the gate of the garden, over against the flaming sword, the symbol of inflexible retributive justice. There, under the outstretched wings of the cherubic forms, poor, trembling sinner man might creep, and again safely enter the garden, or at its gate hold communion with Him who dwells between the Cherubim, and who, from above the Mercy-Seat, talks as a reconciled God with offending man. There, at the gate, before the Cherubim and Mercy-Seat, could Adam and Eve once more *together* talk with God, and with one another. There they did talk with Him. There, as before the Tabernacle, and as in the Temple—*there*, at the gate before the Cherubim, till the increased and succeeding generations receded from the birth-place and homestead of the race, men were accustomed to meet and worship the true God as revealed in the promise. And just as the children of Adam wandered away far from access to this meeting place with God, they became wanderers, and prodigal, and vagabond, and heathenized. "Cain went out from the *presence* of the Lord, and dwelt in the land of Nod, on the east of Eden." There the Jehovah Aleim placed his Tabernacle—Shekinah—in which he placed the Cherubim, the visible symbol of his presence—there, where that symbol was placed, was his spiritual presence enjoyed, at the gate of the garden. There Adam, and Abel, and Seth, and Enos, and the sons of God called on his name—for there it was recorded, and there, from between the Cherubim, he sent out his answers, "And to Seth, to him also there was born a son; and he called his name Enos; *then began men to call upon the name of the Lord.*"

The days of Enos were times of the general apostasy of Cain and his descendants, who forsook the *place* of the worship of their fathers and their brethren—the *place* where Adam and Eve *together* held conference, meeting with God—where Abel offered his acceptable sacrifice—where Adam, Seth, Enos—"men began to call upon the name of the Lord." And have we not here substantially the prayer-meeting? We have *men* of God *calling on the name of the Lord.* This is prayer. The terms of historic record leave no historic doubt. To call on the name of the Lord is no inferential phrase. It represents, and so fixes in the mind, historic fact, prayer. Men prayed. This is more than suggestion. The deduction is natural—easy. Men *together* called on God. This is the social prayer-meeting?

In the early part of the life of Adam, social worship was confined to the family. Adam and Eve conferred with God in Eden, and at its gate after the erection of the Shekinah and the Cherubim. Here Adam and family united in their religious and social devotions. After the race had increased, and Adam's children of the second and third generations were formed into families, Adam, Seth, and Enos, with their families, drawn the more closely together by the influence of the surrounding apostasy, united for the maintenance of the true religion, and for the enjoyment of social fellowship in the communion of saints. This must have been the highest ordinance of religious worship enjoyed. Neither Tabernacle nor Temple services were yet instituted. The head of each family officiated as its priest in offering up its sacrifices, as Noah after coming out from the Ark. Or, individuals, as Abel, offered their offerings for themselves. But now, the "*men*" who "called upon the name of the Lord," with their households, Seth and his younger brothers, Enos and his junior brethren—all these households, meeting together to call on God by prayer, would form a prayer-meeting of great interest, as affording a rallying point where the "sons of God" could enjoy each other's fellowship, sustain the cause of God in jeopardy in evil times, and secure his favor and fellowship in the institutions of his grace. This form of organism being the only visible one by which the church was distinguished from the world—the "sons of God" from the "sons of men"—would be retained so long as the spirit animating Enos should continue, which was probably till the time of Noah, when corruption almost universally prevailed. After the flood, Noah and his sons would probably preserve visible organic worship as it obtained in the days of Enos. His family, with the families of his three sons, like Adam, Seth, and Enos, would as carefully observe their assembling for prayer as retain the worship of the Altar, which, we know from the record, he did.

After the Flood—till Abraham—and during patriarchal times.

That the state of religion began soon after the generations of the flood to decline, is evident from the very brief history of the times. During the period covering the time of Cush and Nimrod, the tower of Babel, the confusion of tongues and dispersions of mankind, to the calling of Abraham, irreligion, idolatry, and corruption of the true worship, greatly prevailed. During this dark period scarcely a trace can be seen of the visible church, as marked in the history of the times, or of the social worship of God in any form. The times of revival came. Abraham is separated from the prevailing idolatry, and appears as a patriarch at the head of a numerous and powerful household, numbering its many hundreds, and all trained in the knowledge and practice of the true religion. He immediately, after migrating from Haran, and pitching his tent in the land promised him, set up the worship of the altar and social prayer. As prophet and head of the church in his household, consisting of scores of families, each with its own family religion, family instruction, and family prayer, he gathered them together, and by system "*trained*" them. As priest, he built his altar, and there, in the presence of his numerous household, forming a congregation of the Lord's worshiping people of many hundreds assembled around the bloody sacrifice, and in awful silence contemplating the way of salvation through the blood of atonement, he trains them in the true worship of the true God.

For, let it be remembered, the patriarchal religion, government, and worship, were both domestic and social. There were single families in which the relations of parents and children, with all their corresponding obligations, were recognized. "Abraham commanded his children and household after him." In his family were parental training on the one hand, and filial obedience on the other, as required by the Fifth Commandment. Here was the plan for the family altar and its worship, morning and evening, a worship incorporated with the religion of the Abrahamic and Mosaic economy, so that *this* was familiar to every pious Hebrew—"Let my prayer be set forth before thee as incense," referring to the morning worship—"And the uplifting of my hands as the evening sacrifice," referring to evening worship.

Many families voluntarily grouped under one head and civil lord—not altogether like the feudal lord, yet in some respects similar, or similar to the chief of a Highland clan of Scottish history—as also, under one head and religious teacher, they formed a household and enjoyed a social and select worship corresponding. Eliezer was head of a single family, where were all its relations and obligations, its worship and family privileges. He was also a member of Abraham's household, not of his family. To him he stood related as a subject, and, in common with others of the household, he sustained the relation of a brother in the household of faith, and of the circumcised in the same covenant with God, enjoying the privileges of social worship, as well as of private family religion.

The school of the altar was not enough for the father of the faithful. He planted a grove where, according to the law regulating the worship of God, no altar could be permitted. "And Abraham planted a grove in Beersheba, and called there on the name of the Lord, the everlasting God." For, in the giving of the law by Moses in the wilderness, the worship of the altar and the grove were clearly distinguished and regulated. "Thou shalt not plant thee a grove of any trees near unto the altar of the Lord thy God, which thou shalt make thee." Deut. xvi. 21. Abraham faithfully observed all God's commands. He faithfully observed the ordinance of the Proseucha, or worship of the grove, as he did the worship of the altar. In all this, as the father of the faithful, he was a pattern of faithfulness. So he taught and trained his children and his household; and so, by the power of his moral and spiritual influence, commanded their affections and obedience after him. Then here, by induction, we know that Isaac, and Jacob, and their children and households, observed the worship of God, as taught and exemplified by their father Abraham.

Though the prayer-meeting, in the latter days of the bondage of the children of Israel in Egypt, may have been more or less neglected, we are certain when the deliverance came, with it the great revival came, and with this the institution of social prayer was revived, and by statute separated, in its observance ever after, from the altar worship, whether under the Tabernacle or Temple service. As the law was given very soon after entering the wilderness, Moses would put into operation that law in regard to both the altar worship and the grove worship. Consequently, that generation, which entered the land promised to Abraham, was a race well trained in all the statutes and ordinances of worship as observed by their fathers.

CHAPTER II.

SUMMARY SKETCH FROM MOSES TO CHRIST.

DIRECT history, in form, makes very little reference to the worship of the grove till the times of the revolt of the ten tribes. We are, however, more than compensated in the abundant moral evidence furnished in another form.

That revolt was quickly followed by a general decline of religion, and by the gross corruption of divinely instituted worship. Among those corruptions was that which sunk the proseucha into oblivion. The humble prayer-meeting, with its spiritual exercises and its sweet communion with God, was lost to those apostate sons of praying fathers. The grove was changed from being the place of quiet and retirement for prayer—as at the river side, where praying women, in after and better times, resorted—to a place for the revels of the noisy worshipers of Baal, and the blood, and smoke, and incense of his bloody sacrifices. Thus that ordinance, which always flourishes where true religion is strong in its vital and spiritual power, was, for political reasons of state policy, suppressed by the leading spirits of the revolt.

The entire silence on the subject of the abuse of the worship of the grove, during the long period from Joshua to Jeroboam, and then afterwards that abuse so often and so prominently denounced, is evidence that it did not prevail during that period of silence. This is the more evident from the record of the lives, and labors, and character of the men of those times—the Judges, the Kings, the

Prophets sent of God, and the Priests, the expounders of the law, and the guardians of the public institutions of religious worship.—And still more, from the character of the writers of the devotional books penned by inspired men, from Moses to Elijah. Here we may find the compensating testimony condensed, and embracing the true history of the state of religion during that eminently historic period of the whole history of that historic people—in their *formulary of worship.* The hymnology of every worshiping people, in every age, in every country, of every religion, true or false, of every creed and kind of forms practised, will reveal the distinctive features of their worship. So we learn from the devotional complexion of the Book of Psalms, whose compilation commenced with Moses, and was carried forward during that entire period, and forward till near the closing of the O. T. canon. These inspired songs, prepared for the use of the church, and representing what should be the character of her religious devotions in all ages, at the same time reflect upon the usages and form of service to which they were at first adapted. Many of the Psalms use a form of expression plainly requiring an application to the social worship of the saints in social meetings, distinct from the family, from the altar, from the tabernacle, and from the temple. Now, if the Book of Psalms, most of which was prepared during the historic period before us, is full of allusions to social exercises, and so much of it adapted to private social devotions, the historical evidence is conclusive, that during that long period the fellowship prayer-meeting was known and observed by the pious people of God, who spoke often one to another, and who, in the familiar language of their manual of social praise, were in the habit of saying one to another, and singing, "All that fear God, come, hear, I'll tell what he did for my soul." "Extol the Lord *with me, let us together* praise his name."

"My God, my soul's cast down in me;
Thee, therefore, mind I will
From Jordan's land, the Hermonites,
And even from Mizar hill"—

the "little" hill of social worship, when far from access to Zion hill.

"Behold, bless ye the Lord, all ye
That his attendants are,
Even you that in God's temple be,
And praise him *nightly* there"—

the prayer-meeting of the priests, who by wards and during the night watches held private meetings out of season, and at hours when no other worship or service, public or private, was held.

"With my whole heart I will God's praise declare,
Where the assemblies of the just, and congregations are."

"Bethsud," is the "private," as well as public assembly, "I am companion to all those who fear, and thee obey"—that is, "I associate with" the fearers of God in select social worship. We might multiply quotations of like character from the book breathing so much of the social and private devotional spirit and form.

With reference to the captivity and return, Jeremiah predicted social prayer: "Then shall *ye* call upon me, and *ye* shall go and pray unto me, and I will hearken unto you. And *ye* shall seek me, and find me, when *ye* shall search for me with all your heart." Jer. xxix. 12, 13. This was fulfilled in Daniel when he set his face to seek the Lord by prayer and supplications, with fasting. Dan. ix. 3. It was fulfilled in Ezra at the river Ahava. It was fulfilled in

Zech. vii. 2: "When they had sent unto the house of God Sherezer and Regem-melech, and their men to pray before the Lord." It was fulfilled as in Mal. iii. 16: "Then they that feared the Lord spake often one to another; and the Lord hearkened and heard" their social prayers.

In seeking historical evidence it is proper to refer to the habits the devout Hebrew captives would carry with them in their captivity. So we find them grouped together by the rivers of Babylon, in solemn, sad devotion—in praise with unstrung harps, while far from temple service—while remembering Jerusalem they send up their prophetic prayers: "Remember, O Lord, the children of Edom." Daniel called his pious and worshiping associates together for select social prayer according to the custom and religious usages of his fathers. "And Daniel went to his house, and made the thing known to Hananiah, Mishael, and Azariah, his companions: that they would desire mercies of the God of heaven concerning this secret; that Daniel and his followers should not perish with the rest of the wise men of Babylon." Can it be doubted by the student of history that Daniel and his friends were familiar with that great principle underlying this call for a special prayer-meeting?—"That if two of you shall agree on earth as touching anything they shall ask, it shall be done for them of my Father which is in heaven. For where two or three are gathered together in my name, there am I in the midst of them." Esther, in her extremity, according to the well-known usages of her people, bade Mordecai "Go, gather together all the Jews that are present in Shushan. I also, and my maidens, will fast likewise." Since prayer is an established concomitant of fasting, this was an example of the prayer-meeting.

Emergencies furnish the surest tests of men's real principles, and their faith in God. When in affliction, they feel the occasion is not opportune for indulging in hypocritical show. If men will ever truly exhibit what they really are, or what they feel they ought to be, it will be when death comes, or when troubles overwhelm like a resistless flood. "In straits they cry to God." This is even nature's law. God's people feel their natures subjected to its control, and by gracious impulses cling to God in all their straits.

Ezra, conducting a column of captives, returning from Babylon, through an enemy's land, dangers besetting them on every side, gathered them together at the river Ahava. Independent of both Priest and Levite to conduct any public service, he proclaimed a fast, that they might afflict themselves before their God, to seek of Him a right way for them, "for the hand of our God is upon all them for good that seek him." "So we fasted and *besought* our God for this; and he was *entreated* of us." In these exercises no official ministrations were required. Neither Temple nor altar was there. This special prayer-meeting was to meet the emergency. The priests and Levites were not, as yet, separated and consecrated, either for offering the regular sacrifices, or for conducting the public worship as divinely instituted. Afterwards, at the organization of the synagogue and its worship, by authority of Ezra the Scribe, the priests and Levites expounded the law to the people. As the priests, the sons of Levi, were the legal expounders of the law, they, at the institution of the synagogue worship, were called in to exercise their official functions. These functions we learn from their commission: "And now, O ye priests, this commandment is for you. And ye shall know that I have sent this commandment unto you, that my covenant might be with Levi. The law of truth was in his mouth; for the priest's lips should keep knowledge, and they should seek the law at his mouth: for he is the messenger of the Lord of hosts." Mal. ii. 1–7. So, when first called by Ezra in setting up the worship of the synagogue (Neh. viii.), "Ezra the priest brought the law before the congregation both of men and women, and all that could hear with understanding, upon the first day of the seventh month. And he read therein before the street that was before the water-gate, from the morning until mid-day, before the men and the women, and those that could understand; and the ears of all the people were attentive unto the book of the law. The priests and the Levites caused the people to understand the law; and the people stood in their place. So, they read in the book, in the law of God, distinctly, and gave the sense, and caused them to understand the reading." From the first institution of the synagogue, its worship was always conducted by official persons—by the ordained, legalized, expounders of the law, to which the official preaching and teaching in the gospel ministrations of the Sabbath corresponds, as illustrated in the Saviour's example. Luke iv. 27.

This synagogue worship, then instituted, and specially for the reading and expounding of the word of God, obtained as the leading ordinance of divinely instituted worship among the Jews till the coming of Christ, when, under his ministrations and his apostles', it was merged into the ordinary weekly public worship of the New Testament, and so passed over and into the new dispensation. For it is conceded on all hands, that the New Testament church, in her worship and order, is modeled, not after the temple, but the synagogue service. The temple with its entire ritual, was typical and abolished. The service of the synagogue was spiritual and moral, and was not abolished, but substantially retained and transferred into the New Testament service. The synagogue worship was, therefore, distinct from the temple service, and was as certainly distinct from the grove or proseucha worship, and so from the prayer-meeting recognized by Malachi, by Christ, by his apostles and the early Christians, who "continued steadfastly in prayers," "in their upper rooms, with the women, the doors being shut," and who "forsook not the assembling of themselves together, as the manner of some was," but observed the ordinance in which every private Christian could enjoy the privilege of "exhorting one another."

It is remarkable that so soon after the revivals and reforms under the teachings of the prophets Haggai and Zachariah, and under the governments of Joshua and Zerubbabel, and later under Ezra and Nehemiah, there should be such a falling away from practical and vital religion as in the time of Malachi. And yet it is as remarkable that there were some, in the midst of general defection among priests and people, who recognized each other as kindred spirits, and by a mutual attraction were drawn together in pious conference. "Then they that feared the Lord spake often one to another; and the Lord hearkened, and heard it, and a book of remembrance was written before him for them that feared the Lord, and that thought upon his name." In the history of these times, we have the most humbling lessons of the depth of human depravity. After the sorest judgments, followed by wonderful deliverances, and these accompanied with warnings, instructions and exhortations, still the tendency of the masses with their leaders was backward from God and the ways of true religion. In these times we have also the cheering historical fact that God, in accordance with the analogy of the divine government, and the dispensations of his grace, preserved a remnant of pious and practical adherents to his cause, who mourned over the defections of the times, and were drawn the more closely together in private religious conference and prayer. "They spake often one to another." The Lord hearkened and answered their prayers. In these select private assemblies, piety was cultivated, and a seed preserved in the church during the waning period, and during the long, dark night which preceded the rising of the Sun of Righteousness with healing in his wings.

CHAPTER III.

FROM CHRIST TO THE REFORMATION.

Revival—Means of—Fruits of—Concerted Social Prayer—Church in the House—Church in the Catacombs—Pliny to Trajan—Pagan Persecutions—The Waldenses—Papal Persecutions—Lessons of this Period.

THE history of the Prayer-meeting at the introduction of Christianity, and in connection with the history of the ministry of Christ and his apostles, and the revival of religion, which so remarkably distinguished the first century of the Christian era, might justly occupy a large space in this historical sketch. Inasmuch as the historic incidents will be found in another connection, and interwoven with the evidences of the divine appointment of the prayer-meeting as an ordinance of grace, references, which might otherwise be greatly extended, will here be brief.

Revival of religion, the means of promoting it, and its fruits will ordinarily appear simultaneously together, maintain their inseparable connection, and move on together harmoniously, as one simple monument and display of divine gracious power. Means produce a revival, in the popular sense as used here. Revival gives increase and power, life, invigorating efficacy to means. And this identifies means with fruits. Means would be nothing but hardening instrumentalities without the grace of the divine Spirit, as a Spirit of life, moving upon the heart renewed, and prompting to the use of means. Earnest resort to means of revival is evidence of the inward impulse of the grace of revival, and at the same time the means and fruit of that revival. Such are the apparent anomalies, and yet the real laws of revival of religion. Revival ordinarily begins with some individual. Its first impulse is felt by some one in whose heart is the grace of the divine Spirit. That first impulse leads to prayer. The social principle, as a religious element of our nature, moved by this first impulse of revival, leads its subject revived to the society of kindred spirits and to social prayer. Two or three are brought together; they agree and ask for the Spirit. The Spirit already prompting to prayer is enjoyed in his enlarged influences more and more in answer to prayer by concert in the social prayer-meeting. Thus the Spirit of God gives revival, and by his grace carries it forward. Revivals during the ministrations of Christ and his apostles furnish historic illustration of these views.

Christ was himself eminently a man of prayer. When he gathered about him a group of disciples, he taught them to pray. He so practised social prayer with his disciples that it formed a custom with them. He went, "as he was wont to do," with his disciples to the Mount of Olives to pray. Prayer with his disciples apart, secluded from the multitudes, was by him and them formed into a religious habit. It was in this school of prayer and religious conference—for their prayer-meetings were conference meetings—that the disciples were trained for that active and glorious work of revival in which they were afterwards employed, and which turned the world upside down. In connection with their prayer-meetings in Jerusalem, in which they waited the promised outpouring of the Spirit, revival came. The Spirit was poured out and greatly enjoyed by them, and by the first Christians, imbued by the same Spirit, and who, "continued steadfastly in prayers." They had a well known social ordinance "called *prayer*."

If anything characterized and distinguished the apostolical Christians, it was devotedness to the cause of Christ as manifested in their steadfast continuance in prayers. Their alms, and, indeed, their whole Christian deportment, which made them living epistles, known and read of all men, made them conspicuous. But the power of prayer—concerted prayer eminently—formed the life-spring and impulsive cause of all that distinguished them, and their revived religion, from all others.

The practice of Christ and his disciples, in meeting together in private rooms—upper rooms—with the women—with the doors shut, for prayer and conference, distinct as to place, time, and form of service, from both Temple and Synagogue, was long retained among the early Christians. Toward the close of the first century, and in the time of the Epistles to the churches, probably vacant, this institution was called "*The church in the house.*" This cannot refer to the family, or the church there: for that is never spoken of as an assembly called out, or called together. "*Ekklesia*" is the proper term for an assemblage convened together for social worship. The Christians of the churches at Rome, at Corinth and Colosse, especially when without pastors, were conspicuous for their steadfastness in prayers, for which they assembled, as did the pentecostal church, in their private houses, in little bands. They observed these Christian conference meetings in their houses for mutual edification, as the principal means of keeping intact their incipient organizations, and of preserving from scattering and from final disintegration. While it was safe to meet in their houses, they did so, "not forsaking the assembling of themselves together; but exhorting one another; and so much the more as they saw the day approaching" when persecutions would set in—remove from them their faithful pastors, make it unsafe to assemble in their public meeting places for the hearing of the word, and even in their private houses for prayer, and so drive them to the caves and dens of the earth, and finally to the "Catacombs, for safety from the rage of Pagan persecution."

With pleasure we here insert a paragraph from Dr. Houston, Ireland—P. 67. "*Fellowship Prayer-meetings*," taken from "*The Church in the Catacombs*," by Charles Maitland, Esq.:

"The records of the Church in the Catacombs, so singularly brought to light in late years, show that when the power of Imperial Rome was wielded against the religion of Christ, his church found a secure shelter among the tombs of believing brethren, and received nourishment and comfort, too, from the private communion of saints in feeding on the word, and in united prayer and praise."

Pliny, writing to the Emperor Trojan, in the year 103, on the subject of pressing the edicts for persecuting the Christians, earnestly dissuades from persistence, assuring him they were a harmless people, chargeable with no crime, only they were in the habit of "meeting together to sing songs"—"*discere carmen*"—"and to worship Christ as God." This was the practice of the Christians throughout all the Roman Provinces; a practice retained from the Apostles' times, of "continuing steadfastly in prayer," the well known term for the prayer-meeting. During the imperial persecutions, from the best evidence gathered from the writings of the Fathers, and the history of the times, we have good reason to infer the continued practice of the persecuted Christians during the periods of the decline of true religion and the rise of the man of sin. This view is confirmed by the historic evidence that "*The Two Witnesses*," who, after the rise of the man of sin, were seen in the ecclesiastical heavens, re-exhibiting apostolical purity in doctrine and worship, the ordinance of the prayer-meeting reappears in its former simplicity. "*The church in the house*" is again frequented, and the humble assembly of private saints gathered together for "exhorting one another"—like the Ark in the city of the wood—is found in the valleys of Piedmont and among the dells of the Alps.

The Waldenses.

The period of the history of the Waldenses, as a distinct and witnessing people appearing on the page of history, brings to view the importance of the prayer-meeting in its historic features and consequence. The church had, by prophetic monition, been forewarned of that terrible power which should make war with the saints, scatter the power of the holy people, cast out of his mouth water as a flood after the woman driven to the wilderness, and that should make war with the remnant of her seed, which keep the commandments of God, and have the testimony of Jesus Christ. She had been warned of the times when her faithful sons must put on the garments of mourning, and retire to the seclusions prepared for the sackcloth wearers, while the holy city should be trodden under foot forty and two months. "And I will give power unto my two witnesses, and they shall prophesy a thousand two hundred and three-score days, clothed in sackcloth."

It is, doubtless, well said by the historian of this wonderful people—"The Waldenses preserved divine truth in its purity, when Christendom was overrun with antichristian corruptions, and were true to their motto, '*Lux in tenebris*,' and maintained a faithful profession, and enjoyed the communion of saints in meetings for prayer and spiritual converse. When the savage persecutions of the papacy destroyed their sanctuaries, and interdicted their public assemblies for worship—when their humble, but devoted 'Barbes' were cut off, or forced into exile—and when, by the rage of the enemy, the Waldenses were expelled in a body out of their native country—in all emergencies they had recourse to meetings for united prayer, as the great means of support and relief under long continued and severe persecution, and as the divinely appointed way of animating the hope of future deliverance. Ecclesiastical history records the marked attention of these early witnesses to this ordinance at different periods of their eventful history; and there can be no doubt that to it, in a large measure, are to be ascribed their remarkable unity in faith, and in godly practice, and their heroic constancy in sufferings. In the latter period of the Waldensian trials, shortly before the dawn of the Reformation, when 'darkness that might be felt' had settled down upon the nations of Europe, when faithful witnesses had been almost wholly exterminated—when the voice of public protest against Rome's idolatry and oppression was nowhere distinctly heard throughout western Christendom, we have on record an affecting testimony to the value which the remnant of these ancient confessors still set upon the social prayer-meeting."

It is recorded, that at that time one lonely *society*, which met in one of the secluded valleys of the Alps—brooding over the low condition of Christendom, and deeply concerned to see if there was any quarter whence deliverance might be expected—after prayerful consideration, dispatched *four* of their number, with instructions to travel north, south, east, and west, to inquire if there were any churches that held fast an evangelical profession, and maintained separation from the general corruption. After an absence of more than a year, these delegates returned with the melancholy intelligence that they had found none. Still these "marked ones," who sighed and mourned for the "abominations of the land," did not relinquish prayer, or "*forsake the assembling of themselves together.*"

History is important mainly for its inductive moral lessons, marking out, in the footprints of the past, the ways of safety, and the ways of danger. Its beacon errors warn us, and its records of truth and virtue shine upon our pathway, and stimulate us to perseverance in the footsteps of "them who through faith and patience inherit the promises." In studying the history of that wonderful people, who, for a thousand years, have, like "the bush that burned and yet was not consumed," survived the fires of persecution, the earnest student will, almost irresistibly, inquire—Where lies the indestructibility of that venerable church of the centuries? How has she outlived the earthquake shocks and revolutions of the ages? And with her surviving identity, how has she preserved, through all the successive cycles of declensions and revivals, her untarnished historic form, whose kindred and affinity all the evangelical churches to this day would assume as theirs? What vital principle, or recuperative element, in her organic structure has been so signally owned and blessed by the Head of the church, as the instrumentality honored in her wonderful preservation? While other means had their happy influences here, yet nothing but a continued series of miracles could have preserved that people through a thousand years of fiery trials, had they abandoned their fellowship meetings for prayer and conference. Whether at times when they enjoyed the gospel with the living ministry, or when scattered as sheep without a shepherd, as often they were—destitute, afflicted, tormented—wandering in deserts, and in mountains, and in dens, and in caves of the earth, these meetings were ever their rallying-points—these their muster-fields—these their burning watch-fires and signals, seen from mountain top to hill top—these the bond that bound in one, from generation to generation, and saved from disintegration. Try it—What church organization, now, with its loose views and looser practice in regard to the prayer-meeting, could, for one generation, survive the fiery ordeal through which that people passed for successive ages? Take any single church among us, boasting of its evangelical character, its unity, its numbers, and its power, place it without the prayer-meeting, under the scathing power that was brought to bear upon the Waldenses, and, like the snow beneath the rays of an August sun, it would soon pass into vapor. What one of the popular churches of the day could stand the fiery trial? Not one. Why, without stated supplies—without the gaudy appendages of a fashionable ecclesiastical organization, in the sunshine days of perfect peace, liberty of conscience, no over-riding civil establishment, what group of emigrants of the same profession, thrown together in the same remote locality, can be held together for a few years only, and by the attraction of principle, and love for one another, can be kept from scattering to the winds? A group of Christians imbued with love to Christ, love to his cause, love to brethren and their fellowship, and possessing within themselves the principle of reciprocal attraction, the inward principle of spiritual gravitation, will be drawn together, as kindred spirits, and then bound together by a weekly prayer-meeting, will, almost infallibly, form a nucleus that will, in a short time, gather around it a permanent and live congregation that will survive trials, and persecutions, and even destitution of pastors, of supplies, and of gaudy accommodations. Such are the historic lessons taught us by a survey of the history of that wonderful people.

On the other hand—how many, perhaps hundreds every year, emigrate from abroad to our Atlantic shores, connect with our Eastern churches, by-and-by take their certificates of membership, and with others, home-born and trained in our midst, settle in the West, and some half dozen of families are thrown within a radius of three or four miles, and because they have no minister to organize and conduct the prayer-meeting, as was the custom under which they were trained, they neglect it, attend "*higher ordinances*" in some other communion, and in a brief time all are gone. The farther use of this lesson we pass now, transferring it to another connection.

CHAPTER IV.

FROM THE REFORMATION TO THE REVOLUTION, 1688.

Continental Reformation—The Church of Scotland—John Knox—His Letter—The General Assembly of 1641—Its prolonged consequences—Prelatic domination—Prayer-meeting spirit brought from Ireland alarmed the Prelatists—Five Articles of Perth—"The Society People."

WE may trace the same lines in the history of the Reformations under Wickliffe, Huss, Jerome, the churches of Bohemia, the Culdees of Britain, the Huguenots of France, the churches of Switzerland, and we find that the prayer-meeting has been the life of them all. So true is this in the history of all those reformations, of their times and of their people, that the armies of the Zuinglians, of the Huguenots, of the Dutch Republics, of the United Netherlands, and others, held their prayer-meetings in their camps, as Cromwell's, in later times; and even in the face of the foe, when drawn up in line of battle, quickly, before joining issue, the soldiers drew their Psalters from their vest pockets, sang a psalm, dropped down on their knees, their firelocks at stand arms—a brief prayer—then up and at them. (Motley's Hist.) These prayer-meetings among the soldiers of the armies of the Dutch Republics, as far back as the times of William the Silent, Prince of Orange, have much to do with the full tide of civil and religious liberty enjoyed by us to-day. Trace back American liberty—all that is noble and Christian in it—along whatever line of history we may, to English Puritans, to Holland or Scotch Presbyterians, we will find its cradle is the prayer-meeting.

A chapter of thrilling interest might be written here, showing, from unquestioned history, that the prayer-meeting has ever been the nursery of civil and religious liberty. It is an institution thoroughly democratic—an institution of the people, for the people, and administered by the people; an institution that recognizes the perfect equality of every one admitted to its privileges—and to these all have a right. It knows no aristocracy—no caste—no class. Here the Prince and the beggar sit down together—here the Pastor and the layman officiate alike—here the male and the female, the old and the young—all that pray, may mingle together in the enjoyment of equal rights and equal powers. This institution of the free in Christ could not live or breathe in the atmosphere of popery. Nor can popery breathe in the atmosphere of the free prayer-meeting. Think of it.—Imagine a prayer-meeting of the Catholic peasantry, in any Catholic country, met together to pray, to sing psalms, to read the Bible, to explain and confer on its blessed teachings! Could it live a year?—a month? Would not the priesthood suppress it in less than a fortnight? And why? Just because it would promote, not only intelligence and piety, but especially because it would foster *liberty, civil* and *religious.* The same reasons for separating the people from all participation in any social religion, not conducted by the priesthood, will separate the people forever from the free privileges of the people's institution—the free prayer-meeting. Why has a Catholic no *family* worship? Why has he no religious worship, as his own, higher than his bead-counting prayers, or his lone *"Ave Maria"?* Because *social* religious rights—*social* religious worship, are all in the hands of the priesthood.

We must pass over, with very brief notice, a long period of the early Continental Reformations. Our space limits us to mere selections and sketches, and admonishes us of the importance of judicious selections here. We shall, therefore, now for a little, turn, for gleanings, to

THE CHURCH OF SCOTLAND.

This noble old church—the mother of us all—not at all particularly singular here, but like most of the daughters of the Protestant Reformation, was born and nursed in the prayer-meeting. Protestantism itself is a social religion—a religion of the people—a religion for the people; it flings away the shackels of Papal tyranny from the conscience, puts the Bible into the hands of all, and opens for the masses free, social intercourse, and unrestricted Christian fellowship; and it points to the social prayer-meeting for its fullest enjoyment. The Church of Scotland seems, from the very incipiency of her organization, to have recognized the claims of the prayer-meeting as a divine ordinance, more distinctly and formally than other churches of the Reformation, which retained more of the shadows of the Romish ritualism.

It is well known to all familiar with its history, that the Church of Scotland received much of its distinctive character and spirit from its leading Reformer, John Knox. While the reformer was a refugee from persecution in his own native land, he wrote from the continent in the year 1557, to his countrymen friendly to the cause of the Reformation, with the express view of calling *the people* to a *leading* and *active* part in the work without, and independently of the ruling powers both of the church and of the state. At this time the people were destitute of reformed pastors to lead them in the cause of Reformation. Calderwood records, in his History of the Church of Scotland, thus:

"In October following, he sent some letters to the Lords, and to particular gentlemen, wherein he proved that the reformation of religion and public enormities did appertain to more than to the clergy and chief rulers. His letters being read, it was concluded, after consultation, that they would prosecute their purpose once intended. That every one might be the more assured of the other, a common band was formed, wherein they promised before God, with their whole power and hazard of their lives, to set forward, and establish the true religion."

Dr. McCrie, in his "Life of Knox," writes of the same letter, (p. 58,) thus:

"In this letter he warmly recommended to every one the careful and frequent reading of the Scriptures. He inculcated the duty of attending to religious instruction and worship in each family. He exhorted the brethren to meet together once every week, if practicable, and gave them directions for conducting their assemblies in the manner best adapted to their mutual improvement, *while destitute of public teachers.* They ought to begin with confession of sins, and invocation of the Divine blessing. A portion of the Scriptures should then be read; and they would find it of great advantage to observe a regular course in their reading, and to join a chapter of the Old and New Testament together. After the reading of the Scriptures, if an exhortation, interpretation, or doubt occur to any brother, he might speak; but he ought to do it with modesty, and a desire to edify or to be edified, carefully avoiding multiplication of words, perplexed interpretation, and wilfulness in reasoning. If, in the course of reading or conference, they met with any difficulties which they could not solve, he advised them to commit these to writing before they separated, that they might submit them to the judgment of the learned; and he signified his own readiness to give them his advice by letters whenever it should be required. Their assemblies ought always to be closed, as well as opened, with prayer. There is every reason to conclude that these directions were punctually complied with; this letter, therefore, may be viewed as an important document regarding the state of the Protestant Church in Scotland, previous to the establishment of the Reformation, and shall be inserted at large in the notes."

In turning over to the letter itself in full, (p. 159, note 25,) we find, farther:

"It shall greatly comfort you to hear that harmony and well-tuned song of the Holy Spirit.—Like as your assemblies ought to begin with confession and invocation of God's Holy Spirit, so would I that they be never finished without thanksgiving."

This letter certainly furnishes a remarkable directory for the government, order, and exercises of the prayer-meeting among the laity. Here are recommended, as agreeable to the teachings of the word of God, prayer, praise, reading the Scriptures, and religious conference; as also the full and free expression of opinion in regard to the meaning of any portion of Scripture that might come before them, without superstitious fear of expounding, as if the exclusive and official prerogative of the clergy. What a glorious deliverance secured by the Protestant Reformation, asserting to every man the right to use the Scriptures, as the noble Bereans did when testing the teachings even of Paul and Silas, who were ordained official expounders of the inspired oracles.

Another historian remarks of this period:

"Especially in many country districts, and in remote localities, the cause of the Reformation was nursed into life and vigor, and the souls of believers were edified by reading the Scriptures, and by united prayer and praise."

Here we may notice a significant incident, which occurred in the time of the Second Reformation in Scotland, and in the General Assembly of 1641. A malcontent, and soon afterward an apostate and bishop, made complaint in regard to some supposed liberties or abuses in these prayer-meetings in regard to expounding Scripture, and also of the practice of families grouping together for family worship. Here prelatic proclivities might pervert a prayer-meeting into the family worship by proxy. The Assembly passed an Act limiting family worship to the members of the household, and forbidding several families from uniting together in worship, directing each to worship separately; also forbidding the laity to expound Scripture in the prayer-meetings. Hetherington, in his History, notices this Act, and refers to the injurious consequences which long followed. While it did not prohibit the prayer-meeting by any means—for that object avowed would have taken off the mask and have revealed the covert prelatic design—yet the ill-disposed abused it to the harm of religion.

Hetherington, giving the occasion of the action of the Assembly, says:

"During the domination of the prelatic party, many religious people had withdrawn from the ministry of men from whom they derived no spiritual instruction; but, to supply the want to the utmost of their power, they had adopted the measure of meeting together in private, and engaging in reading the Scriptures, exhortation and prayer, for their mutual edification. Several who had been in Ireland and other countries for a considerable time, had been so confirmed in this custom, that even after the Assembly, the abolition of prelacy, and the restoration of the purer and simpler mode of Presbyterian worship, they still continued their practice of holding these private religious meetings. The more pious ministers saw nothing offensive or improper in such private meetings of Christian worshippers; but there were others who looked on them with less favorable regard."

It is judiciously remarked by the same author, that the discouragement shown to private fellowship meetings, at this time, produced afterwards the most injurious consequences. He says:

"This unseemly and ill-omened contention may be regarded as the first insertion of the wedge by which the Church of Scotland was afterward rent asunder; and it deserves to be remarked that it was pointed and urged on by a prelatist!"

Here is a remarkable historical incident, the only one of the kind on record, in regard to ecclesiastical action of a reformed and reforming church, which *seems* even to discourage the prayer-meeting, and that, too, led on by a covert enemy, through whose deep design something not suspected or designed by true friends of the Reformation and living piety, was partially accomplished. All evangelical and pious historians of the times concur in lamenting the unfortunate and unhappy mistake of the Assembly of 1641. Though designed by the Assembly to correct some *supposed* irregularities only, enemies took advantage, to the lasting damage of true religion. At the same time, this section of the history of the prayer-meeting attests its importance, its universal prevalence among the Evangelical Reformed Churches, and that neglect of its observance or hostility was confined to the prelatic and ritualistic party, or to enemies of vital and practical godliness.

We suggest farther here: We have a warning of the peril of hasty "declaratory legislation of General Assemblies."

It will, perhaps, throw some light upon this portion of our history, as also upon the general history of the prayer-meeting, as identified always with the history of revival of religion, to notice the connection of this incident of 1641 with a remarkable *revival in Ireland* in 1625, and persecutions following, which drove many persecuted Christians to Scotland for shelter from the rage of the storm. These refugees, of warm-hearted piety, carried over with them their custom in regard to the prayer-meeting.

And to bring it the better to bear on our point just here, it may be well to look back a little farther upon some of the historic events preceding this *revival*, and some of the co-operating causes producing it; as also the effects of the reformations and revivals of those times, together with the surgings of parties and persecutions, and the counter influences of those revolutionary days, affecting for good or for evil the cause of true religion.

The famous "Five Articles of Perth," passed in the General Assembly August 25th, 1618, under the influence and at the dictation of King James, were followed by lengthened and complicated vexations and persecutions in Scotland, which drove multitudes of the people from the ministrations of the dominant party, led by the royal influence, and to their private fellowship meetings, as the means of preserving the suffering cause of truth, and as the only substitute for public ordinances when so grossly corrupted. These "Articles," afterwards, in 1621, received the ratification of Parliament, and were rigidly enforced, and consequently many able and godly ministers were driven from their flocks, and into banishment. Among these were Brice, Glendinning, Ridge, Blair, and others who fled to Ireland. When they arrived there, they found the Province of Ulster—which has so long been the brightest spot on the map of Ireland—in a most deplorable state of ignorance and ungodliness. Their missionary labors—for such they were—were crowned with success. Shortly after they had entered upon their labors, awakenings under the ministrations of Glendinning occurred at "Oldstone," in the district of "Six Mile Water," where a Scottish Calvinist, of prayer-meeting affinities, opened his house for that purpose. Many resorted to the prayer-meetings. Many others were organized over the Province, where the other Scottish ministers labored. So one of the most remarkable revivals occurred, whose fame spread to distant countries, and whose effects are yet manifest in the striking contrast between the moral, spiritual, and physical condition of Ulster and other parts of Ireland.

These prayer-meetings among the people were encouraged by the ministers, and were found to be the strength of their right arm in the glorious revival work then in progress under their ministrations. Out of these private fellowship meetings, held in private houses all over the North of Ireland, grew those "monthly meetings," of such fragrant and extensive fame, first organized and held at Antrim, and known in history by the designation, "Antrim Monthly Meetings," held on the Saturdays or some other day before communions, when ministers and many others from distant parts of the country assembled together for prayer and Christian conference. These aided in making their communions seasons of revival, and dew-like refreshings from on high.

A very judicious and accurate historian, Dr. Houston, of Ireland, drawing from Fleming on the fulfilment of Scripture, and Reid's History of the Presbyterian Church of Ireland, says:

"The remembrance of these hallowed meetings was cherished long afterwards, and when prelatic oppression and the Popish massacre of 1641 served to expel faithful ministers from the North of Ireland, and their attached flocks were deprived of the pure administration of public ordinances and scattered, the prayer-meetings were resorted to as the grand means of supplying their spiritual destitution, and of light and refreshment in the cloudy and dark day.

"In subsequent times, too, the written or traditionary record of the blessed effects of these solemn assemblies has been of eminent advantage to the cause of true and undefiled religion; so that in times of trial, and wherever evangelical religion has been preserved in its purity, and the power of practical godliness has been displayed, these blessings have been sought and obtained by means of associations for united prayer and Christian fellowship."

The persecution in Ireland, in 1641, referred to, drove very many back to Scotland, at a time when earnest religion was being put to the test—a time when many ministers of the Church of Scotland were faltering—as Henry Guthrie, who afterward accepted a bishopric, and who pushed in the Assembly the action in relation to prayer-meetings. At this time the warm-hearted Ulster emigrants threw their influence and the fire of their revived piety into the cause of the meetings in question, and gave new life to the prayer-meetings in Scotland when these ministers, declining towards the prelatic party, aimed their blow at them, and through them at earnest practical godliness. It is in the light of these historic incidents that the action of the Scottish Assembly of 1641 obtains so much prominence in the history of the prayer-meeting. It demonstrates the importance of this ordinance to the life of experimental and practical religion, and to the cause of its revival. Eminently godly ministers, with many of the intelligent and pious laity, retired from persecution in Scotland, carried over to Ireland their zeal in the cause of revival, and for this precious instrumentality, so dear to them in their native land, and by persevering labors and prayers turned almost all the North of Ireland into a spiritual garden, dotted all over with its organized, life-inspiring prayer-meetings.

In the ever-changing tide of affairs, active piety was thrown back into Scotland, making its currents felt among the people. This excited the cold formalists of prelatic proclivity to the insidious attack upon the prayer-meeting in the Assembly of 1641. The importance of this historic incident, in this connection, is our apology for extended notice. Its importance will be enhanced by its connection, in the current of historic events, with the sore trials to which the prayer-meeting and its friends were so soon subjected. Elements were then in commotion which ultimated in that terrible storm of persecution which drove praying people to the fields, to the glens, to the mountains, to the caves of Scotland, there to enjoy the sweet privileges of their fellowship meetings, while their pastors breasted its fury in dungeons, in the fields, or on the scaffold. The dark cloud, bearing in its deathly folds Scotland's "killing time," had now begun to lower. The significance of the stroke of 1641 in the Assembly was but as the distant, low mutterings of fury, pent up and still lying beyond the horizon, soon to develop its power, and direct its arm against a people trained to prayer.

"THE SOCIETY PEOPLE."

In 1660 Charles II. ascended the throne, placed himself at the head of the prelatic party, and soon inaugurated, by system, one of the most dastardly persecutions, blackened with perjury, ever staining the history of modern times. The sequel of this bloody history, closing with the reign of the second James, identifies with and brings to view the particular history of the "Society People," justly entitled to a page in our hurried historic sketch of the prayer-meeting.

In regard to this people, we, with pleasure, insert a page of history borrowed from a living historian of the Reformed Presbyterian Church of Ireland, Rev. Thomas Houston, D. D. We quote from "THE FELLOWSHIP PRAYER-MEETING," pp. 80–84:

"When the prelatic persecution, under Charles II., drove *three hundred* faithful Presbyterian ministers from their pulpits, and hireling curates were intruded upon their reluctant flocks, the value of private social prayer-meetings was again experienced in upholding and comforting the servants of God in evil times. Thus were they fitted for patient endurance of privations and sufferings, and thus they were nerved for the noble conflict in which they engaged against Erastian power. In the latter part of the twenty-eight years' persecution, when under the cruel and arbitrary measures of the Popish and bigoted James, the number of faithful witnesses was greatly reduced; and by indulgences, and every other means that anti-Christian policy could invent, apostasy and defection were encouraged, the few resolute Covenanters who remained had recourse to united prayer, and cultivated fraternal fellowship, as a precious means of preservation and safety amidst manifold danger and suffering. Hence, they were called 'THE SOCIETY PEOPLE;' and the history of this disastrous period, whether as written by persons friendly or unfriendly to their cause, bears unequivocal testimony that it was, in a great measure, owing to their cordial, intimate union, and to their faithful exertions, that the precious truths of the gospel were preserved, and that the civil and religious liberties of Britain were rescued from the grasp of despotic rulers."

Even the prejudiced Wodrow is forced to confess that

"*The Society People*," and not the "*Indulged*," preserved, in perilous times, true Presbyterian principles; and though he blames them for maintaining extreme sentiments, and for extravagant practices, he admits that among them were the honest and faithful martyrs at the period which was significantly designated "*The killing time*." Hetherington, a much more candid and impartial historian, freely acknowledges the eminent advantages reaped by Scotland's suffering Church from association in prayer-meetings, and the obligations under which the nation lies to the example of faithfulness and heroic self-devotion exhibited by "*The Society People*." The following testimony is alike honorable to the head and heart of the writer:

"While Cargill perished on the scaffold, that determined band of Covenanters who had adhered to him were left without a minister—no man for a time daring to take up a position so imminently perilous. In this emergency, those fearless and high-principled men resolved to form themselves into a united body, consisting of '*Societies*' for worship and religious intercourse in those districts where they most abounded; and for the more effectual preservation of their opinions, and security against errors, in the absence of a stated ministry, these smaller societies appointed deputies to attend a General Meeting, which was empowered to deliberate upon all suggestions, and adopt such measures as the exigencies of the times required.

"From the fact that these people, in the absence of a stated ministry, formed themselves into societies for mutual religious intercourse and edification, they came to be designated the '*Society People*'—a term frequently applied to them by Wodrow, as that of '*Cameronians*' has been generally given to them by other historians. Superficial readers are liable to be misled by names, of the origin and application of which they have no accurate conception.

But the affixing of a new name to a party is no sure proof that it has taken new grounds. That 'persecuted Remnant,' as they called themselves, had, indeed, taken up no new principles. The utmost that they can be justly charged with is, merely that they had followed up the leading principles of the Presbyterian and Covenanted Church of Scotland to an extreme point, from which the greater part of Presbyterians recoiled; and that, in doing so, they had used language capable of being interpreted to mean more than they themselves intended. Their honesty of heart, integrity of purpose, and firmness of principle, cannot be denied, and these are noble qualities; and if they did express their sentiments in strong and unguarded language, it ought to be remembered that they did so in the midst of firm and remorseless persecution, ill adapted to make men really cautious in the selection of balanced terms, wherein to express their indignant detestation of that unchristian tyranny which was so fiercely striving to destroy every vestige of both civil and religious liberty. (See 'Hetherington's Hist. Church of Scotland, Vol. II., pp. 122–124.')

"The *Reformed Presbyterian Church* in those countries, which claims to inherit the principles, as it occupies the position, in relation to the civil and ecclesiastical establishments of the land, of the Society People, has carefully maintained, to the present day, the institution of Fellowship Prayer-meetings. Under the Divine favor, this has been to this section of the church a means of safety and extensive blessing. During the eighteenth century, when in these countries, and throughout Continental Europe, evangelical religion everywhere declined, and purity of religious ordinances was generally undervalued, the Covenanting Body held aloft a standard for the truths of the gospel—maintained a faithful discipline—and the lives and conduct of its members were exemplary. These attainments were reached, not only in a state of complete separation from corrupt civil and ecclesiastical systems, but often amidst the positive hostility of persons in authority, and the apathy and opposition of the community, bent on backsliding and defection. The 'Societies' in the Reformed Presbyterian Church have all along seemed to fan the flame of genuine piety among her members, as they have united them in fraternal bonds—been the birth-place of souls, and seminaries for the godly training of the young—and as the 'beds of spices' where the Beloved feeds, and holds delightful communion with his people."

From an intimate acquaintance with this people, whose Fathers were called "*The Society People*"—a people in compact organization now found in England, Scotland, Ireland, the United States, Nova Scotia, Canada and Syria, of whom we are well satisfied, their very existence, their distinctive principles, the compactness of their organization, and their influence among the evangelical churches, are indebted to their systematic and persevering adherence to the letter and spirit of the prayer-meeting more than to all other instrumentalities beside. This is not saying too much. For, like the Waldenses, who, when their beloved and devoted "*Barbes*" were cut off, or exiled, had recourse to their *prayer-meetings*, these "*Society People*" in Scotland, for *eighteen years*, firmly bound together organically, multiplied and grew without a single pastor to break to them the bread of life. So, in Ireland, often, for long periods, destitute of public ordinances, they were held together by their well organized social meetings—their youth well trained and preserved in the church, taking the place of their fathers; and of their entire membership scarcely ever one abandoning his profession. With a tenacity and perseverance unparalleled in the history of churches of modern times, they have, for two hundred years, retained their organization, their distinctive principles, their established usages, and their exemplary lives as professed Christians—and, perhaps, above all, the religious intelligence and evangelical training of their youth and the masses of their people.

For six generations, this people have preserved their organization, with its time-honored distinctive features, amid revolutions and trials that would have disintegrated almost any other people in less than one generation without this ever-present principle and bond of organic unity—their prayer-meeting. It is this that, in the tides of emigration, so deeply draining the energies and members of other denominations, preserves their strength intact. Families migrating and settling in the far West are seldom lost to their communion. They carry with them the principles and practices, ingrained in their religious natures by the prayer-meeting; and wherever even two families can be found together, they organize the prayer-meeting, and rally around it with their children—form at once a nucleus for a congregation—gather in from the society around them and from immigration, and in a reasonable time either secure stated supplies of public ordinances, or migrate elsewhere with hope of better success. To such a people emigration is not to scatter numbers and diminish strength. It is to lengthen their cords and strengthen their stakes—to scatter seed with broader cast in hope of more abundant harvest gathering. Expansion is their very life.

How many thousands of members, and hundreds of thousands of dollars, might larger churches save to their organic strength, if they firmly believed their profession, and loved and exemplified its practice—and especially here, if they carried with them the love and practice of the prayer-meeting!

CHAPTER V.

FROM THE CLOSE OF THE 17TH CENTURY TILL THE GENERAL DECLINE OF RELIGION TOWARD THE CLOSE OF THE 18TH.

Wesley and his followers—Whitefield—Revival in Wales—Reynolds, Harris, Rowlands, etc.—Prayer-Meetings and Revival Identified—Revival and Prayer-Meetings in the English Army—Soldier's Letter from the Army—Cambuslang Revival—Its History Closely Identified with the Prayer-Meeting—History of the Second Cambuslang Communion—Lessons of this Revival—Extends to other Parishes—Reports of Presbyteries on Revivals and Prayer-Meetings—Prayer-Meetings Among Children—Lessons of this History—Baxter's Times, etc—Lessons—Fletcher, Romaine, Berridge, etc.—American Colonies—Edwards' History of Revivals—Reflections.

AT the close of the seventeenth century, and the beginning of the eighteenth, as acknowledged by all historians, the whole kingdom of England was tending rapidly to Infidelity and licentiousness. In the Established Church, and to some extent even among the Dissenters, religion was at a very low ebb. Of the state of things then existing, Bishop Butler says:

"It is come, I know not how, to be taken for granted by many persons that Christianity is not so much as a subject of inquiry; but that it is now at length discovered to be fictitious; and, accordingly, they treat it as if, in the present age, this were an argument among all people of discernment, and nothing remained but to set it up as a principal subject of mirth and ridicule, as it were, bv way of reprisals for its having so long interrupted the pleasures of the world."

Dr. McFarland, in his History of Revivals of the Eighteenth Century, says:

"About the end of the seventeenth, and beginning of the eighteenth century, most of the churches, whether in the United Kingdom or the American Colonies, were in a comparatively low state. Arianism and Deism prevailed in England. In Scotland the old style of preaching was being fast laid aside, and cold, formal addresses, verging toward semi-Arianism, were becoming fashionable."

Stevens, in his History of Methodism, speaking of the same period, says:

"From the Restoration, down to the early part of the eighteenth century, both Churchmen and Non-conformists unite in deploring the decayed condition of religion and morals."

Taylor, in his History of Methodism, says:

"When Wesley appeared, the Anglican Church was an Ecclesiastical system, under which the people of England had lapsed into heathenism; or a state hardly to be distinguished from it."

Dr. Houston, in his History of the Prayer-Meeting, says:

"The awakenings which took place in various parts of England, under the ministry of *Wesley* and *Whitefield*, led to the establishment of social prayer-meetings; and, at this period, when *within* the pale of the National Establishment, and *without* it, all was under the torpor of spiritual death, this organization was a powerful means of exciting earnest minds to pursue after eternal concerns, and to impress them upon the serious attention of others."

While spiritual death thus reigned, a few students at

Oxford formed a *prayer-meeting*, which, by the blessing of God, spread its hallowed influences over that kingdom for a period of one hundred and forty years, down to our own time. Whitefield and Wesley were there. Revived in their humble little *prayer-meeting* they gathered others around them who were warmed by the fire of their burning zeal And in the course of ten years from the organization of that praying circle—a despised little band of students though they were—there went forth earnest men, like apostles, over England, and Wales, and the American Colonies, reviving not only religion in the dead churches, but reviving the prayer-meeting wherever their influence extended; so that from that time forth, the history of revivals and of prayer-meetings became identified and inseparable, as in the preceding times, Reformation and the prayer-meetings had been.

Wesley, whenever he began to organize churches, organized the prayer-meeting, where from ten to twenty members could be grouped together. These "class meetings," subordinated to the most rigid and methodic rules, have been the instrumentality, perhaps, more than any other, in giving to that church compactness, union and increase. Among groups of emigrants cast together in any locality, in any newly-settled country, soon formed into a class-meeting, assembled together weekly, held together by this bond, seldom ever were they turned aside from the church and lost to her communion. With a steadfastness scarcely exceeded by the Scottish Cameronians have they adhered to their profession and to their church. Just here, perhaps, lies the secret of the unparalleled success of the Methodist Church, in its first organization, in all the early settlements of the colonies, and in the new Territories of the West. They were always organized into prayer-meetings, or class-meetings, which held them together while other churches, without prayer-meetings to rally and train their scattered members, soon lost their sheep wandering without *fold* or shepherd. So, history confirms the importance of SOME *fold*, however humble, for the preservation of every flock, however small.

Whitefield, though not so methodic as Wesley, and not so successful in organizing as evangelizing, left behind, wherever he labored, the spirit of the prayer-meeting. Whitefield's revivals, like all true revivals of religion, were characterized by their prayer and by their *prayer-meeting*.

With pleasure, here, we quote a page from Dr. Humphrey's Revival Sketches. He says:

"One of the most important revivals of religion, when the effects are considered, is that which occurred in the 'Principality of Wales,' during the second quarter of the eighteenth century, under Howell Harris and the Rev. Daniel Reynolds; and this was carried forward and fostered by means of private societies for prayer and religious conference. The Welsh, who had been previously left almost wholly neglected and in ignorance by the ministers of the Established Church, when they were awakened embraced the truth in its simplicity, attended upon ordinances administered with a large measure of Scriptural purity, and exhibited a practice becoming the gospel. The *Welsh Calvinistic Methodists*, as they are designated, have continued to be distinguished for a strict adherence to evangelical doctrine, and for godly practice, above any other class of Dissenters in England, and it is an honorable testimony borne to the inhabitants of the Principality, that the time when the last 'census of religious worship' was taken, a much larger proportion of them was found attending upon public ordinances than of the inhabitants of any other part of England. It is related of Harris, who may be considered 'the father' of the body, that 'He frequently attended the meetings which the people held for the purpose of teaching to sing the praises of God, that he might thus have an opportunity of impressing them with a sense of their eternal state. On these occasions many were convinced of their sinfulness. This encouraged Mr. Harris to establish regular meetings of serious persons for religious conversation in several other places; and this was the commencement of the *Private Societies,* which have ever since—taking into consideration the great importance in strictness attached to their observance—formed a principal feature by which the Welsh Calvinistic Methodists may be distinguished from every other denomination of professed Christians.'

"Rowlands availed himself of the same ordinance to extend and perpetuate the revival; and when the Welsh Calvinistic body became organized as a distinct section of the church of Christ, they embodied in their *Constitution and Fundamental Regulations* the ordinance of *Fellowship-Meetings,* and required the members to attend upon them with all diligence. It is, doubtless, owing to the punctuality with which this regulation is observed by the Welsh Calvinists, in the various places where they are scattered, that they are enabled to preserve among them the doctrines of the gospel uncorrupted, and to maintain, above any other religious body in England, a strict Scriptural discipline."

It is worthy of notice here that Dr. Scott, the venerable Commentator, in his impartial vindication of the Synod of Dort, and Harmony of the Confessions of Faith of the Reformed Churches, gives the Confession of the Welsh Calvinistic Church an honorable place.

THE PRAYER-MEETING AND REVIVALS.

Reformation was the *cognomen* formerly used to designate improvement in religion, whether in regard to faith, practice, or vital godliness. The history of reformation and the prayer-meeting have always had a remarkable affinity —they have always been found linked together in their operations like the twin graces—faith and love—the one "working by the other." We now use the term Revival, as nearly a synonym of Reformation. Revival is the Scripture term, and beautifully significant. True revival lives in prayer. Prayer draws power from revival. We need only to follow the way-marks of their remarkable history to be satisfied of their inseparable unity.

Our limits forbid us to attempt, in noticing the progress of revival during a period of over a century and a quarter, more than to bring to view some prominent points in the narrative. We have already noticed the prayer-meeting in the armies of the Protestant Reformers, when in the field battling for civil and religious liberty, and for national and individual life. Let us turn from the peaceful walks of Christian life at home and in the churches, and again look over the tented field for revival and the prayer-meeting.

Shortly after the wonderful revivals in England, Scotland, and Wales, under the labors of Whitefield, Wesley, and their cotemporaries and followers, remarkable revivals were enjoyed in the English armies, both at home and abroad. The remarkable coincidents here, of the resort to the prayer-meeting, under the most unfavorable circumstances, in the army, among the soldiers, in every instance where revival has been enjoyed, are worthy of notice. In the English army in Flanders, about the year 1745, very interesting revivals arrested the attention of the public journals of that period. From these, many important historic gleanings have been gathered and preserved, taken mostly from letters of officers and soldiers of the army.

From these letters, McFarland, in his Revival of the Eighteenth Century, quotes the following:

"Indeed there is a great awakening in our army. There is one John Hairns, a dragoon in Major-General Cope's Regiment; likewise one Clemens, in the First Regiment of Guards; and one Evans, in the Train Artillery, who meet together for searching the Scriptures, for prayer and other duties, as also for rebuking others in following sinful ways, and for setting before them their dreadful state from Scripture and reason. In our last campaign there was open field preaching, and there is now, *in most of all our Regiments, a remarkable awakening.* In this company there are three, who were notoriously wicked, and now desire only to know Christ, and him crucified. There is also a *Society* of *praying* people in this and several other Regiments. *This Society* was erected before the awakening. In Ghent there is another *assembly* of the awakened soldiers."

The following extract is from a soldier's letter:

"REV. SIR:—I received the book which ye sent me.—I hope it will be useful to me, and also to some others of this army, who are ten thousand times more deserving, and who on all occasions seek to do me good. There are a few in this wilderness, where we are deprived of those refreshing ordinances which you have among you, that assemble together; which we believe it to be our duty. There are nearly forty of us, *who meet as often as we can.* But we have not the same opportunities in this campaign we had in the last; and in winter quarters we commonly meet on Sabbath and Wednesday, and oftener when we can. We begin with prayer; we then sing, then read a chapter, we have then prayer again, and questions on practical heads of divinity, such as are in the writings of Mr. Isaac Ambrose. After the question has gone round, duty is gone about, and we conclude with praise. There is a great work of conviction among the men, and I hope that there are also some conversions. If it were not too much trouble, I would be very glad to have your advice concerning our *Society*, and the means whereby we may obtain and preserve the presence of God among us; and concerning myself."

These are very brief specimens of many letters from the armies of those times, furnishing very suggestive illustrations of revival, and the accompanying and ever-present prayer-meeting, wherever and whenever religion makes its power felt. So, in other countries, in other armies of other times, wherever revival has ever made its appearance in the camp, there, invariably, we find, connected with its history, the prayer-meeting.

PROMINENT REVIVALS OF RELIGION AND THE PRAYER-MEETING OF THE LAST AND THIS CENTURY.

In our hurried historic sketch, we can stop but to notice a few only of the many revivals, and their associated prayer-meetings, that have attracted the attention of all the evangelical churches of this country, the churches of the British Isles, and the churches of Protestant Europe.

Soon after Whitefield made his first tour through Scotland, that country was visited with awakening, and a corresponding revived interest in social prayer. This Revival made its first appearance in the church at Cambuslang, from which place it has received the designation by which it has ever since been known and distinguished—"The Cambuslang Revival." It spread over nearly all Scotland, and over much of England and Wales.

We here call attention to a remarkable historic fact, which every reader should bear in mind while making the history of the prayer-meeting a matter of study:—While many and voluminous histories of revivals have been written, published, circulated, read, and studied with intense interest, scarcely the skeleton of a single history, or even a passing formal and designed notice, has ever been given of the prayer-meeting. This belongs to the mere *incidents* of revival history. It is the necessary and impelled prominence of these incidents, so essentially connected with the principal line and design of the narratives from which we glean, that gives our sketch its historic importance.

Dr. McFarland, in his History of the Revivals of the Eighteenth Century, gives a graphic sketch of the Cambuslang Revival. He inserts an interesting letter from the pastor of the congregation, giving a detailed account of the commencement of the work, bearing date May 8, 1742, in which he says:

"On Monday, the fifteenth of February, there was a *general meeting*, at the minister's house, of *particular Societies for prayer*, which had subsisted in the parish for several years before. On Tuesday there was another meeting for prayer in the same place; the occasion of which was a concert with several serious Christians elsewhere about solemn prayer relating to the public interests of the gospel. The people who met for prayer these two days, apprehended that they had been so well employed, and found so much leisure for it, that they appointed a third meeting on Wednesday.

"Among the good fruits already appearing, both in Cambuslang and elsewhere, the following instances seem very encouraging: Desirable evidence of fervent love to one another; the keeping up of divine worship in families; the setting up of *new meetings for prayer, both of old and young*, partly within the parish, where *twelve such Societies are now begun*, and partly elsewhere, among the awakened.

"The sum of all these facts is, that this work—came after such preparations as an extensive concern about religion, gradually increasing, together with extraordinary and fervent prayers in large meetings, and particularly in relation to the success of the gospel."

In the close of the letter, the writer says:

"I leave it with you to judge how far such facts make it evident that the work is from God; that vain persons, who minded no religion, but frequented taverns and frolics, passing their time in filthiness, foolish talking and jesting, or singing paltry songs, do now frequent Christian *societies for prayer*, seek Christian conversation, talk of what concerns the soul, and express their mirth in Psalms, and hymns, and spiritual songs."

In speaking of the wonderful outpouring of the Holy Spirit at the *first communion* after the commencement of the Revival, the writer says:

"You might have seen thousands bathed in tears. In the afternoon the concern was also very great. Much prayer had been previously offered up, and during the whole night you might have heard the different companies praying and giving thanks to God."

In giving the history of the *second* communion, held a few months after, referring to what preceded, he says:

"And there was first one day, and then another, at some distance of time from that, appointed for a general meeting of several *societies for prayer* in the parish, at the manse. The design of these meetings, and the business which they were accordingly employed in—besides singing Psalms and blessing the name of God together—was to ask mercy of the God of heaven to ourselves; to pray for such as, unhappily, opposed this work of God here and in other parts."

From these selections we see how the prayer-meeting was

interwoven with every step in the progress of this Revival. The little groups of *private societies* throughout the parish —their special and general gatherings, as the occasion suggested—their special conferences and consultations, and agreements for concerted prayers, directed to special objects. And then, the fruits following. The writer, speaking of the after-lives of some of the converts, says:

"They have ever since attended fellowship-meetings weekly; and I have been sometimes with them, and have heard them both pray and converse on matters of Christian experience to my great satisfaction."

Again, in another connection, he says:

"They carefully observe seasons fixed for the *concert of prayer*, and join in earnest supplication for the farther spread of the gospel, and the outpouring of the Spirit on the churches.

"To conclude, they abound much in prayer, both secret and domestic; and also in the observance of the *fellowship-meetings*. These are usually held weekly, and the exercises are prayers, praises and Christian conference. In 1731, when I came to this parish, there were only three of these; in 1742 they increased to a dozen or more. In every town or village almost in this country side, where there is any competent number of serious and lively Christians, and where religion is in a thriving state, meetings of this kind exist; and the persevering subjects of the work in 1742 are, if at all near, sure to form a part of them."

Thus far the history of the Cambuslang Revival, and its immediate and local fruits. And what a lesson! More than *twelve prayer-meetings* in one congregation! But there were *serious and lively Christians* there! Can there be many serious and lively Christians in our large congregations—of five hundred and more communicants—and yet have but one prayer-meeting!—that in the church, conducted, too, by the pastor, else it would die!—and then seldom more in number than from thirty to fifty, and, perhaps, four-fifths of these women!

In Cambuslang they had not only more than their dozen vigorous and life-inspiring prayer-meetings, which convened weekly, but they had their general meetings in the church besides. And still more, we are told, they had occasionally "meetings for fasting and prayer." They believed and felt that they were sinners, and acted accordingly.

Our system, as by us practised, will never secure to the church "serious and lively Christians," nor will ever "serious and lively Christians" be satisfied with such system for the name of prayer-meetings. More, here: Such will never bring revivals; nor will revivals, when they come, ever be satisfied with such prayer-meetings.

We may learn something more here in regard to the lessons of history on the importance of the Scriptural prayer-meeting. The fruits of revival may soon be lost if not carefully gathered into the prayer-meeting, and there cared for.

Of this lesson we shall have more elucidation in the reports from other parts of Scotland where the revival spread. Many presbyteries, cities, towns, parishes, and congregations made full and interesting reports of the work from its beginning to its close, and of the results of many years following.

The report from the City of Glasgow has the following:

"In October, 1744, a general concert for weekly and quarterly prayer-meetings began to be observed, and in the year following to become general among the more pious on both sides of the Atlantic. *Many prayer-meetings* and other special means of instruction came thus into operation, and were continued long after, preserving, in the midst of a rapidly growing population, a large measure of practical godliness among professors.

Of *the Parish of Baldernock,* we find the following narrative:

"A school teacher, who had been in the habit of giving religious instructions to his pupils about the time of the Cambuslang revival, soon realized the fruits of his labors. One of his pupils who had been at Cambuslang returned awakened, and asked his teacher whether he would allow two or three of the scholars to meet for prayer and the singing of Psalms. This was readily allowed, and in the course of two weeks, ten or twelve more were awakened and under deep convictions. Some of these were not more than eight or nine years of age, and others twelve or thirteen. And so much were they engrossed with the one thing needful as to meet thrice a day—in the morning, at mid-day, and at night. Several of the grown people were first awakened at Cambuslang, Calden, and Kirkintillock, but the greater part were brought into a state of concern while attending the *prayer-meetings,* which were set up in the parish. These were held among the awakened, twice a week; and almost daily meetings of this kind were held in some place or other. At the second of the general meetings there were nine awakened, at the third four, and at another five or six."

From this example why not encourage children's prayer-meetings? Why may not God still perfect praise to the glory of his grace, out of the mouth of babes?

The Parish of Kirkintillock reports the following very interesting narrative in relation to children's prayer-meetings:

"In the month of April, 1742, about sixteen children in

the town, were observed to meet together in a barn for prayer. Mr. Burnside heard of it, had frequent meetings with them, and they continued to improve. And this being reported, many more were impressed. Soon after, about a hundred and twenty were under a more than ordinary concern, and *praying societies*, as usual, were formed."

Another instance of children's prayer-meetings in connection with the commencement of revival:

"In the *Parish of Kilsith* it was thought to be as the dry place, while all around seemed to be bedewed, when several prayer-meetings had begun to be formed, and several girls, between ten and fourteen years of age had been observed to meet in an out-house for prayer. Soon the general awakening commenced, which was followed by several hundred hopeful converts added to the church there."

The Parish of Muthill, as reported by its pastor, who, speaking of the children's prayer-meeting, says:

"There is also a meeting of themselves in the school-house after the evening exercises, where some hours are spent in prayer to their own edification, and, in some cases, to the conviction of persons standing and listening at the doors and windows. Our praying societies prosper; they are still growing in numbers. The meetings formed of boys and girls give me great satisfaction. They are frequent in their meetings, and the Lord is obviously present with them. One of them, which began after the late communion, has now increased to about twenty members. O, how pleasant it is to have the poor young lambs addressing themselves to God in prayer! Sometimes standing outside the room, listening, I am myself often melted into tears.

"There is another meeting of young ones in a different

corner of the parish. About twenty of them meet twice a week, some of them having a considerable way to travel homeward in the dark."

Noticing the progress of the work still going on among the young, he says farther:

"We have three praying societies, at some distance. One of them, at a place about two miles distant, made me a very agreeable visit on the first Monday of the year—a day that young people especially used to be otherwise employed. We had, I think, upwards of forty of them, and they continued in prayer and other exercises till about ten o'clock at night."

Passing many interesting—indeed thrilling—accounts of prayer-meetings for the young and the old, noticed in the reports of parishes, we stay to notice only one or two more:

"In the *Parish of Crief* not fewer than *eight prayer-meetings* were also set up. Boys were found in the fields engaged in prayer."

"In *Auchterarder*, an adjoining parish, *six prayer-meetings* were formed."

Willison, of Dundee, speaking of that place, says:

"Still their numbers are increasing, and *prayer-meetings* setting up so fast in all places of the town, that our difficulty is to get houses to accommodate them. Blessed be God, we have also a great increase of *praying societies* in this place. I think there will be *above twenty of such societies* here, and in several of them between *twenty* and *thirty* persons, and much time is spent in them."

Of the *Parish of Nigg*, the following is reported:

"A great increase in *meetings for prayer* and *religious conference*. Of this kind were two *General Meetings*, in which *the minister presided*, and *ten special meetings*, in different parts of the parish, and to which numbers were admitted only on their giving satisfactory evidence of their seriousness."

The records of history will be barren of improvement to the student unless their lessons be carefully studied. Unless we look behind the simple facts, and into their hidden philosophy; unless we comprehend the *principle* underlying the facts on the surface—the mere creatures of productive powers, operating according to the laws of cause and effect—we shall have acquired little more than a handful of pebbles, collected from the shore, without even a hieroglyphic inscription on one of them, suggestive of an idea. Still more: Unless we trace, in the history of revivals and the prayer-meeting, the hand of the Spirit of God, and the controlling power of his grace, bringing up from the barren soil of the human heart the spirit of prayer, and from the dead fields of social organisms the gatherings of renovated members, like bone coming to his bone, until all stand together with one heart and one mind, as a great spiritual army in the gathering, in companies for prayer, we shall fail to be instructed. Unless we find illustrations of the teachings of God's word, and the counterpart of its historic lessons in the narrative of these revivals and prayer-meetings, we pursue the story in vain.

Here, however, we are not disappointed. Here we see in history repeated—in its scenes re-enacted—the pentecostal revival and prayer-meeting baptisms. And here, in the similarity of character and fruits pervading the narrative—though centuries intervene—we think we feel the power of the same hand directing both.

From the history of the revivals of religion in Scotland, with their accompanying and revived prayer-meetings, which commenced at Cambuslang, we may learn some very important and seasonable lessons.

First. Revival will bring prayer-meetings into the congregation. Like apostolical gatherings for prayer, *private meetings*, in little select circles, in upper rooms, with the women, the doors being shut. So, also, and as well, general gatherings, in which the minister presides—but these *never demand enough*—revival demands more. A revived state of religion always demands more. It must have "ten special meetings in different parts of the Parish." And as in Dundee congregation, under the ministry of Willison, "*A great increase of prayer-meetings* in this place—about *twenty* of such Societies here—in several, twenty or thirty persons each." Thus, revival brings small groups of the people together in classes—boys, girls, women even—closely and intimately, where they can speak one to another.

Secondly. In revival history we may profitably study the Bible doctrine of the Prayer-meeting. In revival prayer-meetings, exemplifying the Bible teaching especially, we may find aid in correcting the prevailing, and sadly inefficient, system of prayer-meetings. In our churches—in our large congregations particularly—the *rule* is, perhaps, about this: *one-tenth* only of the members receive the benefits of the prayer-meeting, because they have nothing of the kind but the general congregational meeting, conducted by the minister, which fails to meet the demands of living piety. Then, for the want of the "ten private meetings in different parts of the congregation," *nine-tenths* receive no benefit. We are now speaking of the *facts* only of history. The principle underlying is this: The congregational, ministerial, prayer-meeting, because not God's way, wants the vital principle and power of attraction to draw out and hold the masses of the people to its observance.

Thirdly. This history very distinctly, and in no whisper tones, suggests the inquiry—Should not a religious system be abandoned, which fails to secure *nine-tenths* of the end for which it was instituted?—abandoned, as a human device displacing a divine ordinance?—abandoned, as the failure of a human experiment? And, then, should not the Bible system be restored, since its claims, from its revival fruits, have been so signally and repeatedly confirmed?

And here, before pursuing farther the line of history, let us prepare our minds for the inquiry—Are these lessons, of the Cambuslang and cotemporary revivals, peculiar and exclusive; or, are they the lessons of all true revivals? For, if we fail to find the same testimony to the prayer-meeting, and lessons in them all, the claims of truth, and the demands of duty, dictate a suspension of our final decision. Our labor may all be in vain.

A very accurate and discriminating historian of the present century, and of our own country, has well remarked, that "The history of true Revivals of religion is a history of the true church." We may as well, and as truly, add, The history of true revivals of religion is a history of the *Prayer-meeting.*

In England, in Ireland, and in the American Colonies, from the beginning of the 18th century, up to the time of the Cambuslang revival in Scotland, in 1742, we could find in the history of revivals, as also under the ministry of eminent men of those times, much valuable material for our hasty historical sketch. The times and country of Bunyan, Baxter, Flavel, Alliene, Howe, and many others, furnish fruitful reminiscences of the prayer-meeting.

Baxter, writing an account of his charge and of his labors, says: "Every Thursday evening, my neighbors that were most desirous, and had opporunity, met at my house, and there one of them repeated the sermon; and afterwards they proposed what doubts any of them had about the sermon, or any other case of conscience, and I resolved their doubts. And last of all, I caused sometimes one and sometimes another of them to pray, sometimes praying with them myself. Once a week, also, some of the young, who were not prepared to pray in so great an assembly, met among a few more privately, where they spent three hours in prayer together. Every Saturday night they met at some of their houses to repeat the sermon of the last Lord's day, and to pray and prepare themselves for the following day. Once in a few weeks we had a day of humiliation, on one occasion or other.—Our private meetings always were full." Speaking of the effects of this course of religious training, he says: "Some of the poor men competently understood the body of divinity, and were able to judge in difficult controversies. Some of them were so able in prayer that very few ministers equalled them in order and fulness, apt expressions, holy oratory, and fervency. A great number of them were able to pray very appropriately with their families, or with others."

We select this example—one of many of the same kind that might be taken from the practice of many such faithful men as Baxter, and from men of like stamp of that period, and whose congregations were subjected to similar training in regard to social private meetings among the people for prayer and religious conference—a selection which holds up a contrast in principle, in practice, and in fruits, with the order, practice, and fruits of the modern congregational prayer-meetings, in our churches; a contrast from which it is high time we should begin to learn and reform. Baxter had gathered together a few people in his own house, and in other private houses, not in the church only. And this seems to have been the common and the principal form of conducting these social exercises. In these private gatherings the people conducted the exercises, not the pastor exclusively. They talked over and together the sermon of the past Sabbath, like the noble Bereans in their private gatherings. The people generally led in the prayer, Baxter, the pastor, only occasionally. For their better training, they were grouped together in classes, according to their grades of age and attainments. The young, who were not prepared to pray in larger promiscuous meetings, were classed together in juvenile prayer-meetings; there the youth could pray together for "three hours." The private meetings were "always full." In our prayer-meetings, our churches are always lamentably empty, unless under some spasmodic excitement, which passes off like the morning dew. Baxter's people were intelligent, were thoroughly indoctrinated, were mighty in the Scriptures—"some of the poor men competently understood the body of divinity." Our people, alas! too many of them, don't know what they profess—or the principles of the churches of which they are members; and consequently, so unlike Baxter's Christians, they are not so "able in prayer that very few ministers equal them in order and fulness, apt expressions, holy oratory, and fervency." In our churches a few only can be relied on to lead in prayer at all; and perhaps fewer still can make intelligent, fervent, and edifying prayers.

Under the ministrations of such men as Fletcher, Romaine, Berridge, Howel Harris, Wesley, and Whitefield, the masses were trained to social prayer. Groups of the people were attracted together by the power of the social religion of the times. Prayer-meetings were common among the youth; and little children sometimes were drawn together for prayer and conference. Ladies, too, of the aristocracy, were not ashamed to group together in the social circle for prayer. Lady Huntingdon, Hamilton, Chesterfield, Shirley, and others, were prominent in forming female prayer-meetings.

In the American Colonies, about this same period, the prayer-meeting was familiar to all classes of religious people, of earnest and active habits. The Rev. Danforth, of Taunton, Mass., wrote, in 1704–5, "We are much encouraged by a universal and amazing impression made by the Spirit of God on all sorts among us, especially on the young men and women. The young men, instead of their merry meetings, are now forming themselves into regular meetings for prayer, repetitions of sermons, and singing. The profanest among us seem startled at the sudden change upon the rising generation. We need much prayer that these strivings of the Spirit may have a saving issue and effect."

Edwards, in his History of Revivals, answering the objections made to the work in his times, writes: "Another thing that many have disliked, is the *religious meetings of children*, to read and pray together, and perform religious exercises among themselves.—God, in this work, has shown a remarkable regard to little children; never was there such a glorious work amongst persons in their childhood, as has been of late in New England: he has been pleased, in a wonderful manner, to perfect praise out of the mouths of babes and sucklings; and many of them have more of that knowledge and wisdom that please him, and render their religious worship acceptable, than many of the great and learned men of the world.—I have seen many happy effects of children's religious meetings; and God has seemed often remarkably to own them in their meetings, and really descended from heaven to be amongst them: I have known several probable instances of children's being converted at such meetings."

This quotation suggests some reflections: If our prayer-meetings are to be congregational, held in the church, conducted by the pastor, who is expected at every meeting to address the people, as a part of his pastoral labors, by either a studied lecture, or extempore remarks, how long shall it be before we shall have prayer-meetings among the youth, or among the women, or among the people at all? We must first educate the people up to the principle that the prayer-meeting is a divine ordinance—*for them* appointed, *by them* to be controlled, and *by them* to be administered—an ordinance for the benefit of *all the people*, to be enjoyed by them all and by their children. It is a remarkable historic fact, that genuine revivals of religion have always broken in upon these dead and formal, ministerial and official prayer-meetings, and have excited among the people a demand for something more—a demand for the people's social private prayer-meeting—a demand for the meeting in the upper, or the private room—a demand for the meeting for the young men, and for the women, too, where ministerial presence, or the presence of superiors, cannot suppress the gushing spirit of prayer, often like groanings that cannot be uttered.

Edwards, in the close of his work, gives us, in connection with interesting historical facts, some very instructive reflections. He says:

"Before the first great outpouring of the Spirit of God on the Christian church, which began at Jerusalem, the church of God gave themselves to incessant prayer. The inhabitants of our towns are now divided into particular praying Societies; most of the people, young and old, have voluntarily associated themselves in distinct companies for mutual assistance in social worship in private houses; what I intend, therefore, is, that days of prayer should be spent partly in these distinct praying companies. Such a method of keeping a fast as *this* has several times been proved: in the forenoon, after the duties of the family and closet, as early as might be, all the people of the congregation have gathered in their particular religious Societies; companies of men by themselves, and companies of women by themselves; young men by themselves, and young women by themselves, and companies of children in all parts of the town by themselves, as many as were capable of social religious exercises; the boys by themselves, and the girls by themselves; and about the middle of the day, at an appointed hour, all have met together in the house of God to offer up public prayers, and to hear a sermon suited to the occasion; and they have retired from the house of God again into their private Societies, and spent the remaining part of the day in praying together there."

Again, he says:

"There has been of late a great increase of preaching the word, and a great increase of social prayer."

Thus far the unbroken current of historic evidence goes to establish the doctrine we have previously presented on this subject:

First, the divine appointment of the Prayer-meeting as an ordinance of religious worship, indicated by the spirit of true reformation and revival of religion, turning God's people with renewed earnestness, faith, and delight, to social prayer, in which the divine presence is pledged and enjoyed.

Second, that *general* prayer-meetings, of entire congregations, or masses of the people, never satisfy a living church, or a revived people; but more is demanded, and more is always attained in revival—always the social private fellowship meeting of kindred spirits, where one can speak to another—where any one can say, "Come, hear, I'll tell what he did for my soul."

CHAPTER VI.

FROM THE PERIOD OF GENERAL DECLINE, TOWARD THE CLOSE OF THE LAST CENTURY, TILL NEAR THE MIDDLE OF THE PRESENT.

Causes of Decline—Reign of Infidelity—Making common cause with civil and religious liberty—Evangelical Christians alarmed and awakened—Counter influences, though silent and hidden—Church Unions and Divisions—Age of the Organization of Benevolent Associations—Bible, Missionary, Tract Societies—Inscrutible providences—Bible and Missionary effort a harbinger of Revival and Prayer—Revivals toward the close of the last century and beginning of this—Dr. Sprague's Lectures—Revival in the Eastern States—In the South and West—College Prayer-Meetings—Hamden-Sidney College Incidents—Prayer-Meeting Lessons—Jefferson College Prayer-Meetings, in 1823—Their Lessons—College at Princeton, New Jersey—Lessons and Reflections.

SOON after the Cambuslang Revival, and the extensive revivals that quickly followed, spreading over many parts of Europe—in England, Wales, Ireland, and in the American Colonies, the churches, almost everywhere, suffered, for a period of half a century, a gradual and mournful decline. With a few exceptions of local and temporary awakenings, a whole generation passed away without any remarkable revivals of religion, or any marked interest in the prayer-meeting, or indeed in the cause of vital religion.

This half century period embraced the reign of terror which drenched France in blood, and shook, as with an earthquake, every throne of Europe. This was the period of the American and French Revolutions—the period of political agitations and the surging of empires—the period of skilfully directed attacks of open and covert infidelity, threatening to crush out, over all Europe and in this country, Christianity itself. It was during this period that the file-leader of the legions of infidelity, mustering the hosts for the conflict, adopted the characteristic Voltairean motto, and inscribed upon his banner, "Crush the Wretch." It was during this period that the vulgar Pamphleteer, Tom Paine, threw broadcast, over this land, his vulgar issues against the Bible and Christianity.

During this reign of infidelity, and raid of the "Pale horse—Death and Hell following" in train over Continental Europe, perhaps no combination of influences pressed so hard, or could have pressed so hard, upon the vital power of Bible Christianity as the strange and masterly alliance of Infidelity with the cause of human liberty, civil and religious; and at a time, too, when slavery was receiving its strongest defence from the popular churches of both Continents. Could revival of religion and social prayer prevail against such damaging currents without a more than ordinary revealing of the Divine arm?

Still, during this long gloom, and especially toward the close of the last century, the records show some bright spots upon the dark page of those historic times. There were occasional revivals of religion, and revivals of the prayer-meeting. During that same long period of comparative barrenness of revivals, those staid churches, not so subject to changes in doctrine, worship, and forms of religion, and not so subject to spasmodic excitements, still preserved their forms and practice of social prayer. Among most Presbyterians, Reformed Presbyterians especially, prayer-meetings were still observed as denominational forms of religious worship; and cherished, too, as precious divine institutions by which the people of God were preserved in their ecclesiastical organizations, edified and consecrated as a seed to serve God, and to perpetuate his cause in the world. The Reformed Presbyterian could no more dispense with his Social Fellowship Prayer-meeting than with his Family worship, or his public gospel ordinances. The honest Methodist in those days could scarcely easier dispense with his Class-meeting than with his beloved circuit rider, or his endeared Camp-meeting, with its annual heart-stirrings. These denominations, which have incorporated the prayer-meeting in their public creeds, and made it a part of their authorized organic worship, have always more steadily preserved its observance, and reaped more largely of its rich fruits.

And here it may be remarked, that for a century the Reformed Presbyterian and Episcopal Methodist churches, in the midst of all the unions, and divisions, and changes, and extinctions of sects, have maintained the principles and practices, with most of the distinctive features of their fathers, as few, if any, of the other churches have done, whose observance of the prayer-meeting has depended so much more upon the forces of ever-changing circumstances. The prayer-meeting has never failed, when observed in the true spirit of its institution, to operate as a bond, binding together in unity of faith and affection.

HOW INSCRUTABLE IS DIVINE PROVIDENCE!

That God, who makes the very wrath of man to praise him, and who causes all things to work together for good, caused that dark storm-cloud of revolution that passed over most of Christendom during the latter part of the last century, and that deathful march of the pale horse, infidelity, with death directing his course, and hell following in his pathway, to wake up the slumbering churches, and to usher in a new Epoch, the most remarkable of all that has been evolved in the historic Cycles of the Ages. To roll back the floods threatening the very existence of the church, and Christianity, their friends were roused to the necessity of aggressive warfare. The rallying cry rung throughout all evangelical Christendom, and the age of associations, of combined effort in aggressive movements upon the lines of Infidelity, Paganism, and Popery, was ushered in. From the formation of the Missionary Society, in 1792, by Andrew Fuller and others, in England, we may date the era of revivals. Then set in that tide of influences, seen in the formation of Tract, Bible, and Missionary Societies, with other benevolent associations, which now covers the whole face of the Protestant world, and which is to-day sending abroad its healing waters over the perishing nations of the whole earth. The Angel is now seen flying through the midst of heaven, having the everlasting gospel to preach unto them that dwell on the earth, and to every nation, and kindred, and tongue, and people. Now many run to and fro, and knowledge is increased.

That the missionary spirit of modern times, which has revolutionized the church, and which is now turning the world upside-down, caught its inspiration from the revival of religion, no one conversant with the history of the times will doubt. It is equally true that the revival of religion and of missions both received their new impulses from the life-invigorating spirit of prayer—social and concerted prayer, eminently. Their historic connection and spiritual affinity are clearly traceable, awarding to the prayer-meeting that awakening power which has vigorously put into operation those world-renowned agencies which are now so gloriously, under the Captain of our salvation, evangelizing the world.

Dr. Humphrey says, in his "Revival Sketches," p. 45, that "The eminent Andrew Fuller was a leading spirit in establishing the monthly concert of prayer for Foreign Missions, and planting at Serampore the first of modern missions in India."

Again, in regard to missions, he says, p. 116: "This revival, says the author of Mills' Life, was among the most signal expressions of favor to the church. He alludes to the well known fact, that by means of this influence, Mills prevailed to diffuse, through a circle of choice spirits, that zeal for missions which actuated his own breast. On Wednesday afternoons they used to retire for prayer to the bottom of a valley south of the west college: and on Saturday afternoons, when they had more leisure, to the more remote meadow on the bank of the Hoosack, and there, under the hay-stacks, those young Elijahs prayed into existence the embryo of American Missions. They formed a society, unknown to any but themselves, to make inquiries and to organize plans for future missions. They carried this society with them to Andover, where it has roused into missionaries most that have gone to the heathen, and where it is still exerting a powerful influence on the interests of the world. I have been in situations to *know* that from the counsels formed in that sacred conclave—the prayer-meeting in the valley and under the hay-stacks—or from the mind of Mills himself, arose the American Board of Commissioners for Foreign Missions, the American Bible Society, the United Foreign Missionary Society."

All these, and many kindred benevolent agencies of the age, have, confessedly, their origin in the prayer-meeting. The same writer says again, p. 103: "It cannot be denied, that modern missions sprung out of these revivals." Nor can it be denied that revivals are the offspring of prayer. God's Spirit prepares for revival and for mission work, as for every other good work, first by pouring out upon his people a spirit of grace and supplication. This leads them to the prayer-meeting, to ask, in concert, for revival; they are revived, and so fitted for every good work, in answer to prayer.

From even a limited collection of histories of revival, we find a judicious selection and arrangement of historic incidents, in relation to the prayer-meeting, a difficult task. So numerous are the references, and so prominent the place assigned to these conference meetings in collateral history, to select and omit seem but to mar the entire narrative, so full and conclusive. We shall be content with making leading, or representative, selections illustrative of principles.

The author of "Revival Sketches," giving reminiscences of Rev. Jeremiah Hallock, of Connecticut, says: "In 1779, at the age of twenty-one, he was impressed with the sinfulness of his heart, though he had neither seen nor heard of awakenings; and conviction, conversion, and revivals, were terms with which he was unacquainted. Soon after he was called to do military duty, and he and his fellow-soldiers had entered a barn, he found himself surrounded by his young companions and others, exhorting them on the subject of religion, one of whom was then awakened, and afterwards obtained hope. It was the beginning of a revival; meetings were appointed, and became frequent, full, and solemn, and as they had no minister, and Mr. Hallock was the first of the apparent converts, it often devolved on him to lead the meetings. The years immediately succeeding his settlement—1785—were a period of darkness in the churches generally. In 1795, Dr. Griffin was settled in the adjoining parish of New Hartford. They both had tasted the blessedness of revivals, and together they mourned, and wept, and wrestled, for perishing souls and the languishing interests of Zion. One or more of the groves is still pointed out, where they, with neighboring pastors, used to retire from the world to agonize for the descent of the Holy Spirit. The day of mercy was near. At length the revival burst upon them."

Of the beginning of this revival, Hallock himself writes: "This was, indeed, a trying hour. No fond parent ever watched the fever of his child at the hour of its crisis with more anxious and interested feelings, than numbers of God's praying friends watched the work of the Spirit at this critical moment."

When Zion travails, she brings forth her children. So, revivals are the offspring of the travails of God's people in concerted prayer. For, as the writer adds, "The work was now evidently on the increase. Conferences—meaning prayer-meetings—were set up in every part of the parish, and every week, and sometimes every day, would bring the animating news of some one hopefully converted."

These prayer-meetings were called conference meetings, because conference on religious subjects formed a very interesting and important part of their exercises, so often impressive and awakening. Thus, the same, again:

"At a certain conference, in which the conversation turned on the divine purposes, the subject was not attended to now for disputation, but with fear and solemnity. They did not appear to be dry, uninteresting, disputable points, but divine realities, calculated to convict the sinner and refresh the saint. At the close of the meeting a question was asked of this import: 'Does a person who is truly seeking after God, feel afraid that any of his purposes will cut off from salvation?' The question was answered in the negative; and the divine purposes were no more against prayer, than against attention to common matters, and that the only reason why men brought them against prayer was, their having no heart to pray."

The fearers of the Lord will speak often one to another. They will not forsake the assembling of themselves together; but exhorting *one another*—they will admonish *one another* in Psalms, Hymns, and spiritual songs. They will love to say to *one another*, Come, hear, all ye that fear God, and I will declare what he did for my soul.

Dr. Sprague, of Albany, N. Y., gives, in his Lectures on Revivals, a letter from Dr. Hyde, of Lee, Mass., in which the writer says: "The first season of 'refreshing from the presence of the Lord,' which this people enjoyed, commenced in June, 1792, a few days after the event of my ordination. There was at that time no religious excitement in this region of country, nor had I knowledge of any special work of God's grace in any part of the land. The church here was small and feeble, having only twenty-one male members. It was, however, like the primitive Christians, continuing with one accord in prayer. Immediately, on being stationed here as a watchman, I instituted a weekly religious conference, to be holden on each Wednesday, and in succession, at the various school-houses in the town. These were well attended in every district, and furnished me with favorable opportunities to instruct the people. A marvellous work was begun, and it bore the most decisive marks of being *God's work.*"

Rev. Joseph Washburn, Farmington, Conn., writing of revival, (*Rev. Sk.*) says:

"In 1798, God began to appear in power and great glory, in a number of towns in this vicinity. Accounts of these things reached us, and became the subject of conversation among Christians, but appeared to have little or no effect.

"This first appearance of special divine power and grace was in February, 1799. It began in an uncommon attention and concern among the people of God, and a disposition to unite in prayer for the divine presence and a revival of religion.

"Soon after this, numbers in different parts of the congregation began to inquire respecting the meetings, and expressed a wish to attend."

Dr. Shepherd, of Lenox, Mass., writes of a revival in 1799, thus:

"Such were the melancholy prospects of this church while showers of divine grace were falling on other parts of Zion. But in the month of April, several members of the church manifested great anxiety about the state of religion among us, and expressed a desire that meetings might be appointed for religious conference and special prayer for the outpouring of the Spirit. It was done. From that time the work became more general."

Judge Boudinot, writing to Judge Reeve of revival, (*Revival Sk.* p. 165) says:

"The flame at once caught the hearts of the truly pious among us. The next Sabbath morning a number agreed to form a society to meet at nine o'clock, and spend an hour previous to going to church in prayer to God for his blessing on the word. They styled themselves the Aaron and Hur Society, as supporting the hands of their minister. It was not long before the blessed work pervaded every part of the congregation."

One reference only to revivals of this period in the Eastern States. Rev. John B. Preston, Rupert, Vt., July, 1804, says:

"From year to year religion was declining, the church was decreasing in numbers and graces; and iniquity abounded. A little more than a year ago, the darkness reached its height, and appeared scarcely to admit the smallest beam of hope.

"In this hour of extremity, a small number of the few remaining professors agreed to meet once a week for social prayer. At the first the number was very small, sometimes not more than two or three; but they appeared strong in faith and fervent in prayer, the Spirit helping their infirmities with groanings which could not be uttered. The meetings became increasingly solemn, so that, in September, the number of religious conferences, or, rather, prayer-meetings, in different parts of the society, were multiplied to four in a week. A day of fasting and prayer was observed about this time, and attended with a special degree of solemnity. In November, on a sudden, the Spirit of the Lord appeared to come down upon us like a mighty rushing wind. Almost the whole society seemed to be shaken at once. Our prayer-meetings were crowded, and solemn in an amazing degree."

These, but specimen selections out of many, all unite in identifying the prayer-meeting as the uniform instrumentality in promoting revivals, and of testing the state of religion in any locality, or at any period in the history of the church.

Leaving the East as the field of our historical gleanings, we shall turn to the South and West. Here extensive range opens. Dr. Alexander, late of Princeton, Dr. Humphrey, of Mass., with several others, have given many interesting details of extensive revivals in many parts of the South. Virginia, as a field of interest, about the year 1788, furnishes some striking instances of extensive awakenings originating in prayer-meetings.

Dr. Hill, of Winchester, gives the following narrative (*Revival Sketches*, pp. 182–184). Speaking of early religious impressions received from a sainted mother, he says:

"I carried these with me into Hampden-Sidney College, where there was then *not one pious student.* I had no Bible, and dreaded getting one, lest it should be found in my possession. A pious lady near sent me Alliene's Alarm When I got it, I locked my room, and lay on my bed reading it, when a student knocked at the door. And although I gave him no answer, dreading to be found reading such a book, he continued to knock and beat the door until I had to open it. He came in, and seeing the book lying on the bed, seized it, and examining its title, said, 'Why, Hill, do you read such books?' I hesitated, but God enabled me to be decided, and to answer him boldly, but with much emotion, 'Yes, I do.' The young man said, with deep agitation, 'O, Hill, I envy you. You may obtain religion, but I never can. I came here a professor of religion, but through fear I dissembled, and have been carried along with the wicked until I fear there is no hope for me.'

"He told me there were two others who, he believed, were serious. We agreed to take up the subject of religion in earnest, and seek it *together*. We invited the other two, and had a prayer-meeting in my room on the next Saturday afternoon. And O, what a prayer-meeting! We tried to pray, but such prayer I never heard the like of. We knew not how to pray, but tried to do it. It was the first prayer-meeting I had ever heard of. We tried to sing, but it was in a most suppressed manner; for we feared the other students. But they found it out, and gathered round the door, and made such a noise that some of the officers had to come and disperse them. And so serious was the disturbance that the President, the late excellent Rev. Dr. John Blair Smith, had to investigate the matter at prayers that evening, in the prayer hall. When he demanded the reason of the riot, a ringleader in wickedness got up and stated that it was occasioned by three or four of the boys holding a prayer-meeting, and they were determined to have no such doings there.

The good President heard the statement with deep emotion, and looking at the youths charged with the sin of praying, with tears in his eyes, he said, 'Oh, is there such a state of things in this College? Then God has come near to us. My dear young friends, you shall be protected. You shall hold your next prayer-meeting in my parlor, and I will be one of your number.' Sure enough, we had our next meeting in his parlor, and half the College were there. And there began a glorious revival of religion, which pervaded the College, and spread into the country around."

COLLEGE NARRATIVES AND LESSONS.

This College narrative illustrates several things. 1. That true religion, sanctifying our social nature, brings kindred spirits together for the enjoyment of Christian communion. Hill and the other three pious students—the only ones known to have been religiously disposed—were attracted together in a most wonderful way in God's mysterious Providence. They were drawn together by the same common attraction mutually inclining each to seek and delight in the society of religious character. They were drawn together by the same natural feeling of love to social prayer. Here was no force of education, no denominational drill to bias to any ritualistic forms—nothing but the workings of grace upon pious and simple minds, under the influence of love to Christ, love to prayer, love to the company of kindred spirits.

2. The power of social prayer to increase mutual affection, mutual growth in grace, and to prepare for future usefulness. This prayer-meeting produced lasting effects for good upon the minds of the four friends who formed this College prayer-meeting.

3. This case illustrates the power of social prayer in the cause of revivals of religion. This was made instrumental in the conversion of about one-half the students of a col-

lege when it was supposed there was not one pious among them. Many of these afterwards became learned ministers of the gospel. And, besides, from this humble little prayer-meeting commenced many and extensive revivals throughout the country around.

Nor is this an isolated case—a single instance of very rare occurrence. It is only one of many, illustrating an important principle of true religion, and of the power of concerted social prayer, according to the promise of Christ, and the design of this ordinance of grace.

In the summer of 1823, the writer was a student at Jefferson College, Western Pennsylvania. That year witnessed in that College a revival of some interest. With its origin and progress and whole history he was personally and intimately acquainted. It may not be without interest in this connection. During the vacation preceding the summer session, a few of the pious students conferred together on the subject of the conversion of godless and immoral students, many of whom were possessed of fine talents, which, if sanctified by grace, and consecrated to the cause of Christ and religion, would be a great acquisition to that cause. They singled out a few of that class as the special objects of prayer, and agreed that they would organize themselves into a select and special prayer-meeting, for the purpose of pleading Christ's promise. (Matt. xviii. 19): "If two of you shall agree on earth as touching anything that they shall ask, it shall be done for them of my Father which is in heaven." This society had just commenced its meetings, which were held in the private rooms of the students who formed it, when the summer session of the College opened. In the course of a few weeks evidences of awakening began to be manifested, particularly among that class made the special object of the concerted prayers of the recently formed prayer-meeting. And, at the same time, a very marked revival of prayerful zeal and earnestness was seen among the Professors of the College, and professors of religion generally. Religion soon became a topic of general conversation among pious people. Professors of religion among the students embraced occasions for religious conversation with some of those for whose conversion they had been specially pleading in their prayer-meeting. They found, almost to their joyful astonishment, that among some of their fellow-students who had been careless, if not in some instances profane, there was a deep concern already felt. To these they suggested the importance of forming among themselves a separate prayer-meeting for that distinct class. Such society was at once formed of some eight or ten. In a short time, others were found to be awakened, and were encouraged to form a second prayer-meeting of non-professors, now awakened and anxious. And so, as the religious interest increased, societies were formed among the students in their rooms, professors and non-professors, as also among the Christian people of the town, and out among the congregations in the country. Scarcely an evening through the week, or on Sabbaths, that there were not prayer-meetings in town and country.

These numerous prayer-meetings, the concerted prayers and earnest conferences were abundant in their fruits. Besides many additions of the hopeful converts that were added to many congregations in that vicinity, not a few young men who left their homes thoughtless of their soul's eternal interests, and who had never bowed a knee to God, became active in the cause of religion, changed their purposes in regard to a profession and their future life, devoted themselves to the ministry, and became faithful and successful ambassadors for Christ.

One lesson more we may learn from these college narratives and prayer-meeting incidents. No two students, professors of religion, at any college, should suffer themselves to spend one single session without forming a prayer-meeting, and connecting with it some special object of persevering, united prayer. And until this obtains, in spirit and in truth, can we expect our colleges to be really fountains from which streams shall issue gladdening the city of our God? What can be more becoming or more encouraging than for candidates for the ministry, while engaged in preparatory studies, and constantly in contact with promising, though unconverted youths, to form prayer-meetings, and in concert wrestle for the salvation of their fellow-students, who, if by grace were snatched from the control of Satan, might become champions in the cause of Christ?

In this connection we shall detain the reader with one more college reference.

Dr. Green, late President of the College at Princeton, writing to Dr. Sprague, says:

"While I was a member of college, there were but two professors of religion among the students, and not more than five or six who scrupled to use profane language in common conversation. To the influence of the American war succeeded that of the French revolution, still more pernicious. The open and avowed Infidelity of Paine and other writers of the same character produced incalculable injury to religion and morals throughout our whole country."

In this condition of society and of the college, a revival visitation was enjoyed, of which the writer proceeds to make some very interesting statements:

"In about four weeks, there were very few individuals in the college who were not deeply impressed with a sense of the importance of spiritual and eternal things. There was scarcely a room, perhaps not one, which was not a place of earnest, secret devotion. For a time it seemed as if the whole of our charge was pressing into the kingdom of God. The result was, that of one hundred and five students, there were more than forty in regard to whom favorable hopes were entertained that they were the subjects of grace."

In regard to the means used for the promotion of this revival, it is added:

"The few youths who were previously pious, had, for more than a year, been earnestly engaged in prayer for this event. When they perceived the general and increasing seriousness, several of them agreed to speak privately and tenderly to their particular acquaintances on the subject of religion; and what they said was, in almost every instance, not only well received, but those with whom they conversed became earnestly engaged in those exercises, which, it is hoped, have issued in genuine piety.

"In preaching on the Lord's day morning, subjects were selected suited to the existing state of the College—a prayer-meeting was held every Friday evening, at which one of the Professors of Theology commonly made an address. A prayer-meeting was every evening held by the students themselves—smaller and more select associations were held for prayer; the individuals whose minds were anxious, were, as often as they requested it, carefully conversed and prayed with in private."

While in this example we see, as in other cases, the importance of social and concerted prayer, we also have illustrated the importance of conference, not only in the prayer-meeting, but privately and with the special objects of solicitude. Must not every prayer-meeting be necessarily defective without conference? And when they are held pursuant to agreement for special prayer, it would seem important to success to obtain private conference with the objects of our special prayers.

The author of "Revival Sketches" gives a very interesting account of a revival in his own congregation, Pittsfield, Mass., in which he says:

"The narrative would be quite incomplete if I were to close it here. In all revivals God works by means and instrumentalities, and some may be glad to know what course was here adopted.

"Our general course of preaching and incidental labors was as follows: Three discourses on the Sabbath, one of which was always in the evening. Two public lectures on week-day evenings, preceded by a short prayer-meeting a little before sundown; occasional lectures and prayer-meetings in the out-districts, one object of which was to bring as many as we could to attend the central lectures; an inquiry meeting every Monday evening, and a church prayer-meeting at the same hour. Besides these, a great many smaller neighborhood meetings were attended."

The principal lesson of instruction in this reference is, the importance of such arrangement in regard to the prayer-meeting as will bring every family and every individual under its influence, as well as to the enjoyment of the public ordinances of the gospel. No pastor or session of a congregation should rest satisfied with any system of administration that fails to supply all with the privilege of the prayer-meeting; or fails to induce the attendance of all. Every available interest should be given to "the many smaller neighborhood meetings," to induce, if possible, as large an aggregate attendance on the prayer-meetings as on the regular public Sabbath service.

CHAPTER VII.

FROM THE MIDDLE OF THIS CENTURY TILL THE COMMENCEMENT OF THE REVIVAL OF 1857, A PERIOD OF INTENSE POLITICAL AND RELIGIOUS COMMOTION.

The Protestant Reformation a great Revival of Religion and Social Prayer—Revival of this period and American Liberty—Revived Social Prayer—Prepared for the investigation of the subject of the Prayer-Meeting—State of the Country and of Religion when the Revival came—Revival Sketches—Features of this Revival—In its Commencement—Conducted by Union Prayer-meetings—Its spirit rapidly pervaded the country—In its Prayer-meetings "The earth helped the woman"—Xenia Convention—Unparalleled Political agitation, from 1850 to 1860—Intense around the Slavery question—God chose such time for this Revival.

The period of wide-spread revivals and prayer-meetings— 1857–1859.

THIS century, early in its third quarter, witnessed one of the most extensive revivals of religion, and of social prayer, fruitful in results, finding a place in the history of the church since the Reformation. The great Protestant Reformation was itself a great and permanent revival of evangelical religion. It revived *truth*, almost buried in the mass of antichristian corruptions and gross error. It revived *practical godliness*, and turned its converts to *prayer* and other Christian duties, plain and simple, as taught in the word of God and enforced by Christ and his Apostles. It turned away the Christian life and walk from the commandments of men, to the precepts and institutions of Christ. It revived *experimental piety* by pouring out upon the church a spirit of grace and supplications—

by breaking the fetters of superstition and priestcraft from the Christian mind—by introducing into the spiritual liberty with which Christ makes his children free to serve him in spirit and in truth, a broader and deeper exercise of all the Christian graces.

This last general revival, while it may have had its defects, was still attended and followed with gains to the cause both of *truth* and *righteousness*. It prepared the evangelical church, in nearly all its branches, for throwing her influence into the *issue*, when, in the war with rebellion, mighty scales hung quivering in the balance betwixt the cause of liberty and slavery. Had not the church demanded liberty for the slave, in the war waged for slavery extension and perpetuity by the slaveholder, it would have become national and its area widely extended. And had there been no revival in 1858, the church would still have remained, to such an extent, under the leadings of the South, that the war for the Union and for the cause of liberty would have ended in the triumph of slavery, and fall of American liberty, personal, civil and religious.

It awakened in the church a broader and more Christ-like missionary spirit—the poorest of the poor soon had the Bible sent them, and the gospel preached to them as never before since primitive times.

It certainly revived the love and practice of social prayer, and gave a new life to the prayer-meeting. Our very penning of these lines to-day, under all the circumstances which have led thereto, stands as a testimony to the truth of our statement. We believe the state of the church encourages us to write. The subject will be studied, and we have a hope we shall have a careful reading. And we think so, the more because we entertain the abiding hope that still more refreshing times from the presence of the Lord are not far in the future. We, therefore, in this way, lend, at this time, our mite of feeble influence to the cause of revival and the leading instrumentality, under grace, for its promotion. We hopefully make an effort to awaken in the church a deeper interest in the prayer-meeting, and a more earnest inquiry after its Scriptural character and use. As we trace the history of the prayer-meeting nearer our own time, its interest must be increased. And, as an aid to the securing of that interest, it may be important to review

THE STATE OF THE COUNTRY AND OF RELIGION WHEN THE REVIVAL WAS SENT.

Since historians, as well as poets, have their license, we shall avail ourselves of our privilege just here by borrowing some paragraphs from the racy sketches of a trustworthy historian—"Revival Sketches," pp. 276–279. Here we have sketched some of the features of the times immediately preceding the revivals of 1857–1859.

"There was increasing coldness and worldly conformity in the churches. From some of the watch-towers of Zion the alarm, indeed, was sounded. There was weeping in secret places over the general decline, and many prayers were offered for the return of the Spirit. But to the question, 'Watchman, what of the night?' there was no cheering answer. It was very dark, and seemed to be growing darker. As in the days of the prophet, Israel was mad upon her idols, so we had our idols of gold and silver. A *money* mania pervaded not only all our commercial cities, but the whole country more or less, involving all classes. The old paths to competence, by the moderate gains of industry and frugality, were being more and more forsaken, as no longer suited to this progressive age. Speculation in stocks, in city and village lots, in wild lands, in paper villages and flourishing marts of business, and in everything that promised sudden and extravagant gains, had reached the crisis of fever heat, and filled the dreams of thousands upon thousands with uncounted treasures, with fairy mansions, and all the delights of the 'lusts of the flesh, the lusts of the eye, and the pride of life.' Would that it had been but an Arabian night-dream, instead of the actual every-day state of the scrambling multitudes."

And then such a highly inflated and insane grasping for riches could not fail of creating temptations, to an alarming extent, too strong to be resisted, in the large business transactions of the country. Hence those enormous frauds which have made the ears of the nation to tingle, and by which multitudes of widows and orphans have been swindled out of the small hard-earned investments, on which they depended for their daily bread. It was painfully manifest that, without some check to this all-absorbing worldliness, there was no reasonable prospect of such a return of the years of the right hand of the Most High, as we had once enjoyed, under the opening heavens, pouring down the Holy Spirit and reviving his work. The church was fast falling into the current which swept madly on, and threatened, if possible, to swallow up the very elect. To change the figure, we were descending an inclined plane, with all the steam on, and no brakes to check the engine and save the train from being dashed to pieces.

"Just then, in the summer of 1857, God interposed in a way which but few, if any, would have chosen or thought of. When men were saying, 'Soul, thou hast much goods laid up for many years, take thine ease, eat, drink, and be merry;' when they were building their castles in the air, not easy to be numbered; when the common talk on 'Change was of hundreds of thousands and millions; when, in short, all men were saying, 'To-morrow shall be as this day, and more abundant,' then suddenly came the crash, as if thunders from a clear sky had simultaneously broken over the whole land. Like a yawning earthquake, it shook down the palaces of the rich, no less than the humble dwellings of the poor, and swallowed up their substance. Men went to bed dreaming all night of their vast hoarded treasures, and woke up in the morning hopeless bankrupts.

"Happily these overwhelming losses brought many prosperous business men to a stand, who had given themselves no time to think about laying up treasures in heaven; and, under the wise and merciful orderings of Providence, this prepared the way for a new revival epoch, differing in its commencement and some of its aspects from any that had preceded it."

The writer proceeds to mark some of the characteristics distinguishing this revival from all preceding:

"1. In *its commencement.* How and where did it begin? The kingdom of God came not with observation. Such a visit, at such a time, was not looked for. On the contrary, many feared that the financial disasters of the country had so absorbed the minds of the whole people, both in and out of the churches, as to leave no room for the concerns of the soul. But it would seem that the mighty crash was just what was wanted in the great marts of business and speculation to startle men from their golden dreams, and lead them to seek for durable riches and righteousness. The horse-leech epidemic had spread so wide, and reached such a crisis, that no ordinary means could arrest it. There is no reason to believe, I think, that this revival would have commenced as it did, and spread as it has, if the spell which held men in its embrace had not been broken by some sudden and violent convulsion. It came, and the rushing throng of fortune-seekers stood still in amazement. Wall street was shattered and tottering from one end to the other. Every shock threatened wider ruin, and where could the merchant princes and bankers find a place of refuge? Their millions were gone or going, and they had laid up no better portion. A thickening gloom hung over all the cities, and spread over all the country. While the earth reeled, the heavens were shut up.

"It was just then that God put it into the heart of a humble individual to propose a daily prayer-meeting in the lower part of the city of New York, at such a time as would best suit the convenience of business men. At first but few attended, in a little room on the third floor of the Consistory of the Reformed Dutch Church in Fulton Street. But 'behold how great a matter a little fire kindleth.' Soon, to the astonishment of everybody, thronging multitudes filled all the rooms of that building to their utmost capacity. It was a vast daily prayer-meeting, of an hour at twelve o'clock, attended by those of all classes and conditions, and included great numbers of business men, who had never been seen in a prayer-meeting before. It was the Lord's doing, and marvellous in all eyes. Nor could it long be confined within such narrow limits."

Of this meeting the author of "Five Years of Prayer," p. 10, says:

"Among all the records of ancient and modern times, in sacred or secular history, no series of facts is more imposing in their aspect before the Christian mind than the annals of the daily prayer-meetings in the city of New York. They were begun September 23d, 1857, and have continued without the interruption of a day through all the vicissitudes of life in the city, in the midst of war and peace, in the heat of summer and cold of winter, down to the day on which these lines are written, September 23d, 1863, and the Sixth Anniversary has just now been celebrated with the voice of supplication, thanksgiving and praise."

OUR REVIVAL SKETCHES PROCEED.

"The fire from heaven that kindled the flame then, spread rapidly in all directions. The call to prayer became louder throughout the city than it ever was before. It daily filled some of the largest churches; it gathered thousands into one of the vast theatres; it reached the Free Academy; the fire and the police departments opened their doors for daily prayer. Rooms were opened by merchants in their stores, in which their clerks met for prayer; and the waiters in one of the large hotels had their daily prayer-meeting. Even Jews participated in the great revival movement, and attended the meetings in various parts of the city. Such, in brief, was the commencement of this marvellous work of the Spirit. The oldest Christians stood still and exclaimed, 'We never saw it on this fashion;' and may I not ask, Who ever did? Of such a simultaneous movement we have no recorded example.

"2. They were *Union* prayer-meetings, attended by all who chose, without respect to denominational differences. This was a new feature in the revival. The middle walls of partition had never before been so thoroughly broken down. Evangelical Christians of every name found they could come together and pray for the outpouring of the Spirit without any sacrifice of church order, and were astonished that they had not sooner found out 'how good and how pleasant it is for brethren to dwell together in unity' at a throne of grace. O, how it liberalized the sectarian spirit! how it enlarged the heart! how it tended to unite the whole household of faith in one common brotherhood! Let it be our united prayer, that Satan may never more get an advantage of us by rebuilding the walls which have so long kept us apart to our mutual discredit and loss. Have we not all one Lord, one faith, one God and Father, who is above all, through all, and in us all? And shall we ever hesitate to unite in praying for the descent of the Holy Spirit, whenever and wherever we can enjoy the privilege?

"3. Another remarkable feature in this revival, is the *rapidity* with which the spirit of united prayer spread from city to city, and from State to State, gathering the vast multitudes who, in a few weeks, were everywhere seen crowding the meetings, giving unmistakable evidence that God was in the midst of them. His presence and power were manifest as never before, in making New York, Philadelphia, Cincinnati, and almost all our large cities centres of this great movement, radiating the spiritual light and warmth which they were first to enjoy, upon all the regions round about. Thus the *united prayer-meetings and the revivals spread* with wonderful rapidity to hundreds of places, from the centre to the circumference. It has been variously estimated that there were within one year, between three and five hundred thousand converts.

"4. *The earth came in and helped the woman* as never before since she fled from the great red dragon into the wilderness. Thirty years ago, it was difficult to get even a short paragraph of religious intelligence into a secular city paper. Such a thing as a notice of a revival, we may almost say, was never heard of through such a channel. The best that could be done was chiefly accomplished with singular tact and perseverance by a minister well and widely known at the time, as bent on doing good in every possible way. At first it was a volunteer and gratuitous service, collecting and writing out short articles, handing them to the editors, and getting them inserted more as special favors to the man, than to their readers and patrons. Finding how much good he was doing in this way, a number of religious men contributed moderate sums to sustain him, and this was all that could be done to reach the masses of newspaper readers. I believe I might say it took a whole year to get the amount of two columns into any secular city paper, when revivals in almost every part of the country were going on with mighty power.

"But how astonishing the change! Scarcely had the *Union prayer-meetings* been set up in New York, Boston, and other cities, when the same papers, of their own accord, devoted whole, closely-crowded columns, weekly and daily, to this new religious phenomenon, vying with each other who should most minutely chronicle the progress of these meetings, and spread the news widest. In fact, for some time, they took the lead of the religious papers in this department of intelligence. The change was so sudden and so surprising, that we could hardly believe our own eyes in reading the dailies. This was a great advance upon what had ever before been witnessed."

We remember, very distinctly, that, when in the convention at Xenia, Ohio, May, 1858, a reporter from Cincinnati, for the *Gazette*, manifested a deep interest in the proceedings of the meeting, especially in the religious devotions. With commendable respect for the worship, he always laid down his pencil and took part with the worshipers in the prayers and singing. Often he appeared delighted to ecstasy. So much was he moved by the songs of praise, in which he with earnest and full voice joined, that during an interval of the convention he called in a book store, and asked for a copy of the soul-moving hymns sung in the meetings. The bookseller replied, "Sir, you have those hymns in your Bible. They are just the Book of Psalms in an old metrical version, used by the churches represented in the convention." Here he remarked with deep interest, that he had never heard sung songs so fully appropriate to revival meetings. Every morning we had full and interesting reports of the doings of every preceding day's sessions of the convention.

These things presented to us, and, so far as we know, to every member of the hundreds of the convention, a new and strange feature of the times—strange to see so deep and earnest an interest in the political press in those solemn and soul-stirring exercises. And this was the more remarkable, as that period was one of most intense political excitement.

And here we feel constrained to add to the sketch of the times immediately preceding this revival as drawn by the author of *Revival Sketches*, as already so largely quoted. That was an epoch not only of financial excitement, greatly absorbing the public mind, turning it away from the concerns of eternity and the soul; but it was a time of deep, intense, and all-absorbing political stir. Perhaps never since the French Revolution was religion so put to the test as by the political agitations from 1850 to 1860. Much as financial interests affect the human mind, and much as Mammon can steal away the heart from Christ, yet there is one other thing which more deeply and more firmly takes hold of human nature as an absorbing and controlling power, which sometimes overrides all other temporal interests. The love of gain could never have plunged this country into the late rebellion and civil war. But the maddening spell of political excitement did so involve this country. She was in the whirlpool of an incipient civil struggle, just at the very time the Spirit of God was poured out on this land, so that just from the scenes of the prayer-meeting were hundreds of our brave sons summoned to the sanguinary field of fratricidal carnage.

Let it be remembered that the period from 1850 to 1860 is styled by historians as "the era of slave hunting." It was the era of "the Nebraska-Kansas struggle." It was the era of "the Dred-Scott case in the Supreme Court." It was the era of "the pistol and the bludgeon," in high places and low. It was the era of "Sumner and Brooks' gutta-percha logic," of blood-stained floor of an American Senate, and freedom of speech lying prostate at the feet of the slave-dealer, in the halls of American legislation. It was the era of "the Impending Crisis," and of the "Irrepressible Conflict." It was the era of "the John Brown raid," and summary execution. It was the era of fierce and war-boding presidential campaigning—Lincoln and Douglas, and Breckenridge and Bell.

How could such a time be favorable to revival and the prayer-meeting? Only as the journey to Damascus, with a heart madly set on the blood and the life of innocent men and women, was an acceptable time with God for the display of the power of his grace in the conversion of Saul of Tarsus, a chief sinner.

Yet God chose that dark hour for the display of his grace in reviving the churches—in calling the earnest attention of all classes, in all departments of society—in many countries—on the high seas, and in the armies and navies of many nations, to the prayer-meeting; and in such way that the public mind was everywhere turned to those meetings as the centres of interest and influences everywhere felt and acknowledged. From various sources we have abundant testimony to the happy influences of the prayer-meeting among the soldiers of the Union army. The reports of chaplains, of delegates of the Christian Commission, and from many visitors, both ministers and laymen, furnish abundant materials for the history of revival and the inseparable prayer-meeting.

CHAPTER VIII.

PRAYER-MEETINGS IN THE ARMY, HOSPITALS, AND NAVY.

Agencies Employed—Bible Society—Tract Society—Christian Commission—Letters from Soldiers in the Camp—From a Chaplain—Prayer-Meetings in Hospitals—Testimony to the Prayer-Meeting—Prayer-Meetings among Seamen—Benevolence of the Age in Marine Hospital, the Post Society, the Sailors' Home, the Marine Church—Sailors' Narratives—Ship Niagara—Chaplain's Letters—Religious Interest of Commodore McKean, and his example in behalf of the Prayer-Meeting—Lessons—The Old War-Ship North Carolina—A Place for Prayer-Meetings—The Ohio and her Prayer-Meetings—U. S. Ship St. Louis—A Sailor's Letter to Dr. Stewart—Reflections upon the important Lessons of this Chapter.

Prayer-meetings among the Soldiers.

THE impression has, perhaps, been very general, that the camp is a very unfavorable place for the development of Christian graces, for the conversion of sinners, or for the reform of those addicted to habits of vice. The heart of Christian benevolence has seldom been so deeply sounded as during the late campaign for the suppression of rebellion against the government of our country. The Sanitary and Christian Commissions drew their hundreds of thousands of dollars in voluntary contributions from the masses of the Christian and patriotic people. And while the temporal comforts of the soldier was a matter of deep solicitude, perhaps it is not too much to say his spiritual interests excited far more of the Christian sympathy of a Christian people. Efforts, unparalleled in the history of all former wars, were made to supply the army with religious reading matter. The Bible Society, the Tract Society, and other agencies, issued by the millions copies of reading matter. And yet these Bibles and tracts, good books, and every variety of religious publications, were of little avail alone. It was the concurrent testimony of Chaplains, Agents of the Christian Commission, and other Christian men and women, who visited the army on errands of spiritual benevolence, that, with all the outlay of Christian charity in this way, if there should be no prayer, there would be no good done. It would be seed scattered by the way-side. But when the prayer-meetings were opened, and the prayers of God's people went out with these, and in behalf of the soldiers, then hearts were moved and encouraged, and filled with hope and joy.

A soldier, who, in addition to patriotic motives, was moved to enlist that he might have opportunity of laboring for the salvation of the poor soldiers in the army, makes the following statement: "When he got into his regiment, after very diligent inquiry, he could find only one pious man, but he was of kindred spirit. They were only two, but they were resolved on a prayer-meeting. It was begun in much fear and trembling, and against not a little opposition and ridicule. They had no help but God; 'and, Oh,' said he, 'how did He answer and help us!' He converted four of our fellow-soldiers—the four most unlikely that we could have picked out. We felt all the time that some one would be converted, but were almost overcome when these four came out for Christ."

One who had visited the Army of the Potomac, to promote the spiritual interests of the soldiers, said, on his return:

"You can have no idea of the eagerness of the men for religious reading. You cannot take a wagon, with religious tracts and religious newspapers, and drive into one of these camps, and begin to distribute them, but you will be almost devoured. Hundreds of men will come running from all directions, stretching out their hands and pleading for something good to read. In one of the regiments there is a genuine revival going forward at this present time. They have meetings every night. One night is a prayer-meeting; the next night is an inquiry meeting; the next a meeting for the relation of religious experience; and so all through the week."

Thus, where there is strong desire for religious reading matter, and especially where there is revival of religion, or even any live religion at all, there soon will the prayer-meeting be.

A soldier once communicated to his praying friends the following:

"You will, perhaps, remember, that I, some time ago, asked prayer for a regiment. I want to tell you what has been, and is now, its spiritual condition. Vice and immorality prevailed in it to an alarming extent. Soon after I asked prayer in their behalf, four of the soldiers resolved to establish, if possible, a prayer-meeting in camp. At the first meeting only these four were present. At the second meeting thirty-three attended. At the third, three hundred were present, and at the fourth, nearly all the regiment, except those who were on guard or other duty."

"The chaplain of a Maine regiment stated, in the daily prayer-meeting, that God was pouring down his Spirit upon the regiment, and about twenty-five of the men had been hopefully converted within three weeks. Among them was an old man aged sixty-eight years. He was a soldier in the war of 1812 and has always lived a moral life, but wholly unconcerned on the subject of religion.

It was very touching to hear him talk or pray in the prayer-meeting. He blesses God that he came into the army, for he thinks if he had remained at home, he would have lived and died in his sins, without repentance. All the newly converted men took part in their regimental prayer-meetings."

A soldier in a New York regiment, writing from a fort to which his regiment had been sent, says:

"On Saturday evening we hunted up some half dozen young men, who were professing Christians, and appointed a prayer-meeting for Sabbath morning, at half past six o'clock; and on Sabbath morning, at that time, there were gathered some dozen or more at the southwest bastion, which we had permission to use for the purpose. It was a pleasant reviving meeting, and it shed its influence over us during the whole day. At night, at eight o'clock, we had another meeting of the kind, at which there were, I think, more than twenty present, and among them two of the captains, one of whom is a professing Christian, and at that time joined in the exercises with us. We met again last evening, and the exercises were conducted by one of the captains, who is a Christian. We have these meetings now every evening in the week, and more than once a day on Sabbath. We hope and pray they may do much good to those who are out of the ark and without hope, and we pray God to use it to his own glory and to that effect."

Another soldier, writing from Beaufort, S. C., April 27, 1863, says:

"I can name several regiments in which daily prayer-meetings have been sustained for several weeks, even without a chaplain. In two regiments there have been one hundred and fifty conversions each. In other regiments, one hundred, eighty, and so on, down in numbers. In this place is a daily evening prayer-meeting, held in the large Episcopal Church, at which from three to five hundred soldiers attend. And they come, not from curiosity, not to escape the confinement of the camp, but to take part in the meeting, to pray, to bear witness for what the Lord has done for them, to invite others to come to Jesus, and to encourage one another in the Christian course."

"One of the most faithful chaplains in the army of the Union was the Rev. Mr. Wyatt, a clergyman of the Reformed Presbyterian Church, who, after passing unhurt through the battles of James Island, Antietam, Fredericksburgh, and others of the severest conflicts of the war, died in the officers' hospital, at Memphis, Tennessee, July 10th, 1863. In a report, which he made to the Synod with which he was connected, he stated that fourteen hundred men had been under his immediate care during his chaplaincy; that eight hundred of these had fallen on the field of battle, or of their wounds subsequently, while a few only had died of disease. Among these, he adds, several had been converted to God after they joined the regiment, and of the religious men in the regiment, many presented the highest types of Christian character. On the evening before the assault at James Island, near Charleston, in 1862, he held a prayer-meeting with his men, a goodly number of soldiers being in attendance; and his heart was moved to speak very tenderly to them, because he knew that many of them would not see the setting of to-morrow's sun. He said afterward, in picking up the wounded and visiting them in their hospitals, he found some three or four who thought they became Christians that night in that prayer-meeting."

PRAYER-MEETINGS IN THE HOSPITALS.

"The chaplain of one of our large hospitals, in the vicinity of the metropolis, said: There is much religious anxiety among the men. Many express hope—say twenty-five or thirty—that they have lately passed from death unto life. Our prayer-meetings are very interesting, and nearly one-third of the inmates of the hospital attend. It would be sure to move your hearts if you could see those men come into our meetings. Some come in on crutches, some on sticks and canes; some with bandages around their heads; some with broken arms, and some with broken legs; some blind, some sick—too sick to be out of bed, but creeping into the prayer-meetings because they are so anxious on the subject of religion that they cannot stay away. They long to know how they can be saved. They long to know how they can have religion. They ask for religious reading with an intensity of interest of which you can have very vague conceptions. I have come for religious reading to-day, and I am in this meeting to solicit your prayers in behalf of these anxious men."

What a testimony we have here in behalf of the prayer-meeting! Men in earnest concern about their soul's salvation—creeping into the prayer-meeting when sick—too sick to be out of bed—earnest for religious reading—earnest to have a place in the united prayers of Christians assembled in the prayer-meeting. Some things we surely learn here: 1. The prayer-meeting is always a point of attraction, and deep interest, to the awakened and earnest sinner. 2. The prayer-meeting furnishes a very accurate discriminating test of character. The live Christian loves its enjoyments, the spiritually dead have no delights there.

A chaplain in a hospital says:

"I am crowded to death with my duties, and truly they are privileges; for I think a hospital one of the best places to do good in, of the whole field of work. God is truly blessing us in this hospital. Prayer-meetings in different wards every night, except Saturday night, are well attended. A healthy interest is growing."

"One who had been visiting a hospital for which we had often been asked to pray, said he wished all in this meeting could have been there. It was an affecting sight to see these men come hobbling down on their crutches and sticks, in great numbers, to attend the place of prayer. A more solemn prayer-meeting is not often attended. Great numbers were deeply moved during the meeting, and many tears were seen falling. Then, when tattoo beat, which was a signal to close the service, you ought to have seen how anxious the men were that it should be extended." Extracted from "Five Years of Prayer," pp. 200–214.

These extract gleanings from the army and hospitals, exhibit rather exceptions than the general rule. Iniquity and irreligion rather than prayer-meetings, or respect for religion in any way, were too common. But wherever religion had a hold upon the soldiers in the camps, there the prayer-meeting had a place, and *there*, cherished with affectionate concern, and *there* illustrating a *law* of true religion, whose Author is the Spirit of God, namely—That wherever grace is implanted in the heart, the subject is led to pray. Wherever religion is revived in any community or society, *there* will be *social prayer*. As the vapors of the clouds are, by a certain law of nature, condensed, and descend in rain-drops and showers, so will the attractive power of the social principle, when sanctified and constrained by love, draw sweetly, yet irresistibly, Christians revived together for prayer and religious conference. Thus it was in the camps. When a few pious soldiers were thrown together in a regiment, though from different and extreme points of the land, they soon, by some mysterious influence, were thrown together, and linked, as kindred spirits, by kindred ties, in sacred fellowship, seeking for its enjoyment—the social prayer-meeting.

PRAYER-MEETINGS AMONG SEAMEN.

The interest taken in the spiritual welfare of seamen is, perhaps, one of the distinguishing features of the age. When we consider the obstacles in the way, and the nature of the field itself, scarcely any other department of missionary labor has been more signally crowned with success than that which contemplates the sailor, the marine, and the entire naval department. Recent missionary enterprise has made the Marine Hospital, the Port Society, the Sailors' Home, the Mariners' Church, familiar institutions to active Christians of modern times. These things belong to the age of missions and Bible Societies. And in connection with these will be found material for Revival Sketches and Prayer-Meeting Narrative.

"The pastor of one of the Mariners' Churches in the city of New York, stated, not long since, that within four years he had admitted to the communion of his church more than five hundred persons, more than three hundred of whom were seamen, and that there were members of his church on twenty-two ships of war belonging to the United States naval service, and that on seven of them are held daily prayer-meetings.

"A statement published in 1863 says, 'that number has so increased under the divine blessing, that on our seventh anniversary, in March, 1863, the membership had reached over seven hundred and sixty. During that period, we have good reason to believe, that full one thousand souls have been hopefully converted, as the result of the combined labors of the pastor, the missionaries, and the membership of the Church and Port Society.' On a single cruise of one of our national vessels, there were seventy hopeful conversions, and the daily prayer-meeting was constantly maintained for the space of two years."

A Saturday evening prayer-meeting has been for some time organized and sustained in the New York Sailors' Home. Here, in connection with the prayer-meetings, interesting awakenings and revivals have often been enjoyed. Thrilling incidents of prayer-meeting revivals might here be recorded far beyond what our space would warrant.

The following are among some of the impressive statements made in the New York daily prayer-meeting:

"A sailor arose in the back part of the room, and said the Lord had mercy on him in answer to prayer. He was awakened at sea, when far from any means of grace or communications with his friends, and converted on board ship, before reaching a port. He did not know what to make of it when religious anxiety first came upon him. He, however, could find no rest till he found it in coming to Christ. He thought, at first, that he could never live religiously on shipboard; but he had found that he could not keep hid, that he hoped he had become a Christian. He told his shipmates of the great change, and boldly declared to them that hereafter he would be on the Lord's side. He found it more easy than he expected to stand up for Christ. No one ridiculed or opposed him, and in this he was disappointed. But not till he came into port could he understand why the Lord had sent his Spirit to convince him of sin while at sea. He found that he had been made the subject of special and daily prayer. His brothers and sisters and the daily prayer-meetings had carried his case to the throne of grace, and now he could understand why, away at sea, he had been convinced that he was a sinner, and needed a Saviour."

In this narrative we have a very illustrative instance of the power of persevering, concerted, social prayer. "If two of you shall agree on earth as touching anything that they shall ask, it shall be done for them of my Father which is in heaven."

A ship's captain, in very earnest terms, described the change which had come over his spirit as follows:

"I had a pious sister who urged me to come to this meeting. I told her, 'No, you don't catch me in a prayer-meeting, or any little room like this. Have I not paced the quarter-deck of a ship? Humph! I go to a prayer-meeting! Not I; when I go to a meeting, I will go into a *church*—a *church*, mind you, and not a small lecture-room.' But she insisted and urged, and somehow I got in here, I don't know how. And when I had been here only a very short time, at the first meeting, O what a change came over me! I had been puffed up, and was a great man in my own estimation. I felt I was a man of importance; I was a proud sinner. But in a few minutes, in that first hour in this meeting, I had such a sense of my own littleness as I never had before. I never dreamed that I was such a little creature. My importance was all gone. O, I tell you, it was a blessed place to me before I got out of it, this despised Fulton street prayer-meeting; for though I had not said it, I had, in my heart, despised it."

"One who had come in from sea, arose in the meeting and said, 'About one year ago, I stood up in this meeting and requested your prayers. I stated that I was about going on the steamship Hermann, on her voyage to San Francisco, and I desired that your prayers might go with us. For three weeks after we left this port we tried to get up a daily prayer-meeting on board. We met with opposition; but finally the opposition gave way, and our meetings commenced. Soon the Holy Spirit was poured out. Many were converted; and though I was ignorant, and when the Lord converted me on ship-board I could neither read nor write, yet the Lord enabled me to be useful, and I was enabled to guide many inquiring souls to Christ. When we arrived at San Francisco we attended meetings there.' "

We have before us two very interesting letters from Rev. C. S. Stewart, D. D., Chaplain, dated on board the U. S. Ship Niagara, one April, 1861; the other November, 1861. They contain much historical matter in regard to the prayer-meeting in connection with revival and religious interest experienced on board a man-of-war. They were directed to the *New York Observer*, and are introduced by the author of " Five Years' Prayer," p. 236, in the following notice:

" On the 1st of July, 1860, the U. S. Ship Niagara, Captain McKean, sailed from the port of New York, with the Japanese Ambassadors on board, to take them to their own country. Immediately, on her return, about a year after, she was ordered to the Southern waters in the service of the government, with the same officers and crew on board, and remained more than a year longer. During all this time the ship was literally a Bethel, religious services being constantly maintained. Numerous conversions took place both among the officers and seamen. The captain was a man of decided piety, who gave every encouragement to the religious services."

The first letter proceeds:

" By the time the Niagara reached Japan, the number of avowed Christians on board, among the fore-mast hands, had increased from nine to upward of twenty. The visit of the ship at Kanagawa, for a week, afforded to these an opportunity of happy and refreshing intercourse with the missionaries there. The freedom of the mission houses, and the hospitality promptly and most kindly extended by them, were gratefully appreciated, while their Christian fellowship and brotherly love cheered the hearts and confirmed the faith of the new disciples of a common Lord. Two or three prayer-meetings, on successive evenings, at the mission houses, in which the sailors chiefly took part, and one on board the Niagara the night before we left, to which all the missionaries, both ladies and gentlemen, came, although a gale was blowing at the time, seemed to be greatly enjoyed by and blessed to all parties."

The vessel, on its return, stopped at Cape Town, where very interesting social and Christian intercourse was enjoyed with the missionaries of the place. As in Japan, the chief entertainment was in the frequent prayer-meetings held during the short stay.

"Soon after leaving Table Bay, on the 9th of March, there were evidences of increased seriousness on board. The nightly prayer-meetings were attended by greater numbers, and an unaccustomed spirit of prayer manifested; and now, for more than a month past, we have been in the enjoyment of a season of grace more marked and more general than at any other period in our cruise. From twenty-five to thirty have again been added to our number, including six officers, besides those already mentioned; these are of different ranks, from that of lieutenant down. Two nights ago, fifteen of the crew, at one time, publicly avowed their purpose of henceforth serving the Lord as the first duty of life, and the prayer-meeting has become the centre of attraction every night to a large number on board.

"This state of things has had a marked effect on the whole ship's company; and it is freely confessed, by those who have the best opportunities for judging, that they never knew so great a change for the better to take place in a month anywhere, either at sea or on shore."

In the second letter, dated "U. S. Flagship Niagara, Mouth of the Mississippi, Nov. 2, 1861," we have the following:

"The Niagara, as you may recollect, arrived from Japan in April, in a state of much religious interest. Some fifty of the ship's company, embracing officers as well as seamen, had been hopefully converted during her absence—the greater number within a few weeks just preceding. The influences leading to this happy result were still prevailing, but were almost unavoidably stayed by the circumstances awaiting our arrival. No intelligence from the United States had reached us for many months; we were ignorant of the secession of any of them, and little prepared for the shock of the first words reaching us from a pilot-boat, as she swept under our stern: 'The Union is gone!' 'We are at war!' 'Fighting has begun!' Nearly half the commissioned officers of the Niagara refused to take the oath of allegiance required from them, and abruptly left the ship, as secessionists, the same day.

"That the good work in progress on board should have suffered a check by such disturbing causes was not a surprise. For a time this was the fact, so far as regarded new cases of conversion; but the faith, hope, and *spirit of prayer* of those already on the Lord's side continued in lively exercise, and at the end of a few weeks the presence of the Spirit was again manifested in the conviction and inquiring state of one and another here and there, among both officers and crew. Hopeful conversions have again occurred up to the present time, and within the last two months twelve more have been added to the number of professed disciples, and have openly joined our band of praying men. It certainly is an interesting sign of the times, that there are found, among the most promising young officers of our service, those who have the independence and decision of character not only to avow themselves to their messmates and fellow officers to be followers of the blessed Saviour, but also unhesitatingly to identify themselves as such, at our nightly prayer and conference meetings, with the humblest sailor under them who loves the Lord, as members of a common brotherhood.

"With a commander-in-chief deeply interested in the best good of all under him—himself an humble and consistent follower of Christ; with a fine set of officers generally, so many of them of the same mind of our chief, and so large a number of professed Christians and converts among the crew, the combined influence on all on board has been most marked and most salutary. We have a happy ship; one that is a model in good discipline, good order, and, consequently, in contentment. Commodore McKean, as you well know, is a man of prayer, and during our whole cruise has been found, night after night, at our prayer and conference meetings on the forward deck, occupying the same plank for a seat with the common sailors, uniting in the songs of praise and in the prayers of the humblest of them, and himself often leading us to the feet of Jesus at the throne of grace. His promotion has produced no change in this respect; he was in his accustomed place the first night after receiving it, and I know not when I have been more touched than when, at the close of the meeting, he motioned to me to withhold the usual benediction for a moment, that he might, as I soon discovered, solicit the prayers of his brother sailors and fellow Christians, lowly as their position in comparison with his is, that he might have grace and strength from the Hearer of prayer to discharge the responsibilities newly devolved upon him to the glory of God and the best interests and honor of his country."

In these letters, which must command the interest of

every pious and intelligent reader taking an interest in the cause of living religion, we may learn some impressive and profitable lessons. 1. As kindred spirits are mutually attracted to association congenial, so, eminently, grace leads converted sinners to associate with the converted in exercises congenial to the gracious soul. And here, in the prayer-meeting, the congenial fellowship and exercises are found. 2. This pleasant exercise is the more attractive to the active working Christian, because it is found to be, by God's appointment, and in all Christian experience, and under all circumstances, the specific and appropriate means of promoting and sustaining revival of religion. 3. Whether on sea or land, in camp or church, the state of religion and progress of grace are always known by the condition of the prayer-meeting, as the most natural and easily discriminating test.

From the following extracts, taken from recorded reminiscences of the old war ship North Carolina, we may learn the foot-prints of the work of the Spirit of God in revival, by tracing the lines of prayer, and the selected objects in the concerted prayers of the prayer-meeting. And what a striking similarity here, in the realization of the power of the Spirit of God accompanying the prayer-meeting as a means of grace, to the symbolical representation of Ezekiel, in his vision of the wheels, the living creatures, and the Spirit moving on in concert with them both! "And when the living creatures went, the wheels went by them; and when the living creatures were lifted up from the earth, the wheels were lifted up. Whithersoever the Spirit was to go, they went; thither was their Spirit to go; and the wheels were lifted up over against them: for the Spirit of the living creatures was in the wheels. When those went, these went; and when those stood, these stood; and when those were lifted up from the earth, the wheels were lifted up over against them; for the Spirit of the living creature was in the wheels." Wherever prayer, with other means of grace, goes, there the Spirit of God goes with converting and reviving power; for the Spirit of God is always in prayer.

"For several years the United States Ship North Carolina, a very large vessel, has been lying at the Brooklyn Navy Yard, used as a Receiving-ship for seamen. During the greater part of the time, many hundred men have been on board, waiting to be sent to other vessels. A ship thus stationed at the entrance to the sea, in which thousands of sailors sojourn for a time, would naturally be an object of interest and a subject of prayer with those who have the spiritual interests of seamen at heart: and God has heard and answered prayer on behalf of this vessel. More than once the spirit of revival has been kindled, and many souls have been converted on board. We give below some of the reports which have been made from time to time of the state of things on board this ship.

"Rev. Dr. Stewart said one day in the Fulton Street meeting, he had often requested prayers for the men of the sea on the North Carolina. When last he mentioned the case of that ship in this meeting there were but few men on board: now there are about five hundred. The work of grace goes steadily forward, and from night to night there are some who are coming out on the Lord's side. Never did the men of this old ship stand in more need of prayer than now, that God would not stay his hand, but bring many to repentance.

"Another gentleman said he had been to one of the prayer-meetings on the North Carolina. There was a good number present, and the presence and power of the Holy Spirit was most manifest. He heard a most touching letter read from one of the seamen, who had been sent from the

North Carolina to the Ohio at Boston, giving a cheering account of the progress of the work of grace on the Ohio. The writer says that they have not the presence or aid of clergymen or Christians from the shore, as in the Brooklyn Navy Yard; yet they have the wonderful workings of the Holy Spirit among the men of the ship, and daily there are added to the numbers of believers those who they trust shall be saved."

In speaking of the prayer-meetings held on the vessel, it is added:

"One thing was remarkable in the prayers of all these men: they prayed for the conversion of all the men at sea, and for the blessing of God upon all on shore whoever prayed for them. There was something," continued the speaker, 'that made me feel that it was a great privilege to be remembered in the prayers of those men, for one could not resist the impression that these prayers would be heard.'

"At another time a chaplain of the Navy said the revival on the North Carolina, with which he was almost daily conversant, was wonderful, and without a parallel, so far as he knew, in the naval service of any nation. At the last three or four of the daily prayer-meetings which he had attended on board, not less than fifteen had come out and confessed themselves to be on the Lord's side. The hopeful conversions of the last few weeks are about eighty, and it now seems to pervade more or less the whole ship's company, numbering from nine hundred to one thousand men. No man, who can be a witness for himself, can have a doubt of the genuineness of the work. No power but Almighty power, could produce such results as are now seen on board of this man-of-war. You would not know what is going on in the minds of these really fine and noble men, till you speak to them on the subject of religion, or go into their prayer-meetings, and hear them pray; then you will feel that the Holy Spirit is at work in his silent, but mysterious and amazing power, upon the hearts of these men. The work of God's grace and mercy on board our ships of the Naval service is a blessing to the nation and to the world, for those men will be missionaries wherever they go, on sea or on land."

"The following letter to Rev. Mr. Jones, of the Mariner's Church, New York, speaking of a revival on board the United States Ship St. Louis, was written by the pious sailor who was the means of the establishment of the daily evening prayer-meetings on board the North Carolina, and which resulted in the ingathering into the fold of Christ of such a company of earnest, faithful men, who are scattered now through several ships of war. In reading it, Mr. Jones remarked that there were members of his church on board eighteen of the armed vessels of the United States:"

From this letter, above noticed, we extract the following:

"SAN JUAN DE NICARAGUA, *Dec.* 26, 1859.

"Looking from this advanced point, I can trace the commencement of this work to the first days of October—at that time the Lord having evidently heard our prayers. Most of the converted take, at once, an active part in our meetings, and some have already begun missionary labor among us."—"Another, two days after his conversion, and his confessing Christ before men, conducted a noon prayer-meeting in the main-top. Once he had the disposition of the enraged tiger, now of the gentle lamb; once his mouth was full of bitterness and cursing, now of prayer and praise. Oh, that I could impart to you a faint, yet correct, idea of the spirituality and blessedness of our meetings of late! Oh, what solemn meetings! several officers present and a large portion of the crew. Great joy flowing from a sense of the Saviour's pardoning love."

"Of the result of this revival, so far, there have been nineteen hopeful conversions. Our officers are all kind to us. We have privileges extended to us that praying men on board other ships do not enjoy. On Christmas day Captain Poor called all hands to prayer on the quarter-deck, and in the afternoon and evening we had our own prayer-meetings. All hands to prayer on the quarter-deck is an uncommon order from an officer commanding a ship of war."

One extract more in this connection, and we shall close this interesting part of our history of the prayer-meeting among seamen:

"The following letter was addressed to Rev. Dr. Stewart, of the Navy, by a young sailor, bred regularly to the sea, without any advantages of education or position other than those of a common seaman:"

"U. S. FRIGATE—*Jan.* 4, 1860.

"When I first came to this ship, I went to the captain and asked him to grant me the privilege of having prayer-meetings on board. His answer to me was 'No!' My hopes for good failed me, but God held me up. There were only two of us, W—— and myself. I did not know how I should keep on without the meetings I had enjoyed on board the North Carolina. Little did I know of the love of Jesus. He heard my feeble cry and blessed me. Jesus is, indeed, the sailor's friend. When we had been out about six weeks, I fell into conversation one day with the ship's painter. I thank God for it. Through the blessing of the Holy Spirit, I was thus made the means of leading him to Jesus. Then W—— E—— and I went up into the main-top every evening, and knelt together in prayer to God, that He would open a way for us to do good, and would add to our number. Soon our little flock increased to seven, and I thought then we might have a private meeting on deck, where we could get together, sing our hymns, and offer our prayers to God. We met between two guns, and kept on in this way for some time, till two more were added to us; and at last, as our number had thus increased, we went down on the gun-deck. Here we took a bold stand. The place we chose was by the main hatch, in the midst of the deck; on both sides of us were the ship's company, going on in sin, and we in the midst of them praising God. We still hold our meetings regularly there. We were not granted the privilege; we took this on our own responsibility. We have no aid from officers or men. The captain, and officers, and most of the men, seem against us; still the power of God is wonderfully manifest. Our stand is so strong that none now trouble or disturb us, and the captain does not stop us. It looks as if God had placed us there for a light to others, and the men seem to regard it as a hallowed place. None come to it to trouble us. Here we have had two more added to the little band who meet together for prayer and praise. Dear brother, we send a special request to all the followers of the Lord Jesus, for prayer that the Holy Spirit may be felt in power in this ship."

In this last extract we have a much needed moral lesson of duty, and of Christian consistency with Christian profession. We have also a spiritual lesson in regard to the divine faithfulness to divine promise, and the power of divine grace in making prayer, faith, and the faithful use of divinely appointed means, successful in the conversion of sinners, and gathering of saints together in holy fellowship, and edifying them in holiness and comfort.

The moral and spiritual lessons of these extracts are these:

1. This young sailor, with one only kindred spirit, was thrown away upon the high seas, among the enemies of religion, far from his much loved North Carolina and her happy prayer-meetings, and his beloved friends, with whom he had so often enjoyed the sweet fellowship of saints.

2. On his new ship, and from his new captain, he met at once almost crushing discouragements in his first attempt to form a prayer-meeting. And there, in all that ship's company, not *one more* than the *minimum number* to secure the promise to a prayer-meeting. *Two only* to make a prayer-meeting. "There were only two of us, W—— and myself." But *two* or *three* will do.

3. Notwithstanding the discouragements—"two only"—and these refused permission by the captain, they go up to the main-top every evening, and there have prayer-meeting. There they ask God to open for them the way for doing good. What an interesting example of strong faith with telling works!

4. Their feeble and almost hopeless effort was crowned with success. Soon to the little flock—to the *two—seven* were added. Now they are *nine*—too large a number to find pleasant accommodation in their little upper room—"the main-top." Then the nine meet on deck, between two guns. This persevering boldness is soon rewarded. Two more are soon added to the nine. Now they are eleven disciples. This is really quite a prayer-meeting. Once more they make a bold advance. They now bring their meeting to the main hatch, in the midst of the deck. Soon two more are added. The prayer-meeting of two on

the main-top, is now grown to a meeting of *thirteen*, in the midst of the deck, at the main hatch—one more than the number of disciples Christ had with him in his weekly prayer-meeting in the upper room, the doors being shut. Here are now *thirteen* disciples, and Christ, making, in the sailor boy's prayer-meeting, *fourteen*, one more than in Christ's primitive meetings. The sailor's effort was a success. It has a moral. Can we not apply it to matters of vital interest, and of almost every day's occurrence—to matters producing most serious consequences for good or for evil to the cause of Christ?

Christian families, members of the church, are, by hundreds, every year, emigrating to the wild West, scattering over immense territory fast settling up by the constant tide from the East, and so depleting our old churches, and making it a matter of some doubt whether, on the whole, the church is gaining much, if anything, in numbers, just now. It might be a successful way of improving our historical lesson here, to follow some of these emigrations, and so have before us fact sketches from which to learn. We shall suppose two cases of not at all improbable occurrence. In the State, or Territory, and county of ———, *six families* of our church, in regular standing in some of our eastern churches, and regularly certified as members thereof, settle down in the same vicinity. Two of them settle at the cross roads, or in the new village in said county. The other four settle, each out from the centre, one mile and a half in four opposite directions, making a circumference whose diameter is three miles. These four families will have each one mile and a half to travel to enjoy the privilege of meeting with their brethren for prayer and conference in the centre of their locality. An equal number, under similar circumstances and in like manner, settle in the State, or Territory, and county of ———.

Immediately, after thus settling down in their new homes, the first group seek and form an acquaintance with each other—which thing they will soon do if they are under the influence of the attractive principle implied in the letters of certificate and dismissal they carry with them, or if they are of like spirit with the sailor boy and his kindred spirit friend, who went together every evening to the main-top. They at once organize themselves into a prayer-meeting. They establish their rules, and mutually agree to observe them. Every Sabbath day, when they cannot secure a supply of the preaching of the gospel, they meet in the centre for prayer and Christian conference. Also, weekly, on week-day or evening, they meet for the same object, whether supplied with the preaching of the gospel on the Sabbath or not. There, punctual to their rules, and faithful to their brotherly covenant and church obligations, each endeavors to be in his place in the prayer-meeting on week-day and Sabbath. And as each feels an interest in the success of the society, in the prospect of an organized and settled congregation, in the prosperity of the cause of Christ, in their own and their children's spiritual advantage; as also, in the salvation of sinners and the welfare of their neighbors, with whom they are every day associated, they will all—like Moses to Hobab—say to those around them, "Come with us, and we will do thee good." And so, like the sailor boy, on every proper occasion, by word and by Christian deeds, laboring and persevering, they will gain others, and their numbers must increase. Soon the six families should become a score. That bond which holds them together, they and their children will, by the blessing of God, draw within its folds an enlarged band, ripe for a congregational organization. This organization—like the sailor boy's prosperity—will stimulate still more, and soon they can have five prayer-meetings, one in the centre, and one in each of the four extreme points, each of these still gathering around it, as did the first, and as the sailor boy's prayer-meeting did, and thus everything will be upward and onward, for *there* faith *will* be, and *there* God *will* work with them and for them.

To such a people the ordinances of the gospel will soon be all supplied regularly, and their congregation become self-sustaining. Still more: their youth, with the youth of all the fanilies of the church settling among them from time to time, and of those influenced to join them, will be kept from the world and preserved to the church. And still farther here: all who incorporate with them in good faith, together with their children, will be trained for and retained in the church as pillars; or, if emigrating elsewhere, will form certain and reliable nuclei for other prosperous and solid congregations.

It may here be replied: Few families thrown together in new localities have the principle, or moral courage, attracting and holding them together in this way. Perhaps too true; and the more to be lamented. It might be said, too, and justly, there are few such sailors as this pious youth, from the prayer-meetings of the North Carolina. For good reasons, it may, indeed, be so said of too many of our families thrown together in new settlements. They were never well indoctrinated in the faith of their own church, or in the faith of the Bible. Especially, they have never been trained in our sailor's faith and practice in regard to the prayer-meeting. They are fixed in the faith and love of nothing of the kind, and, therefore, in the market for anything that may happen to form their surroundings.

The other six families:—Let us follow them to their locality, and mark their course and progress. They take the common popular course: they and their families glide along with the current. They form no particular acquaintance with each other. They organize no prayer-meeting. Of course they have no Sabbath school. They have nothing of the denominational kind. They worship on the Sabbath with the most convenient assemblies, with little reference to their matter and forms of worship. Their children incorporate with the most convenient Sabbath schools—perhaps with the "Sunday" School Union. Perhaps, at best, these six families and their very inviting locality come to the knowledge of the Home Mission Board. A missionary is sent them. He may succeed in bringing them out to hear him on the Sabbath. He may succeed in bringing the better part of them out to a prayer-meeting, while he remains with them to lead in the meeting, as they were wont to see in their old home churches. But the three or four weeks of supply pass by, and the young preacher is gone. To meet by themselves on the silent Sabbaths, and to conduct a prayer-meeting, without a minister to lead—these things are not to their mind; and then their youth and children must be in their places in the Sabbath school, from which they cannot withdraw them.

Next quarter, or perhaps at the end of six months, the Board sends them a month's supply. The missionary again wends his way to this fine field, where thousands are locating, and where many churches are directing their attention and their resources, as to "a centre of influence." But he finds our six families, at best, *statu quo;* or, if any additional families have, in the meantime, settled in the bounds, they are discouraged, and the youth of all alienated from the church. So this routine of missionary rallying and Board expenditure, in a majority of cases, ends in a failure.

There is another page in the history of these two groups. The Home Mission Board claims a brief chapter here in connection with these two young mission stations. When six families, as in the cases supposed, sustain a living prayer-meeting, they cannot fail to sustain an efficient Sabbath school. The other failing in the one, will as certainly fail in the other. With quarterly or monthly supply, one will grow up and ripen into a self-sustaining congregation; the other will die, and all missionary expenditure in money and labor be lost. Here, let our Mission Boards know, lies the secret of the dwindling, failing, and dying of so many mission stations, and the absorption and waste of so much expenditure. Here lies the secret of so much of that mournful falling off of our youth to the world, and of our members to other communions, or into apostasy.

Let it not be said, there is no help for these things. There is help for them; but not in the prevailing and popular regimen of the times. There is help in God. There is help, through grace, in the divine institutions. If *two* weak sailor boys could, by the live prayer-meeting, in a few short months, increase their number seven-fold, what might *six* families of the right spirit effect in almost any new and rapidly populating locality? How soon might the whole face of our Home Mission field be changed, if all our emigrants were trained to the prayer-meeting, as were those two sailor boys! If all our people were trained in the principles of the church and the Bible, and believed and loved them, every group of settlers, in our broad Home Mission fields in the rapidly populating new countries, would be like our sailor boy and like our *first six families*—a success and acquisition to our Home Mission cause. If our people, settling up our Home Mission fields, were right on this in their faith, their training, and practice, it would be worth more to the cause than all our present expenditure, in both men and money. Oh, when will the church learn to be wise!

CHAPTER IX.

CONCERTED PRAYER—AND PRAYER-MEETINGS AMONG THE MISSIONARIES.

Prayer-meeting interest awakened in India—Origin of the Week of Prayer—Missionaries ask for Concerted Prayer at Home—Universal Concerted Prayer among the Churches—Bombay—Poona—Letter of a Ship Captain—General Principles.

Concerted prayer, and prayer-meetings among the missionaries.

SOME time after the opening of the Fulton Street daily prayer-meeting, a more than usual religious interest was felt among the missionaries in almost every foreign field. In Sealkote, in Lodiana, Bombay, and, indeed, in almost every Mission Station in India, the subject of revival, and the call for more earnest united prayer, became a more prominent concern, awakening general attention. This soon drew out correspondence among the missionaries themselves, and with the churches at home, on the subject of the absorbing interest of the times. While the awakening of the churches to the revived prayer-meetings was pervading the entire evangelical church, in all her branches, at home, the missionaries abroad prepared and sent their call to the whole church for concerted prayer, upon a scale of comprehension, for its grandeur of conception, its simplicity, its scriptural character, its practicability and promise of rich and permanent fruits, perhaps never conceived and carried into effect in any previous age. The move was most heartily seconded, and most promptly carried out in letter and spirit. Everywhere throughout all Christendom the hearty response was sent up. Now, since the second week of January, 1860, the Week of Prayer has become almost as familiar, to the live Christian, as the weekly Sabbath.

That suggestion for a week of universal concerted prayer was the fruit of revival, and prayer-meetings previously giving character to the spirit of the religious times in this country. The wonderful gatherings of daily concerts, as in New York, in Philadelphia, the Fulton Street and Sansom Street gatherings, and as in all the cities and towns in all parts of the country, were then of world-wide fame. The long-to-be-remembered Xenia Convention had been held. In every corner of the land the prayer-meeting was an every day matter of greeting. The result of that suggestion—the establishment of that annual concert—may form the electric chain which shall yet convey, in some future time, the life-currents of the past down into the church in a more glorious revival. It may yet be the instrument, and may furnish the occasion, of calling to remembrance "the year of the right hand of the Most High." Nothing so powerfully moved the returned captives, when standing before their new house, as the remembrance of the glory of their former house. And what now gives deeper emotional feelings, to many fathers in the church, than the remembrance of the happy revival times, the happy convention times, the happy prayer-meeting times, the happy union times of that year of grace, 1858?

Thrilling chapters could be written—and some have been—giving a narrative of requests sent by missionaries to prayer-meetings at home for special and concerted prayers in behalf of objects of great interest to the mission cause—as for the conversion of sons of missionaries sent home for education with earnest solicitude for preparation for mission work in a foreign field. Many such cases of great interest have occurred; that of Dr. Newton, of Lodiana, who had sent his son home, is one deserving a perpetual record. Our space forbids to enter it here in full. That son was for a time, after being sent to this country, unpromising and reckless, indeed, almost a confirmed infidel. The intelligence of his downward course, which nearly crushed a fond and praying mother, and saddened the heart of an eminently godly father, who had dedicated him to God for the work of the ministry in a foreign field. Long had fond anticipations been cherished by the father of living to see with him, side by side in the work of the mission, a dear son to cheer in a foreign land, and close the eyes of a dying father, and then take up the mantle and carry on the Lord's work after he should be taken home to rest. Notwithstanding the thickness of that dark cloud that for a time hung over the hopes of the anxious parents in a foreign field, and of friends at home, that father realized his hopes. Earnest solicitations by letter had been sent home to the prayer-meetings for united prayer on his behalf. At the same time the parents set apart a week for fasting and prayer, during which they together earnestly pressed the same object at a throne of grace. Each day they wept, and prayed, and fasted before God in behalf of their reckless son. About the same time at home, in the daily prayer-meetings, many prayers were turned to the same object. The whole course and current of the life of this reckless youth was turned in a new direction. He consecrated himself, soul and body, to God and to the cause of missions. After due preparation he set sail for India, where, joining his venerated father, he labored side by side with him, and where he is still, since the death of his father, spared to do battle with the powers of darkness.

A letter from Bombay, written by a missionary there,

bearing date June, 1859, directed to the Fulton Street Prayer-meeting, soliciting the prayers of the meeting in behalf of the writer and the mission, was read in the meeting and produced a deep sensation. The reception of the letter and the result in the prayer-meeting was in due time made known at Bombay. Another letter was soon on its way home bearing intelligence of the state of revivals and of prayer-meetings, not only at Bombay, but many other mission stations. The following are some extracts taken from that letter:

"Just about the time that the letter above mentioned reached its destination, and the attention of the Fulton Street Union Prayer-meeting was specially directed toward Bombay, two daily Union Prayer-meetings were established here, one at seven o'clock in the morning, in the Church of Scotland's Missionary Institution, in the native town; the other at one o'clock in the Scotch Church in the fort, and designated the Business Men's Mid-day Union Prayer-meeting—all government officers, and those of our merchants, professional men, etc., being in the fort. It has been my great privilege to take part in the establishment of these meetings, and it has been my precious privilege to bear a humble part in the maintenance of them to the present time. Shortly after the commencement of these two meetings, another was established by the native Christians in their own language. We have now, therefore, three daily Union Prayer-meetings in Bombay. I can bear testimony that such praying as is heard in these Union meetings, has never been heard before in this city during the fourteen years of my connection with it. God's people have been taught by the Spirit how to pray, and strengthened by the Spirit to continue instant in prayer. This spirit of prayer is the earnest of blessings which it is transporting to anticipate. In addition to the daily

20*

prayer-meetings, we have seven or eight weekly prayer-meetings, and three monthly concerts.

"In the city of Poona, distant about one hundred miles from Bombay, a weekly Union Prayer-meeting has been recently established, which is well attended, and increasing in interest and power. I attended this meeting lately, while on a visit to Poona, and can testify to the earnest spirit of prayer that prevails in it. There are two or three other prayer-meetings in Poona, and a monthly concert.

"At Ahmednugger, about seventy miles from Poona, a great spirit of prayer prevails. The Annual Meeting of the American Mission was held there from the 19th to the 26th of last month. All the American missionaries of this presidency, with one exception, were present.

"A great and interesting spirit of prayer prevails in other parts of India. I cannot lengthen this letter by a reference to all the places where daily Union Prayer-meetings have been established; but I cannot refrain from noticing the very interesting circumstances in which such a meeting has been established in Calcutta."

The writer then proceeds to give a deeply interesting account of the commencement of a series of meetings for prayer at Calcutta, in the first of which he says:

"During the meeting numbers were deeply affected to tears. All went away as if sorry that the meeting was at an end, feeling that it was good to have been there, and hungering and thirsting after a renewal of similar meetings."

The following narration was given in one of the Fulton Street meetings:

"A ship captain, recently returned from a long voyage, said he had called at an island in the course of the voyage, 14,000 miles sailing from here, one which he had known well in former times as an island of cannibals. He stood off and on for some time, uncertain whether to land or not. He considered it dangerous to attempt it. Finally, one evening, he ventured to land with a few of his men; and what do you think we found? We found a prayer-meeting. It was a meeting of sixty young people, all the children of heathen parents; but thirty of these were now Christians. They had been visited by missionaries from some of the neighboring Christian islands, and I found them and heard them singing the same tunes which I have heard here to-day. Only think of it, said the officer, 14,000 miles away I heard heathen youth singing your tunes, and praying to God on an island where I dared not land when I first hove in sight! I tell you that it affected me greatly. I thought of what God is doing in answer to prayer. I have come home more deeply impressed than ever I was before with the power of prayer."

It may be well to notice here, in this connection, that, so far as the history of prayer-meetings is concerned, in the army, among seamen, in union meetings and religious conventions, in the great annual gatherings, as the week of prayer, on the second week of January, and among the missionaries in foreign fields—all are embraced in the same general principles sanctioning them, and clearly stated in the Bible. They all belong to a distinct class of prayer-meetings, outside of ecclesiastical organization. All the ends contemplated in all these specified meetings are sanctioned in God's word as the legitimate objects of Christian effort, and concerted social prayer a legitimate means of obtaining them. In a proper, yet qualified sense, all the prayer-meetings of *this class* are extraordinary, growing out of the circumstances and occasions suggesting them. They are not a part of the ecclesiastical organization of any particular congregation or church, and, therefore, not under the control of any congregation, session, or higher church court. They belong to the church catholic, or to all Christians. They seem to be well adapted to the divided and scattered state of the church. They are platforms on which all Christians can stand, and rallying centres around which all can gather for the enjoyment of an extended Christian fellowship, and for holding counsel in regard to all that concerns the glory of God, the cause of religion and the church, the salvation of sinners, and the welfare of the race.

This is not the connection in which to discuss the divine warrant for prayer-meetings of this class. Their authorization has been noticed elsewhere; yet it is proper to notice the distinction referred to, inasmuch as we are about to bring under review a class of prayer-meetings distinct, more intimately connected with the church organic, and with her internal and household work, more immediately under the notice of her courts, her officers, her congregations, and her members. As revivals find a place in General Assemblies, in Synods, in Presbyteries, in Sessions, in congregations, and in select praying circles, so the prayer-meeting, side by side, will, of necessity, find a place in all these. Still more, as the ordinances of religious worship appointed by the Head of the Church are to be kept pure and entire, and to be observed always, whether in times of revival or times of backsliding, so is the prayer-meeting, as an ordinance of worship, to be observed ordinarily in every congregation. In this view, mainly, of the prayer-meeting, we shall now follow its history during a period of great religious interest. The church has, or should have, her own prayer-meetings. She needs them in seasons of revival. She needs them when the love of many waxes cold. She needs them when the enemy comes in like a flood. She needs them when any perilous time shall come.

In the year 1857, the prayer-meeting was revived in all the evangelical churches in Europe and America, just at the time when it was revived among the seamen, in religious and union conventions, and in Foreign Mission fields. And while, with men, it may be impossible to determine when, or where, or with whom, precisely, the revivals of that period first commenced—yet the historian may trace, by the prayer-meeting, their manifestations, their progress, the means employed in promoting them, and their fruits.

CHAPTER X.

THE PRAYER-MEETING AMONG THE CHURCHES.

American Writers—" Five Years of Prayer "—*N. Y. Observer*—Premature Impressions—Revival in Ireland—Prof. Gibson, of Belfast—References to Year of Grace—Revival Awakenings in Ireland as Early as 1855—Early Prayer-Meeting and Sabbath School Movements—" The Believers' Fellowship Meeting "—Revival in Connor—Prayer-Meetings for a Quarter of a Century—Facts and Reflections—Revivals and Prayer-Meetings move forward over the Churches together—State of Revivals and the Prayer-Meetings brought before the General Assembly—Progress of Prayer-Meeting Revival through the North of Ireland—Reports from Congregations—Genuineness of the Revivals—Testimony of Pastors—Churches and Sabbath Schools thronged—Arianism and other prevailing errors decline as Prayer-Meetings and Revivals Progress—" Psalms never so much prized "—Rev. Magill's Report of Dundrod—Prayer-Meetings and Suppression of Immorality—Drunkards Reformed—Wonderful increase of Prayer-Meetings—Lessons and Reflections suggested confirming the Views taken of the Prayer-Meeting—Fruits of Revivals in Ireland and America Compared—Revival in Ireland propagated by Prayer-Meetings in the Church—Report of the Presbytery of Ahoghill—Congregational Reports of Prayer-Meetings—Remarkable Record of the state of Evangelical Religion and the Prayer-meeting from 1857 to 1859.

AMERICAN writers have made, at least, enough of the Fulton Street Union Prayer-meeting, and of the extent of its influence; and, perhaps, too much of its originality and priority. We are not sure that it is entitled to all that is claimed for it, or for the *New York Observer*, in waking up the Presbyterian churches of Ireland and Scotland. Nor are we sure that American writers have not given more to human-devised agencies, and less to divine institutions, than European laborers and writers. The *animus* American seems to rise above the surface in the following, from S. J. Prime's "Five Years of Prayer," p. 269:

"The Connor enlightenment, so far as practicable, was kept unnoticed and unknown. It seems to have been so gradual and gentle, like the dew on the mown grass, that the parties did not feel *constrained* for a time to compel others to come in. One member of the flock wandered a little away beyond the parochial limits, and, touched with a live coal from the altar himself, his words, and tears, and prayers, kindled a flaming fire in the hearts of others, and *impelled* them to go and beseech sinners to flee from the wrath to come. Besides, tidings of the American revival reached this country. Our church courts directed ministers to consider the subject and preach on it. This was generally done throughout our presbytery, and, I presume, throughout the congregations of our Synod. American newspapers, especially the *New York Observer*, were regularly read by some of us, and thus the subject kept fresh and prominent before the mind."

Two impressions in regard to the beginning of the revival and revived prayer-meetings of this period may have been premature. First. That the revival began in this country, and then extended its influence to Europe. Second. That the revival began with the Fulton Street Union Prayer-meeting, New York. Facts of history, and reports of the actors of the times seem to indicate a work of grace in progress in Ireland, in connection with the prayer-meetings and other ordinary means of grace, some time before the sudden rise of the Fulton Street meetings, whose light blazed so brightly over the world.

A distinction is certainly due to the facts of history. The revival in Ireland began in the churches under the earnest administration of the ordinary institutions of grace given to the church as divinely appointed means of revival, and was conducted mostly in the same way, and never became so ostentatious and noisy. So, also, its effects were more permanent and lasting. The American revival began outside of the church—rather led and controlled the church, than otherwise, and was, perhaps, consequently not so evangelical or permanent as revivals originating in the church, and controlled by her influence.

Professor Gibson, of Belfast, Ireland, in his "Year of Grace"—a work from which we shall draw largely—says:

"The great awakening of last year, though it has culminated in a form which has attracted the attention of the churches, is not in its remoter origin a thing of yesterday. For many years a purifying and preparatory process has been going forward, especially in that communion which has so largely shared the gracious influence. A return to the 'old paths' of orthodoxy was speedily followed by auspicious indications of returning life; and the Presbyterian church of Ulster, immediately on the consummation of an ecclesiastical union between its two great sections, about twenty years ago, at length arose to its true position as a missionary institute to Jew and Gentile—a witness for the truth to all nations. By the good hand of God a generation of energetic and devoted ministers was raised up, with many of whom the burden of their prayers has ever been, 'O Lord, revive thy work.'"

"It is right it should be known," says the Rev. S. M. Dill, of Ballymena, "that this movement has not come among us quite so suddenly as people at a distance might be led to suppose. I am able to testify that there has been a gradual, but perceptible improvement in the state of religion throughout this district for some years. Ministers were led to speak to the people with greater earnestness about the things which belong to their peace. Attendance on the public ordinances of religion had considerably increased. Open air preaching was extensively practised. Sabbath schools were greatly multiplied. Prayer-meetings were growing up in many districts."

That the revival of religion and of the prayer-meeting had passed its incipiency before the fall of 1857, and had made encouraging progress in many parts of Ireland, is evident from the state of religion above referred to, and its condition previously. A reliable writer, referring to this previous state of things, says:

"From my first entrance on the work of the ministry, I believed that the faithful use of the means of grace should be followed by their appropriate effects as certainly as the tillage of a field is followed by a crop, or as diligence in any profession is rewarded with success; and bitter, therefore, was my disappointment as year after year passed and still no fruit appeared. In grief I wondered at what I considered the *mysterious* withholding of the Spirit, and set myself to account for it. What alarmed me most was the disinclination, almost hostility, of the people to hold prayer-meetings. I had nearly begun to cease hoping. I felt as if I were almost quite alone—no one mourning or praying with me. I told them that I was appalled at their apparent determination to have no prayer-meetings and to seek no revival; that the showers were going around us and around us, and not a drop falling our way, and that we would be left utterly reprobate, a visible monument of the consequences of despising gospel privileges."

Again, speaking of the succeeding period, after the revival of the prayer-meetings had set in, he adds:

"Some whom I had never seen at a prayer-meeting, and who would have said they had not time to attend for a couple of hours once a month, have, since the revival commenced, attended often twice daily, in some instances with three or four sons, during the best working hours of the summer day. I knew there were always a few, very few, I feared, praying people in the several congregations in the neighborhood; and attempts were always made to keep up prayer-meetings in my own; but up to the very week of the bursting forth of the revival, there appeared no general desire nor felt need of such a thing."

In the winter of 1855, extra evening meetings were appointed at Connor for the benefit of the masses without, because the church was so thronged at the usual services by the members of the church that few besides, could find accommodation. These meetings, toward spring, became very interesting. The idea took hold of many that a great revival was at hand. Many prayers were offered up in public and in private for its realization. So deep was the impression upon the minds of staid men, that, at the close of one of the meetings, one exclaimed to the pastor with almost prophetic pathos, "You will yet see good days in Connor." Such was the state of things early in that year, in the place destined in a few years to become the centre of wide-spread revival of religion and the prayer-meeting.

About the same time other congregations introduced extra exercises with the view of extending and deepening an interest in matters of religion. At the close of a Sabbath evening exercise in Ballamma, the pastor said to a young man:

"Could you not gather, at least, six of your careless neighbors, either parents or children, to your own house, or some other convenient place, on the Sabbath, and spend an hour with them, reading and searching the word of God? The young man hesitated for a moment, but promised to try. From that trial, made in faith, originated the Tannybrake Sabbath school, and in connection with it, two years subsequently, a prayer-meeting, which yielded some of the first fruits of the great awakening."

The subsequent spring, the Sabbath school was re-opened, with an accession to its teachers, and under more favorable auspices. It was soon in a flourishing state, and marked with great religious earnestness, both among the teachers and the taught. In this state of things, the parents of the Sabbath school children were brought in, and at the close of the school a meeting was held for prayer, reading the Scriptures, and religious conference. Some discouragements, for a time, attended this prayer-meeting. It was called in the neighborhood, "The Sabbath School Teachers' Prayer-meeting." It has since been better known in history as "The Tannybrake Sabbath School Prayer-meeting." Owing to the localities of four of its leading members, and for the sake of convenience, the place of meeting was changed to a little school house near to Connor, County Antrim, and received the significant name from that time forth of "The Believers' Fellowship Meeting." They here agreed upon a special object of prayer. That object—"That God would bless the means of grace in Connor, the Sabbath school and prayer-meeting, with revival of religion"—was, pursuant to the agreement, perseveringly pressed in their concerted prayers, till, at length, they were wonderfully answered.

"For more than a quarter of century the prayer-meeting had existed in that locality, while similar meetings had, in other districts, after many ineffectual efforts to maintain them, languished and revived, languished again, and died. Once the meeting in question was so far reduced in numbers, that only two came together to call upon the name of the Lord. Still they continued to pray on, and by degrees the little company increased, until it became two bands."

Some facts here are worthy of special note:

1. The prayer-meetings, which seem to have been common over the greater part of the North of Ireland, had, for a quarter of a century, been in a declining state—some had actually died. Everywhere religion was in a confessedly low state; for here was the outstanding evidence: the prayer-meetings—the never-failing thermometer, certain in its thermal indications, now very low—declared to all, a cold and dead state of the religious atmosphere. 2. The district of Connor—like Philadelphia, among the seven declining churches of Asia Minor—still, for a quarter of a century, had kept alive the prayer-meetings, and the praying ones still struggled on, "continuing steadfastly in prayer," though at one time "only two" met in the prayer-meeting. 3. When the great awakening came, here first the showers began to pour down their refreshings—Connor became the great Fulton Street of the Revival in Ireland in 1857. Why was this place distinguished, like the fleece, bedewed with such significant promise? And does not this suggest the inquiry—Can prayer-meetings—earnest prayer-meetings—fail, sooner or later, to secure the blessing of revival, where that is perseveringly sought? Where will revival be sought but among a praying people? Can any praying people live together in convenient vicinity, and not be gathered together by the attractive power of the spirit of prayer, to have and enjoy the prayer-meeting? The history of Connor, its living prayer-meeting, and its consequent revival, show that a praying people, keeping alive the prayer-meeting perseveringly, will, in due time, enjoy the blessing of revival.

Speaking of "The Believers' Fellowship meeting," near

Connor, in County Antrim, the author of the "Year of Grace," proceeds to say of the Revival in Ireland:

"The fellowship meeting," above referred to, "was established almost simultaneously with those concerts of prayer, begun by a similar agency, in America, whose influence was so extensively felt throughout the great Western Continent The society soon ceased to be a secret one; and slowly one kindred spirit after another was introduced, on the recommendation of some of the original members."

This prayer-meeting, which took its origin from the religious influence of the church, after its notoriety became wide-spread, was opened to all, and became the centre of extended operations in conducting the revival through the course of its after progress. It became the place of concentred interest, where, like the Fulton Street Meeting, special prayer was frequently offered in behalf of persons whose names were reported to the meeting. During this period, "a great impulse was given to consideration and seriousness, intensifying and extending these general precursors of conviction and revival. The old prayer-meetings began to be thronged, and many new ones established. No difficulty now to find persons to take part in them. The winter was past; the time of the singing of birds had come. Humble, grateful, loving, joyous converts multiplied."

These are given as the evidences of revival of religion in the church of Connor; the conversion of sinners and the revival of prayer-meetings, for—

"Meetings for Christian converse and prayer began to spread. In a short time the community was altogether changed in its outward aspects, and pervading seriousness prevailed."

This state of things, prevailing through the churches,

was brought before the General Assembly, where action was taken, which had for its object encouragement in the great work, and counsel to the churches for conducting to a happy issue. This action of the Assembly gave a more wide-spread notoriety, at home and abroad, and clothed the work—the revival and the prayer-meetings—with a *quasi* ecclesiastical character.

PROGRESS OF THE PRAYER-MEETING REVIVAL THROUGH THE NORTH OF IRELAND.

Some youth, awakened in the Connor fellowship meeting, passed over into the adjoining district of Ahoghill, and there organized the prayer-meeting, and introduced the practice of concerted prayer for special objects. This was soon followed by blessed fruits in that district; thus we have it stated:

"Thereafter prayer-meetings began to multiply. The new converts, with other Christians, whose hearts the Lord stirred, engaged in the work of prayer and exhortation with unquenchable zeal. Thus the work spread daily; and daily fresh interest was awakened. Common houses, and even large churches, were not able to contain the multitudes that assembled, so that often the highway and the open field, in the cold evenings of spring, were the scenes of deeply interesting meetings."

The religious movement, indeed, everywhere throughout the country, seems to have shaped its character after the pattern of Connor, where, as we learn, there were one hundred prayer-meetings every week. A few months ago the bellowing of anger, and cursing, and blasphemy, resounded along the roads from parties returning from the markets, and especially on Saturday night, or, rather, on Sabbath mornings. Now the sweet song is heard floating on the night air from persons returning from the prayer-meetings.

Speaking of the evidences of the genuineness of this work, the author of "The Year of Grace" says:

"It is known by the feeling of deep solemnity that pervades the neighborhood—by the vast increase of family religion—by the absence of hitherto prevailing sins—by the keeping up of prayer-meetings in almost every locality—by the great increase in the attendance on the ordinances of God's house—and by the large accessions which have been made to the communicants' roll in all our churches."

The same, speaking of the evidences of the genuineness of the work in Ballymena, says:

"The greatest blessing is not the blessing seen, though there is enough to disprove every doubter. Sabbath schools have been increased and invigorated. A town mission has been instituted. Prayer-meetings are very numerous, and family worship generally observed."

Again, evidences of the character of this work among rural classes:

"It is not, however, mere feeling which distinguishes these individuals; their spirit, their lives, their walk, bespeak the marvellous revolution in their history. Is love of the Bible a proof of conversion? There is one who keeps it at her pillow, another who carries it in his pocket, for a hurried glance amid the business of the field. The summer before last, in a bog, were seen, in the hands of different parties, while resting from the labor of cutting turf, five packs of cards; last summer as many Bibles were their companions in toil. Is fellowship with one another, another mark of grace? Numerous are the little prayer-meetings held in the cottages, where neighbors assemble to read and pray with one another."

Testimony of liquor dealers to the revival and the prayer-meeting:

"There are drunkards reclaimed by something more

potent than the pledge; their burning lust has been cooled by the blood of the cross; and not a few of these lift up a warning voice among us against what they invariably call the *devil's cup.* So strong is the testimony borne by the Spirit against the use of intoxicating drinks, that four public houses in the parish have closed, and those publicans who remain in the trade find their occupation almost gone. I know one, who, a few months ago, heartily cursed the revival and the prayer-meetings, for 'they had done him up.'"

Rev. S. M. Dill, closing a letter in which he gives an account of the character of the work in his district, says:

"Happy am I to say that most cheering evidences of God's work continue in our district; everywhere meetings for prayer and Scripture reading—great thirst for hearing the word—increased attendance on the house of God and at the communion table—and seriousness and anxiety about the concerns of the soul."

A report from Coleraine, giving an account of the work there, and closing with evidences of its character, says:

"Full sanctuaries, full Sabbath schools, full prayer-meetings, brotherly love, increased liberality, and additions by hundreds to the communion of the churches—these are the fruits that remain to witness to the character of the work, which will make the summer of 1859 to be long remembered in Coleraine."

The Rev. John Stewart, pastor of the congregation of Ballycarry, writes the following narrative:

"Here was erected the first Presbyterian Church in Ireland. Here the Rev. Edward Brice, in 1613, unfurled the banner of Scotland's covenant, and began preaching the everlasting gospel. Two faithful and godly ministers were his successors, and there for eighty long years the church lay under the incubus of Arianism—the frozen zone of Christianity. God reserved here a goodly remnant which adhered to the Synod of Ulster, when, in 1829, their minister and a portion of his flock openly abandoned the faith of God's people. Since that time our church, like the house of David, has waxed stronger and stronger, and 'Unitarianism,' as the heresy is now called, like the house of Saul, has waxed weaker and weaker. God's gracious 'REVIVAL,' which commenced early in May last, has still more added to our members. Through the mighty working of the Holy Spirit on the hearts of sinners, forty souls have been brought from under that Christless system (Arianism) into the communion of our church, and God has bestowed on some of them, both males and females, wonderful power of prayer, and fluency of expression.

"After more than seven months' experience, I can boldly and fearlessly bear my testimony to the blessed fruits and marvellous results of this mighty movement. Amongst ourselves here, in this extensive district, God's right hand and holy arm have won many victories. Never was there such a summer as the last; never such an autumn; never such a winter, as far as it has gone. Hundreds have been savingly converted to the Lord. The first effect of the revival was, that 'fear came upon *every soul.*' Then was our church filled to suffocation, and we were obliged to take to the open fields to declare the message of mercy to a hungering and thirsting population. I had pastor's work to do. I had living men and living women before me. They came to the sanctuary on the sole errand of obtaining the bread of life. Every Sabbath was a day of sweet refreshing. *On every week-day evening* 'they that feared the Lord spake to one another, and the Lord hearkened and heard' them (in their daily prayer-meetings), and there were added daily to the church 'such as should be saved.'"

The Rev. William Magill, pastor of the church of Dundrod, in closing a long report of the revival in his charge, bears this testimony to the prayer-meeting:

"Prayer-meetings are appointed in the several districts of the congregation, but wherever there is an earnest seeking soul, the people meet for prayer. The songs of Zion, the Psalms of David, those glorious Psalms, never so much prized as now, ascend from almost every house. And in the still summer evening, strains of heavenly music seem to float on the tremulous air. Imagination is busy, and no wonder, and men pause on the highway to catch the sweet sounds, now soft and low, rising and falling, and now ringing like the chimes of church-bells. They thought the angels were above and around them. They thought they heard the festive chimes of heaven, the pealing of the bells of the city of God, as the heavenly hosts proclaimed the triumphs which their Lord was achieving over his foes on earth."

Rev. Brown, of Newtonlimavady, reports the effects of revival there, as follows:

"The effects I shall sum up in a few words: Drinking of ardent spirits was scarcely known in town for the months of June, July, and August. Of those impressed, not more than one or two have gone back to intemperance. Party spirit and quarreling are all but dead. The assistant Barrister has almost nothing to do on the Crown day. Prayer-meetings are held in every hamlet of the country, and in every street of the town, almost every evening, and sometimes twice on the same evening, in different places, by the same persons. Scarcely a young man, above the age of fourteen, either in town or country, will refuse to pray publicly in any meeting; and sometimes little boys, of nine or ten years old, astonish their grandfathers by the beauty and fervor of their devotions. The daily meeting is well attended, and the early zeal appears scarcely aught abated."

Another, in reporting results, says:

"We have two united meetings for prayer every day, in one of which the laity take a prominent part. The ministers are at once helped and refreshed. In addition to these united meetings, there are Presbyterian meetings, in which the various congregations unite, and also *in each congregation one meeting in a week for their* own members, and others who may join them, all of which are well attended."

Rev. J. P. Willson, of Cookstown, says:

"Within a district four miles round, hundreds have been added to the communion of the church. Family worship has been established where it was never observed before; people come out to the house of God in greater numbers, and listen with more marked attention; *district prayer-meetings are multiplied;* drunkards have been reformed; and neighborhoods have totally changed their character. The people have settled down to an earnest, sober, prayerful use of the means of grace."

Another:

"I am now busily engaged visiting in the country; and the downright reality of the glorious revival is demonstrated in the extraordinary transformation of character which I witness in many families, who, from being the most careless, are now ready for every good work. I never enjoyed such real pleasure from any former visitation of my people. Nothing amazes me more than the number of the prayer-meetings established everywhere over the country. Neither my brethren nor myself have had anything to do with the formation or sustenance of them. All false delicacy and shame are laid aside in matters of religion, and men and boys that could not be induced to pray before others, now do so with effect and profit."

The following is an interesting report:

"It is no exaggeration to say that the attendance at our houses of worship is double what it was last year, and that attention to the services of the sanctuary fills every heart. There is a new feature manifest in our assemblies—the people evidently come to hear, and to learn, that they may obey. On the last administration of the sacrament in our congregations, there was, at least, one-third of an addition to our communicants' roll, and this increase consisted principally of young converts. Prayer-meetings are in active operation in our bounds, and there is not anything connected with the whole movement so astonishing as the fervent, eloquent, and well-conceived prayers put forth on these occasions by young converts, whose education and opportunities for mental improvement have been so limited. A few Sabbaths ago, I made an appeal to my people for some money to procure a congregational library, that knowledge might be increased among our youth; and I was met in a way I did not expect; all were inclined to give. Had the subject been mooted among us some years ago, not one in twenty would have responded to the call."

After grouping together a number of extracts of great interest, and all, more or less, bearing the same testimony to the inseparable connection between revival and the prayer-meeting—the latter always given as an evidence of a healthy state of religion—we may here, before proceeding farther in this connection, notice some of the leading facts bearing upon our subject. They are fact demonstrations of the truth we are laboring to urge upon the consideration of our readers—the vital importance of the prayer-meeting to the cause of religion, whether personal or social.

1. These extracts show, without exception, that true revival of religion stirs the heart of the revived to the ardent love and the habitual practice of prayer—brings to the closet, to the family altar, and to the social prayer-meeting invariably. When Saul of Tarsus was converted, the Lord, who knew infallibly the best evidence of true religion, and of revival of religion, sent down from heaven his testimony, which silenced all fears, "Behold, he prayeth." So all these witnesses before us give decisive evidence of the unquestioned character of the revivals in their churches—earnest and numerous prayer-meetings.

2. With the manifestation of the spirit of prayer in revival, and the consequent outgrowth of prayer-meetings, concerted prayer for special objects prevailed. Revived Christians, moved by the power of life-giving grace, are drawn together for prayer, and by the same gracious impulses they are inclined to unite their prayers upon some common object of spiritual solicitude in their social prayer-meetings. They often "agree on earth touching something that they shall ask, assured that it shall be given them of their Father in heaven." This exemplifies the spirit of true revival, and applies one of the efficient instrumentalities appointed for the promotion and extension of the cause of true religion. God hears and answers prayer, but most signally concerted social prayer. It need not be matter of surprise that congregations should hold their prayer-meetings—cold and aimless prayer-meetings—from year to year, and at the end of long years have no evidence of any known fruits of prayer and of prayer-meetings. And why? Mainly, because they never unitedly desired, and never, by previous agreement, importunately pressed an

object of prayer upon the ear of a prayer-hearing God.

3. Another feature of these historic extracts: Wherever prayer-meetings prevail in congregations, there will vigorous Sabbath schools be sustained, and earnest attention given to the religious training of the youth. There will be town missions, or some such benevolent enterprises for the benefit of the masses. There will be effort and interest in every good cause in which the spirit of revived religion enlists every one under its life-inspiring influence. These references very distinctly show that just in proportion as any people take an interest in the prayer-meeting, so are they found active in every other Christian and benevolent enterprise. So, on the other hand, these show that where there is no interest manifested in the prayer-meeting, little well-directed public spirit will appear in the cause of religion and the church.

4. These extracts demonstrate the efficiency of the prayer-meeting as an instrument of moral reform. Drunkenness and the liquor traffic fall before its influence as Dagon before the Ark of the God of Israel. Here is a reforming agency more potent in reclaiming the drunkard than either pledge or Good Templar Lodge. Four public houses close in one parish. One publican remaining in the trade, finds the profits of his occupation almost gone, and curses the prayer-meeting because "they had done him up." Instead of packs of cards being carried by the poor turf-diggers, the Bible is made the pocket companion in toil, and placed under the pillow, at night, where rests the toil-wearied head. The angry passions of party spirit and political excitement, are alike allayed by the Christ-like spirit of social prayer.

5. These prayer-meetings were correctives of the grossest Arianism, and of kindred heresies which had long pros-

trated the strength of the church and the power of vital godliness. Too many popular revivals have been productive of the grossest errors and corruptions, as also divisions and disintegrations of churches. Such were many of the revivals in our western country, about the close of last century and the beginning of this, as in Kentucky and some other of the Western States. Out of Kentucky revival sprung New-Light Arianism and a large growth of Shakers — disciples of Anna Lee — headed by Barton Stone, Houston, McNamar, and others.

These revivals and revived prayer-meetings of Ireland were productive of very different fruits. They were characterized by very different sowings. Instead of the tares of the enemy, the seed of Scotland's Reformation, under the banner of Scotland's Covenant, was liberally sown, broad-cast over the fields, by these revival prayer-meetings; and the result was, that where, "for eighty long years, the church lay under the incubus of Arianism—the frozen zone of a nominal Christianity, these souls have been brought from under that Christless system into the communion of the church." In these revival prayer-meetings were explained and sung "the songs of Zion, the Psalms of David, those glorious Psalms, never so much prized as now, ascending from almost every house." Under such popular influence how could heresy thrive? How could pure religion decline? But where Sectarian songs, imbued with Arianism and other Sectarian heresy, were made the sources of the inspiration of revival and of the prayer-meetings, how could it be otherwise than the reaping of a luxuriant harvest of heresy?

6. The salutary effects of these revival prayer-meetings, as here presented, in arresting the current of waywardness among the youth, and of training them for exemplary

usefulness in the church, are brought out to view so as to throw around them more than ordinary interest. "Scarcely a young man above the age of fourteen, either in town or country, will refuse to pray publicly in any meeting; and sometimes little boys, of nine or ten years old, astonish their grandfathers by the beauty and fervor of their devotions." Here we have the practical demonstration of the truth already assumed, that the prayer-meeting is the normal school of the church. Out of these prayer-meetings flow—as from the river of God—streams gladdening the church. Not only do such fellowship-trained youths, like living waters, exert a healing influence among surrounding youth; but, especially, they go forth from the normal school, well trained educators, fitted for all the extensive variety of labors devolving upon the laity in the church, in all the relations they may be called to sustain. Nine-tenths of the young men who lead in the prayer-meetings, it will be found, give promise to become fit material for the ruling eldership, and for other leading posts with their important work. Out of this class must the Sabbath school find its conductors and teachers. Out of this class must every Christian enterprise find its most substantial defenders and active supporters.

7. These prayer-meeting revivals excite in their subjects an earnest desire for knowledge. Says one from whom we quote: "A few Sabbaths ago, I made an appeal to my people for some money to procure a congregational library, that knowledge might be increased among our youth, and I was met in a way I did not expect; all were inclined to give. Had the subject been mooted among us some years ago, not one in twenty would have responded to the call." Revival and Christian conference inspire thirst for knowledge. This begets a taste for reading; and this

again a desire for books; and these, all together, foster a spirit of Christian liberality.

The justness of the remarks just made, suggested by the statements contained in the preceding extracts, will be further confirmed by the subsequent references:

"From the first I had *classes* for inquirers and converts, which were greatly needed and much blessed. At the close of every prayer-meeting, (and they were held in the church five evenings each week during the months of July and August,) persons anxious about their souls were invited to remain, and warning, instruction, and encouragement were given, as might be required. Many meetings for prayer, conducted by members of the church, were at the same time held throughout the country. These still continue, to the number of about *twenty* each week. They are well attended, and have helped greatly to confirm the souls of the disciples."

This example suggests the propriety, First: Of general prayer-meetings in every congregation, held in the church, with the minister presiding, either for the whole congregation, or for "classes," as the circumstances may require; and also, Second: Of particular meetings in the several districts, to be conducted by the members of the church, and for their special benefit. This arrangement, if wisely made, will bring the prayer-meeting to the door of every member, and will be more likely to secure its benefits to a larger portion of the masses of the whole people.

The following reference, taken from a statement of Rev. Andrew Long, of Monreagh, confirms greatly the correctness, as well as the importance, of these views of the prayer-meeting:

"Since the beginning of the great awakening, we have had congregations on week-days, during the autumn, varying from five hundred to one thousand; whereas, about twelve months ago, it would have been very difficult to collect two hundred persons even, on any occasion. Formerly, I was under the necessity of giving up a *monthly congregational* prayer-meeting, the attendance was so miserable; and the only way in which I could maintain the semblance of it was by holding district meetings, and thus itinerating through our bounds; and even then very few of them came together. But no sooner did the Holy Spirit breathe on the dead bones than eight weekly and two bi-weekly district meetings sprung up spontaneously. And in addition to these, we have one week-day and two Lord's day union prayer-meetings, which are numerously attended.

"A short time ago I was visiting from house to house in a distant district of the congregation, and in the evening called upon a respectable family to pay my last visit that day. In a little while after I entered, the voice of Psalms in the distance fell upon my ear. On inquiring 'what meaneth this?' I was informed that it was a little prayer-meeting in the other end of the house, attended by five young men who are members of the district meeting, and assemble weekly, besides, to pray specially for a more abundant outpouring of the Holy Spirit upon the land; I at once joined the little band in the small 'upper room.' One of the young men, whose duty it was to engage in prayer, modestly declined doing so in my presence, saying he was 'but a babe, and weak.' I encouraged him, and at length he poured forth a sweet, simple prayer, in which I was not forgotten."

In this item of history we have very distinctly marked:

1. In revival of religion the Holy Spirit, breathing upon the dry bones, breathes into them the life of prayer, re-

vives the spirit of social prayer, and the practice of the prayer-meeting observance.

2. When religion is revived in a congregation the people demand the *district prayer-meeting* for their own benefit. The spontaneous cravings of the revived spiritual nature demand the fellowship of kindred spirits in the little upper rooms where Christ is wont to come and breathe upon his disciples. How distinctive this of true Christian character, and of a healthy state of religion!

3. Revival calls out class prayer-meetings. Young men seek the fellowship of young men in the prayer-meeting. Boys seek the fellowship of boys. Females seek the fellowship of females in these fellowship-meetings. Here the social nature, sanctified by grace, finds its fullest and purest exercise, and its sweetest social enjoyments.

We shall trouble the reader with but a few more historical illustrations of the happy results of a revival of religion upon congregations, and of the inseparable connection of the prayer-meeting with a revived state of religion.

Rev. R. Dunlop, reporting the change resulting from revival in Monaghan, says:

"But now, there is not a district where more hopeful cases can be pointed out, where greater changes have been wrought in the moral and religious life, where greater anxiety continues to be manifested, or where *prayer-meetings* are more numerously attended."

Here, as always, the prayer-meeting stands out the ever-attendant evidence of true revival.

In a more general report of several churches, we notice the following:

"Special meetings were immediately established in the Presbyterian churches, and the neighborhood was deeply moved. In the congregations of Bailisborough there are few houses in which family worship is not maintained. Through the district generally there is a marked improvement. Meetings are held for prayer and Christian fellowship, sometimes in the houses of those who formerly neglected gospel ordinances altogether, and several such meetings are also held among the female members of the church. Two congregational libraries are being organized. Two public houses have been closed—one for the want of trade, the other for conscience' sake."

"*How the Revival was propagated.*—I am no advocate for forcing religion upon those who are unwilling to receive it. In my judgment, we have had far too much of that in Ireland already. I do not think the gospel can be propagated by storm. But I think that the legitimate and *inoffensive* means of 'revival meetings' should be used in every neighborhood to call attention to the subject. It has been by these means, and *through a chain of Presbyterian churches*, that the revival has come so near us; and may we not hope that the experience which the church has acquired during the past year may enable it to conduct such meetings with fewer drawbacks to their utility?"

Another, in giving evidences of the genuineness of this revival, from its likeness to the apostolic revival, says:

"What steadfastness 'in fellowship'! To talk with one another of the preciousness of Christ, and of the great salvation; to strengthen each other's hearts; help each other's infirmities; to stimulate each other to a still greater readiness to work for their blessed Master; and, as they travel on to their eternal home, to lighten the toil and trial of the pilgrimage by speaking to one another in Psalms, hymns, and spiritual songs; and, oftentimes, with hearts too full for utterance, to pour out their common supplications before the throne—these are the delightful and abounding evidences that the new children of the covenant are knit together in an endearing and indissoluble alliance.—Let the heaven-directed aspirations presented at those brief seasons, snatched from worldly occupations for spiritual converse—the many social gatherings now sanctified by the word and prayer—and the distinctness, importunity, and expectancy exhibited by those who have been divinely taught to pray, bear witness to the extent to which the Spirit has been given as a Spirit of grace and supplication."

REPORT OF THE PRESBYTERY OF AHOGHILL.

Presented to the Synod, May 17, 1859, and valuable as the first public testimony of a church court with reference to the Revival in Ireland, and the prominent importance of the prayer-meeting:

"An extraordinary interest began to be awakened; prayer-meetings multiplied; crowds flocked to these refreshing streams; nor were ordinary houses able to accommodate the eager multitudes that assembled to hear the burning prayers, and to listen to the plain but heart-stirring addresses of the converted brethren, and those ministers and laymen whose hearts the Lord moved to engage in this important work. The open field, or the public way-side, even in the cold evenings of spring, were the scenes of deeply interesting meetings, over which angels hovered with joy. The prayer-meetings held in the first and second Presbyterian churches were crowded to excess, although held on the same evening and at the same hour. For several miles around multitudes flocked to these meetings for prayer and exhortation. Our lay brethren from Connor, at the first, gave, and continue from time to time still to give, a powerful impetus to the good work.

"Never, in these localities, was there such a time of

secret and public prayer; in all directions prayer-meetings have sprung up, and that without number. They are conducted in a manner of deepest solemnity, and with a burning earnestness for the outpouring of the Holy Spirit, and for the conversion of souls. These meetings have been signally honored of the Lord. The Spirit has descended in power.

"On this revival work, so far as it has as yet developed itself, there is written, 'Holiness to the Lord.' Even upon that portion of the public who make no claim to be religious, a deep, solemnizing influence has been exercised. Many of them are thoughtful and inquiring, attending the prayer-meetings with evident interest, and, it is to be hoped, with profit. But, among the awakened and converted, other delightful fruits are growing up with rapidity to maturity. Prayer has received a powerful stimulus—not only secret, but family and public prayer is one of those heavenly fruits.

"It is truly astonishing the liberty that many, very many, both male and female, have got in public prayer. It is most refreshing to hear the holy, earnest, edifying prayers which many babes in Christ are now offering at the family altar, and at the public prayer-meeting. It is nothing uncommon to hear the voice of prayer wafted on the wings of the wind from the adjoining field. The Bible is studied, and prized, and loved, more than it ever was before. It is felt to be 'more precious than gold, yea, than much fine gold, and to be sweeter than the honey, yea, than the honey that droppeth from the comb.'

"Never was there, in this locality, such holy, and importunate, and believing prayer offered up by members, in the name of the holy child Jesus, for the outpouring of the Holy Spirit"

CONGREGATIONAL REPORTS OF PRAYER-MEETINGS.

In connection with the General Assembly of the Presbyterian Church in Ireland, there are some five hundred and twenty congregations. Of these, at the request of the author of "The Year of Grace," about three hundred reported on the history and character of the Revival. And of this latter number, about one hundred and seventy-six report the number of prayer-meetings in each of these congregations, the whole numbering about 2,000. This will make, in the aggregate, over *eleven prayer-meetings* in each congregation. In the one hundred and seventy-six congregations reporting the number of their prayer-meetings, three is the lowest, and eighty the highest, numbei reported of any one congregation. This highest number is from the Berry Street church, in the city of Belfast, presumed to be one of the largest in the Presbyterian communion. Presuming its number of members to be twelve hundred, then the district prayer-meetings of that congregation would be one for every *fifteen members*. This state of things, in a large congregation, seems to be something like what the state of affairs should be in a healthy state of religion. Those fifteen members, with their children, and members of their respective families, not in communion, would make eighty prayer-meetings of some *thirty persons each*, enough to fill comfortably any upper room for prayer, with the women, after the manner of apostolical times.

From the three hundred and forty-four congregations not reporting the number of their prayer-meetings, the following statements are gleaned: In Ballycarry, prayer-meetings are universal: in the several districts one thousand attend the prayer-meetings. In Ballymena, the prayer-meetings pervade town and country. In Fisherwick Place, the prayer-meeting, with difficulty sustained before, has an increase of from three to five hundred, and besides, the young people have prayer-meetings among themselves. In the Carrickfergus Saltworks, the men meet for prayer seven hundred feet under ground. In Connor, from which place no report is made of the *number* of prayer-meetings, the return contains the statement, that there is a net-work of prayer-meetings, embracing the whole extent of that district of country. In Lecumpher, according to its report, district prayer-meetings, embracing the whole extent of the congregation, are held in the houses of the rich, and cottages of the poor. In the first congregation of Drum, the prayer-meetings are often thronged to inconvenience in the rural districts.

The Presbyterian congregations in the County of Antrim, returning the number of their prayer-meetings, report four hundred and seventy-two. In the County Down, they report three hundred and sixty-eight prayer-meetings. In the County of Derry, two hundred and five are reported. And thus the meetings of some seven or eight counties are returned.

These reports show a remarkable state of religion in the Presbyterian Church of Ireland. Can any of the larger churches in the United States show such a record? Could they, at any period, during the Revival of 1857–1859? The state of religion in any particular church will be better known from the state and number of its own prayer-meetings, among its own members, than from the outside, noisy, popular and exciting gatherings of the masses, headed by a few of the active spirits of the several churches, in the world-renowned Union Prayer-meetings.

We know they had their "Open-air Meetings" in Ireland. We remember the Weekly Union Prayer-meetings held in Music Hall, in the Capitol of Ulster; the City Mayor in the chair, with a hundred ministers of all denominations filling the platform. And again, another week, the Lord Bishop in the chair, while the surging crowds without failed to find admittance. We have heard of the immense gatherings, on the grounds of the Botanic Garden, numbering *thirty or forty thousand*—such assemblage as was never before seen in the North of Ireland. Of this, more again.

These "demonstrations" may not be the best evidence of the gracious presence of Him who was not in the great and strong wind, rending the mountains and breaking the rocks, nor in the earthquake, nor in the fire, but in the still small voice. In the closet, at the family altar, and in the prayer-meeting, we shall find the better tests of the spiritual state of any church.

CHAPTER XI.

REVIVALS AND PRAYER-MEETINGS IN SCOTLAND, WALES, ENGLAND, FRANCE, AND GERMANY.

The Scottish Guardian—Prayer-meetings in Glasgow—Fishing Villages of the North—Reports to the Free Church General Assembly—Humphrey Jones and David Morgan—England and Wales—Origin of the Prayer-meeting Revivals in Wales—Prayer-meeting characteristics of the Welsh churches—Prayer-meetings in France and Germany—Dr. Frederick Monod—In Paris.

The Revival and Prayer-meetings in Scotland.

SO far as we know, the history of the general revivals that occurred ten years ago, has been given more in detail in the United States, and in Ireland, than in any other portions of the church. The gleaning of Prayer-meeting history from Scottish field, in these latter years of revival, is somewhat meagre. Reference to the prayer-meeting is incidental only, and especially so in connection with the church. Here, as everywhere else, the history of the prayer-meeting is, as yet, unwritten.

The Revival of 1857 had progressed some time in Ireland and in this country before it made its appearance in Scotland. In August, 1859, the Scottish Guardian had the following notice of the beginnings of the revival in Glasgow and its vicinity:

"The Holy Spirit has been manifesting His gracious power in a remarkable manner in this neighborhood during the last few days. Our readers are aware that ever since the news of the great revival in America reached Scotland, *prayer-meetings* for the special purpose of imploring a similar blessing, have been held in Glasgow, as well as in other places. The intelligence which has reached us recently leaves no room to doubt that those prayers have been heard. We have heard—we trust, with gratitude—that God has been pleased, from the very beginning of these prayer-meetings, to use them as the means of converting souls, and quickening his own people; and latterly—at least in the meeting of the Religious Institution Rooms, with which we are best acquainted—the attendance has been decidedly on the increase, and anxious souls frequently remain, at the close of the services, to seek counsel and direction from the ministers and others who take part in these meetings. Christian men and women appear to be attaining to greater faith in the power of prayer; and petitions from Christian parents for their children, children for their parents, brothers and sisters for brothers and sisters, and friends for friends, have been becoming more common. There is already evidence that some of these prayers have been heard."

Rev. Hamilton H. Macgill, Home Secretary of the United Presbyterian Church, in a communication published in the "Evangelical Christendom," bears the following interesting and important testimony to the connection between the revival and the prayers of God's people:

"The invariable testimony of the brethren is, that a spirit of prayerfulness preceded the revival. In Burghead, one of the fishing villages of the North, the first special part noticed, as preceding the revival, was the following: that at a prayer-meeting, held in the house of a Christian woman, laid for the last thirty years on a bed of affliction, the burden of the prayers, at her request, was for the outpouring of the Spirit, for the quickening of God's people and the conversion of sinners. Ere long the careless fishing people were awakened, and many of them converted to the Lord; while the entire community, with few exceptions, was moved, and not a few, formerly without the pale of the church, came forward to confess the faith. There have been cases in which nothing but almost total deadness existed before the blessing came, but in many places the preparation for the blessing was deep humiliation among the people of God, and much earnestness in crying for the descent of the Spirit. 'Where there were God's own faithful saints,' says Mr. Gordon Forlong, 'I have generally seen a spirit of prayer combined with faithful testimony.' Another layman, like Mr. Forlong, largely acquainted with the history of the revival, Mr. Reginald Radcliffe, puts the single word *prayer* opposite the query about *preparation*, as certainly the full and significant reply."

In May, 1861, the following report on the Revival was made to the Free Church General Assembly:

"This is, in some respects, the most important and interesting report that was ever laid on the table of the General Assembly. If, as has been said, a living soul is of more value than a dead world, what joy has there been in heaven over souls that have been made alive in Scotland since we met here last year! In consequence of instructions from last General Assembly, the Committee on Religion and Morals transmitted a circular to every minister and probationer in a charge or station throughout the Free Church. In reply to that circular, I have received one hundred and sixty-nine returns. Of these, eighty-six reported decided awakening and revival in the congregations of which they report. It is important to bear in mind that, besides the returns we have received, we know that there are many congregations where there has been revival, though not reported to us. We have reason to know that, while the returns we have received give a very pleasing idea of the state of religion throughout the country, they by no means give us an adequate knowledge of the state of religion. We find, indeed, that since the returns were sent in to me, awakening has taken place in a number of localities.

"It is very interesting to find that these reports are spread over the whole country, from Shetland to Solway. The revival with which God has been pleased to bless us extends over the length and breadth of the land. Moderator, you, and the fathers and the brethren around me, are aware that in former times Scotland has been visited with revival and awakening, but I believe that on these occasions the revival and awakening was partial—confined to particular localities. It seems a blessed characteristic of the revival in our times, that it is wide-spread. We trust that through God's sovereign grace it will yet prevail over the whole of Scotland. The indications in the reports that I have are exceedingly cheering; even where no revival is reported, it is reported that there is *much prayer*, much earnest listening to the word of God, much earnest expectation and desire for the blessing; and I find that these things, in almost every instance, have preceded the awakening; and I scarcely know of any instance where the awakening has not been preceded by this *spirit of prayer* and expectation.

"There seems in many—almost every instance—to have been a preparatory work. In our own church, we have been looking, for many years past, for such a revival. Many now present must remember our exercises in Music Hall, before we had the privilege of meeting where we are now assembled. They must recollect the earnest prayers for revival that were then offered up in conference and addresses connected with the revival. Then, in many of our congregations, there was a gradual increase of the *spirit of prayer*, and increased expectation of revival. There was increased attention to the preaching of the Word, *increased attendance at prayer-meetings*, and an *increase of the exercise of prayer in our social circles*, in our families, and in secret; and when the Lord had thus prepared us for receiving the blessing, it pleased him to pour it out very remarkably and very abundantly. I cannot help observing, that one great means of awakening seems to have been the communication of intelligence of what the Lord had done in other places. I find in almost all the reports that this was done with the most blessed results. The information interested the people, and brought the thing home to them; they felt it was a reality; it excited a desire to partake of the benefit, and led them to use the means God has appointed for obtaining the benefit. I believe we can scarcely ascribe too much influence to the communication of religious intelligence in England about the results in which we this day rejoice.

"Perhaps in no part of the world have the effects of the revival and the actual visitation of the Spirit been more permanent than in Scotland. The revival spirit has pervaded many portions of that land, and corresponding fruit has been exhibited even to the present time. Wherever the *spirit of prayer* has been preserved, there God has been present by the awakening and converting influences of His grace accompanying the faithful labors of His people."

REVIVAL AND THE PRAYER-MEETING IN ENGLAND AND WALES.

The great revival which swept over the North of Ireland in 1859, and which pervaded the South and West of Scotland during the two following years, although visiting some portions of England, did not become so general here. Many of the ministers of the metropolis and great numbers of Christian laymen of various denominations, visited Ireland while the revival there was going on with greatest power, and they returned not only to tell what they had seen and felt, but to communicate the sacred influence to others with whom they came in contact. In this way, as well as by the growing principle of piety and activity, the Christians of London were led to devise ways and means of reaching the vast population of that great city, who were living outside of the circle of religious influences. *Meetings for prayer and Christian instruction* were greatly increased; the various classes of the previously neglected were reached by specific efforts designed for their benefit. But there has not been at any time such a manifestation of the presence and the power of the Spirit in the conversion of souls as has been witnessed in other places.

"*Wales*, on the other hand, has experienced some of the most wonderful displays of God's grace that have been witnessed in these latter days, and nowhere has the availing power of the effectual, *fervent prayer* of the righteous been more marvellously illustrated. The work, indeed, commenced about the same time as in Ireland, although, owing to the diversity of the language, and the comparatively little intercourse ordinarily carried on with this part of Great Britain, there were fewer visitors, and much less was known of what was then transpiring. Revivals were enjoyed in some localities in 1858; and, in 1859, the same wonderful scenes were transpiring in Ireland. It was not until the commencement of the year 1860 that the facts became generally known. During the first year of the revival the number of converts to the various denominations of Orthodox Christians, was estimated at from thirty, to thirty-five thousand. It is known, from reliable sources, that twenty-five thousand were added to the Welsh Calvinistic churches.

"It is said that the work commenced chiefly by the instrumentality of Humphrey Jones and David Morgan. Mr. Jones had emigrated to the United States, and having witnessed much of the revival work in that country, he was now anxious, on his return to his native place, to witness a similar outpouring of God's Holy Spirit there. We are told that he addressed discourses to professing Christians, chiefly with a view to rouse them to greater life and activity, maintaining that an *awakened church* is to be the principal instrument in converting the world. It is said that the first intercourse between these two men was most solemn. Being engaged in the same work, they interchanged views and feelings very freely. Mr. Jones spoke to Mr. Morgan very strongly on the state of religion in the country, the deadness of the churches, and *the necessity of more earnest prayer*. The character of the ministry was dwelt upon; the gospel should be preached with more directness and energy, *to be followed up by personal labors among the people.*

"Mr. Morgan was at first prejudiced against Mr. Jones' proceedings; but what he said to him had such a powerful effect upon his mind that he could get no sleep for several nights, but *continued in earnest prayer for the guidance of the Spirit.* Mr. Morgan went again to see Mr. Jones, and said, '*We cannot do much harm by keeping prayer-meetings*, and trying to rouse the country, even if there be nothing but man in it, after all.' 'You cannot do any harm,' Mr. Jones replied, 'and if you try it, you will not be long before God will be with you.'

"The following week, the two churches, Wesleyan and Calvinistic Methodists, united to keep *prayer-meetings* every night alternately, and we soon had a proof that the

Lord was willing to accept our offerings, for there was a sweet-smelling savor accompanying them. Old backsliders began to return. Men came in crowds from the mountains, and all the country round, to our meetings, until we were afraid the chapel would come down; men who were never seen in any place of worship, except in church at a christening or a funeral, and who knew nothing of worshiping God.

"Mr. Morgan was by this time full of the spirit of revival, and was fully occupied during the day, as well as every evening, in holding *prayer-meetings* and conversing with inquirers."

Similar cases produced similar effects, and the revival made rapid progress. Other ministers entered the great field, baptized with the same spirit of earnestness and zeal for the Master's glory and the salvation of souls.

THE ORIGIN OF THE PRAYER-MEETING REVIVAL IN WALES.

Rev. William Griffiths writes, February 10th, 1860:

"At our annual assembly, held at Aberdeen, in June, 1858, it was proposed and unanimously resolved that the first Sabbath in the following August should be set apart by all the churches and congregations of our association, *to pray unitedly* and earnestly for the outpouring of God's Spirit. I went home, and stated the resolution to my people, and some unusual feelings thrilled through the minds of all present. When the stated Sabbath arrived, we were blessed with remarkable earnestness at the throne of grace for the descent of the Holy Spirit to revive the church and convert the world. Ever since that memorable Sabbath, the *prayer-meetings presented a new aspect;* they gradually increased in warmth and number during the following months. This continued to February last, when it pleased Jehovah to pour down his Spirit from on high, as on the day of Pentecost. At this period it was advisable to publish *prayer-meetings daily,* and the attendance constantly increased for months, and continues doing so to the present time. At the close of each meeting we announced a Society (church) Meeting, and new converts came forward daily. The heavenly fire still continues to burn, and the flames have spread throughout the country at large. All religious denominations are cordially united in *social prayer-meetings,* and the descent of the divine influences among us is evident. The writer of these lines (to God be the praise) has had the great honor of giving the right hand of fellowship to more than six hundred and fifty new candidates for membership in our churches in this district since February last, and that in a comparatively small circle, too."

The following letter is from the Rev. R. Killin, incumbent of St. David's, Festinaig, dated February 14th, 1860:

"In order to give you a correct idea of the work, I must lead you back to the beginning of the year 1859. Hearing at that time of what was taking place in America, South Wales, and Ireland, *weekly prayer-meetings* were held for the outpouring of the Spirit upon us in this neighborhood. These have continued to the present time. They have been well attended from the beginning, and a blessing seems to rest upon them. Indeed, a deep feeling seemed to pervade the whole neighborhood during last winter and the following spring, until the general elections took place in May, which dried up our spirits for a time, though we continued our meetings.

"I ought to have mentioned that prayer-meetings were held in some of the quarries twice a week, during the dinner hour, last summer and autumn, at one of which, held on the 4th of October, I had the pleasure to assist, accompanied by the rector of Festinaig. The following Sabbath was a memorable day here, in many respects. A large open air *prayer-meeting* was held in one of the quarries, which deeply affected many. Some young people broke out rejoicing, in a *prayer-meeting* held among themselves in one of the chapels. There was an unusual solemnity of feeling in the church, and some of my people assembled in a cottage afterward, and held a *prayer-meeting,* which continued till midnight. The week following will be remembered as long as we live. Three *prayer-meetings* were held on a mountain, on successive days, at which the quarrymen attended; and *prayer-meetings* were held in every place of worship every night in the week, when scores of people joined the different denominations of Christians. I never heard such prayers before, although I have been accustomed to *prayer-meetings* from my early days."

A correspondent in the *Welsh Standard* thus refers to the movement in this district:

"I rejoice to be able to inform your numerous readers that a most powerful revival has just broken out in Bethesda, and the various chapels adjacent thereto. On Saturday, September 3d, *prayer-meetings* were held at two and six o'clock in the evening, and most remarkable meetings they were. God was truly among us. We have felt the Spirit of God in such meetings before; but nothing to what we experienced in these wonderful gatherings. After the meetings had passed away, loud praises were heard in the surrounding fields till midnight—one of the most wonderful things we ever witnessed. Besides the lateness of the hour, it rained heavily; still, hundreds of people ran to the place whence issued this unwonted sound. It was found that several of those recently converted had retired to a field in the vicinity of Bethesda, and that, being overpowered by the Spirit of God, they poured out their hearts joyfully before a throne of divine grace. In the present movement we have been greatly struck by the fact that so much of the *spirit of prayer* has possessed the Lord's people. They draw the heaven of heavens, as it were, into every *prayer-meeting;* hence such congregations as were never before seen are brought together on these occasions."

The following is from the History of the Revival in Wales, by Rev. John Venn:

"Without disparaging the pulpit, or in any way degrading the offices instituted by Christ in his church, it must strike all that *prayer*, oral, *united prayer*, has been greatly honored of God as a means of commencing and extending the present movement. The exact *place of prayer* in the great machinery of moral means has been better understood, and the belief in its efficiency has been more fully acted upon now than at any former time."

A correspondent says:

"We expected that the great outpouring of the Spirit would come by means of preaching. It was so in former days, it may be so again, and is so now, to some extent. Thank God, the ministry has not lost its power; but still, it is quite clear that the Holy Spirit's influences, at the present time, is communicated by means of *prayer*. Having heard from the pulpit of the unsearchable riches of Christ, we desire to receive them, and this has led us to our knees to seek and to enjoy. What a traffic there is between heaven and earth; prayers ascend, and the blessings descend in great abundance!"

Another correspondent, near Bangor, says:

"In several of the chapels, *prayer-meetings* are held at

five o'clock in the morning, and again in the quarries during the dinner hour, besides the Sabbath. It would be almost impossible for men in the present state to enjoy more communion with God. The house of clay can hardly stand more. I know many young persons and others who have spent whole nights in prayer in the out-houses, barns, and woods, even when the cold weather had set in. They seem to forget that they are in the flesh.

"I am persuaded that the means blessed of God to create and carry on the revival in most places, if not in ALL, is PRAYER. You can trace its origin and progress, in every locality, to prayer, especially the prayers of the new converts, after they have commenced their career. The broken sentences coming from the hearts of those under conviction, and the simple, child-like prayers of young believers, tell most powerfully on all present. Be they converted or unconverted, they cannot help being moved to tears; to the former, they are tears of joy; to the latter, they are produced by a sense of danger.

"I cannot say that any indications of a revival could be observed here previous to the very day on which it took place. Our denomination throughout South Wales devoted, however, the first Sabbath of last August to pray for the outpouring of the Holy Spirit. *There was no preaching*, PRAYER ONLY. I believe there has been more praying for this great blessing ever since. At all events, the Lord is now doing great things by means of the prayer-meeting."—*Rev. E. Jones.*

"Prayer-meetings have been the principal means with us of awakening the churches. In many places union prayer-meetings have been very useful in drawing the public mind toward the great question of salvation. I have been endeavoring, for some time, to induce all the congregation, the irreligious as well as the religious portion, to attend the prayer-meetings. In order to this, we have held a prayer-meeting for many weeks past, immediately before the Sabbath evening service, commencing at half-past five o'clock. By this arrangement, we have succeeded in having all the congregation, some time, to attend the prayer-meetings, and great good has been the result. Prayer-meetings have been held on the Sabbath, sometimes without preaching, and have been highly useful, when the people were, in some measure, prepared for them. In most places prayer-meetings have been held for weeks together; and in no instance have such means been persevered in, in the right spirit, without a signal proof of the Divine approbation. But to keep up the interest of the people in such protracted meetings, much depends on their conductors—they must be full of the spirit of prayer themselves. Prayer, faith in God's word, singleness of purpose, earnestness and perseverance, never fail of their object at a throne of grace; God may be nearer us than we sometimes dare believe."—*Rev. W. Evans.*

PRAYER-MEETING REVIVALS IN FRANCE AND GERMANY.

In the religious history of France and Germany, the material is very limited from which to gather prayer-meeting incidents. Still, in that general awakening of 1857–1859, France and Germany had some share. Among the evangelical churches of both countries, there were some evidences of revival, and as in all other instances of the outpouring of the Holy Spirit, the prayer-meeting formed the prominent feature of the work.

Rev. Dr. Frederick Monod gives the following intelligence:

"It is with deep emotion that, under the head 'DOMESTIC,' we, for the first time, write the words, 'Religious Revival.' We know that there have been some manifestations of an awakening in several places, but we had hitherto received no direct intelligence on the subject, and in such matters we are unwilling to speak from hearsay. Here, at last, is an abstract from a letter written by a Christian entitled to all confidence. We pray God that this blessed experience of the power of prayer may not be lost among us, but that it may prove the first fruits of an abundant harvest. The Lord, in order to grant it, is only waiting for the prayers of faith. There is neither in the word nor in the providence of God anything that can stand in the way of our obtaining for our France an outpouring of the Spirit, like unto that which for the last two years has been reviving the churches of God in the United States. The obstacles are only in ourselves. Here is our abstract:

"'The Lord is now beginning a reviving work of grace among my people. On our communion Sabbath in September, a few friends, to whom I had been reading the American work on the "Power of Prayer," asked me whether I would open my house every evening for a *prayer-meeting.* I heartily consented. We began that very night. There were six of us—all men. The first week our number did not increase. Nothing occurred worthy of special notice, only we were greatly refreshed and strengthened in our souls. The second week a school-mistress and three young ladies expressed a wish to join with us. We prayed for them, and during one of our meetings their hearts were melted under the power of the Holy Spirit; they shed many tears, confessed their sins, and a few days afterward found peace. It was a moment of such solemnity as I had never known before.

"'From that time the impulse was given; our faith in the power of prayer was strengthened, and we lived a new life. Backsliding souls came among us and were restored to their first love and their first joy. All the persons for whom we prayed, received a blessing. What we have asked the Lord to give, He has given. Wednesday last, especially, was a day of rich blessing; three persons asked an interest in our prayers. Among them was a woman, a very devil, a plague to her family, the chief promoter of all worldliness in our village, turning her house into a dancing saloon. That woman asked for our prayers. We must confess that, at the first moment, our faith failed. I, most of all, was staggered. However, I took courage. I told the persons that were met together for prayer—about twenty in number—that upon the issue of the struggle upon which we were about to enter depended the whole course of the revival which was just beginning in the midst of us; that, if we were conquered, our faith would be broken, and it would be all over with us. I reminded them of the Saviour's promise, "Whatsoever ye shall ask the Father in my name, that will I do." We cried to the Lord in great anguish. After two hours of wrestling, we were all broken down; but we had conquered. The poor sinner opened her mouth to cry for mercy.'"

"It is not necessary," writes a friend, "to go to America, or to Ireland, to behold the wonderful effects of the grace of God; all that is necessary is to pray with faith in the name of Jesus."

In Paris there was considerable awakening, commencing at first among the English almost exclusively, and conducted by friends of the cause from England. Soon the attention of the French was arrested. Immense crowds were gathered together, moved by the awakening influences brought to bear upon them. On one occasion three thousand children, with their relations, crowded the Cirque Napoleon, and hung upon the burning words of

Mr. Radcliffe, from England. The work here was conducted after the general mode of conducting revivals everywhere else—they sing, and pray, and alternate by brief remarks upon appropriate portions of Scripture, or by general conference adapted to the circumstances.

"Rev. Dr. Sawtelle, of the American Chapel at Havre, being one day in the Fulton Street meeting, stated that as he was stepping on board the steamer, to come to this country, he had an earnest request given him to be presented to this meeting, and that request he had come here to urge. He also wished prayer for his own field of labor. He said the influence of this meeting was felt in France. He knew the spirit of prayer was waking up the world. We see the dawning of a day of prayer."

The churches in Germany, in 1857–1860, were strangers to such revival and prayer-meetings as were, at that period, familiar to the American, Irish, and Scottish churches. We reserve, for another connection, a notice of a most remarkable awakening, with its accompanying prayer-meetings, which occurred in the early part of the year 1861, at the Orphan Asylum in Elberfeld, Germany.

CHAPTER XII.

REMARKABLE PRAYER-MEETING AND REVIVAL INCIDENTS.

Incidents of Elberfeld—Remarkable incidents of a Backslider, Townsend Street Church, Belfast—Remarkable Prayer-meeting Conversion—Blesses God for the 51st Psalm, and for all the Psalms memorized in the Sabbath School and Bible Class—"What would we have done without the Psalms?"—Bungener's France before the Revolution, Vol. I., p. 110—Narrative from "Work in the Wynds"—Noble Testimony to the fitness of the Psalms for Revival—"Their deep soil can be turned over and over again, while hymns bear scarcely a single plowing"—Prayer-meetings near Belfast—Incidents at Ballinahinch, Maghera, Ballykelly—Incidents in connection with Orangemen and Catholics—Broughshane Incidents—Ladies' Prayer-meetings.

WE shall begin this chapter of prayer-meeting incidents with the Elberfeld Orphan Asylum case, just now noticed in the close of the last. It furnishes an example of the most striking kind, illustrating the ever-present prayer-meeting wherever the Holy Spirit breathes upon any people the spirit and life of revival. No law of nature, or of grace, is more uniform in its operations than the law of the Spirit in the work of reviving grace, bringing its subjects together for prayer and conference. Grace makes the heart of its subject say: "All that fear God, come, hear, I'll tell what he did for my soul."

The account is taken from a paper published at Elberfeld:

"The work began with the 'Week of Prayer,' at the opening of the year 1860. This week of prayer was observed extensively at Elberfeld, and earnest prayer-meetings were held at Arrenberg. Petitions were offered for the Orphan House, where many of the children at the time caused much anxiety by their perverseness. And, lo! the spirit of prayer entered mightily into the House, and especially after this refractoriness and opposite disposition showed itself in some of them. On the afternoon of the 13th of January, one of the largest girls was noticed to sit quietly among the others, taking no share in their play, but evidently in anxious thought. In the evening she came to the superintendent of the House, complained of great anxiety for her soul, and desired to open her heart to him. He pointed her to the Saviour, who, having begun his good work by a revelation of her sinfulness, would still farther help her. The child was quiet in her work, and continually in meditation and prayer. On the following Sabbath the same unrest was renewed, but the Lord had mercy on her childish prayers, and sent her a joyful faith and blessed peace. Soon after the 13th of January, a second girl came to the superintendent, complaining of her sins, and expressed the wish to pray each evening alone. She begged for the key to an empty chamber for this purpose, which was given her; beyond this, the thing remained a secret. Soon, however, there were several other girls who wished to talk with the superintendent concerning the welfare of their souls. All were recommended to the Lord in prayer; with some he prayed alone, and not only bore them, as also the other children, daily on his heart to the Lord in prayer, but engaged those already under conviction in prayer with him for the others. After this little number had earnestly prayed for their thoughtless companions, the superintendent disclosed the affair to a dear friend, and heard, to his great joy, that he also had remembered in particular the Orphan House, and rejoiced heartily at the good news.

"On the 28th of January, the superintendent was called

from supper in the evening by a boy, who begged him to go to one of his companions, who lay upon the cellar stairs, and cried with a loud voice, 'Dear Saviour, forgive all my sins.' He was struggling under deep consciousness of sin. To the boys who had assembled about him, he expressed the earnest wish, 'Would to God you all were compelled to prostrate yourselves before the Lord.' Later in the evening the superintendent allowed the anxious boy, and two others who wept because of their sins, to come and pray with him. While engaged in this manner, four other boys, likewise in deep anxiety, came into the kitchen, and cried to God for mercy. There were now seven boys so deeply affected by their consciousness of sin, that after they had retired to rest, they could not sleep. They rose, dressed themselves, and went into the boys' sitting room, and, in the presence of one of the inspectors, who had also risen, they spent the night in prayer and supplication. The next morning, they felt themselves so united with the Lord, that they could bear quietly the scorn, ridicule, and even persecution of others. During each recess of the day they united again in prayer; read portions of Scripture, which they *explained one to another;* sang and prayed freely from the heart. Soon others, also in great anxiety, were joined to these seven boys, and on the following evening, in an empty room that had been opened for this little prayer-meeting, sixteen boys were found upon their knees, or oftener lying on their faces; and a loud, united call was heard for grace and mercy, for the forgiveness of their sins, and a pouring out of the Holy Spirit, not only for themselves, but for other children and the whole house.

"On the 31st of January, the fourth day after this first awakening among the boys had taken place, after the tasks of the children had been performed, this little chamber was entirely filled with boys who wished to pray together. One of them rose and said to the others, 'You know that hypocrisy is a great sin. It is written that the hypocrite shall not enter into the kingdom of heaven. Whoever, therefore, among us, is not in earnest, had better go away.' But no one left. A boy fourteen years of age then offered a touching, passionate prayer, which every one, in astonishment, could but feel *the Spirit alone had called forth.* Afterward the twenty-first chapter of Revelation was read, upon which a boy ten years of age *discoursed* in such a manner that we could but ask, 'From whence hath this one these things?' The superintendent, who had been present the whole time, now knelt down and prayed with them. At first they all listened, but at last became so moved that each prayed aloud what was in his heart. In the evening, at nine o'clock, a united prayer-meeting was held, which those children were allowed to attend who felt constrained to unite with the adults in prayer. More than thirty boys, and the same number of girls, were present."

Some things here are worthy of note: *First,* these earnest and awakened children seem to have caught, really, the spirit of prayer. The Divine Spirit, the Author of prayer, seems to have made intercession within them, *inspiring desires, and so making prayer for them;* for "the Spirit alone had called forth" that touching prayer. *Second,* these children, in their prayer-meeting, "explained one to another" the Scriptures they read. One "discoursed" on the twenty-first chapter of Revelation. In obedience to apostolic injunction ruling the exercises of the prayer-meeting, they "exhorted one another."

"After the meeting, the anxious children entered the kitchen, where they threw themselves upon their knees, and prayed for a pure heart, for obedience, and a gentle disposition, that from this time forth their behavior might be only a source of rejoicing to their teachers. One boy, fourteen years old, who, until this time, ridiculed the whole affair, and had said, 'If they all are converted, I will not be;' and declared openly he had no longer any conscience, had gone to bed before the prayer-meeting, and remarked to those who slept with him, 'While the others are making such a noise with their prayers, we will take a quiet nap'! But he could not sleep. The awakened children were praying for him continually. When he heard that his dearest friend, an apprentice, who, on account of sickness, was for a time in the Orphan House, had also united himself with the praying circle, he said, 'Now, my strength is half broken.' At last he got up and went to the kitchen. There he saw his friend in the midst of the other boys, upon his knees, and heard that they prayed for him. In a moment he was upon his knees, cried aloud, and fell into violent convulsions, so that it became necessary to carry him back to bed. A great anxiety for his soul had taken possession of him, and he believed himself to have committed the sin against the Holy Ghost. The convulsions continued more than three hours. He was speechless during this time, but had full consciousness. On the next morning, all power of resistance was gone, but as yet no true faith was apparent. Toward eleven o'clock the convulsions were renewed, and continued until one. At four o'clock he said, 'Now I can believe.' He had, during this time, a hungering for spiritual food. The children and teachers must sing with him, and also pray, or read passages from the Bible continually. He pointed out with his own cramped, trembling hands, portions of Scripture to be read to him. Among these was the Twenty-third Psalm. As he heard the last words, 'goodness and mercy,' he seemed transported with delight.

"This wonderful work of the Lord made the deepest

impression upon all the children; and many others, with those already awakened, prayed in such a manner that we were continually reminded of the words, 'And there were added daily unto the church such as should be saved.' Afternoons we saw a circle of thirty-seven boys who all prayed. There were among them children of all the confessions which were represented in the House, for the Spirit worketh freely.

"Since the Lord had so richly blessed this work, a prayer-meeting was appointed at eight o'clock in the evening, when we might thank the Lord for the wonders of his grace. Besides grown persons, sixty boys and an equal number of girls took part in it. After the opening hymn, the person in charge of the meeting prayed, and was immediately followed by one of the teachers. A portion of the Bible was then read by one of the inspectors, which he wished to follow up with prayer; but this he was unable to do, for, as soon as the assembly rose, a boy of twelve years of age began to pray. He prayed so fervently that the souls of all present were moved. It was, indeed, the first time that a child in the Orphan House had prayed openly and from the heart. After him three or four other boys prayed, and at last the one who had been in convulsions the preceding evening.

"On the following evening—Sabbath, the 3d of February—another prayer-meeting was held. The interest was greater than before. Several children, and among them one girl, prayed in such a feeling manner, and with such child-like simplicity, that all were moved. During the prayer-meeting a great deal of feeling was manifested among the little girls, who had gone to bed attended by one of the teachers. Toward eleven o'clock three girls came to the superintendent, with whom he must pray alone. Before he had closed, he was told that the girls in the sleeping-room desired to see him, that he might pray with them. As soon as he was able to go there, how great was his astonishment! Nearly all the girls from the neighboring chambers had come together, weeping loudly, on their knees in bed, by the sides of the bed, and all about in the corners. Everywhere was heard a cry for grace and mercy.

"On the 4th of February, the children desired another prayer-meeting in the evening, which was appointed. A converted boy, seventeen years of age, whose conduct heretofore had been far from upright, made the closing prayer. Also, in this meeting, it was necessary to take several children from the room. Among them was a young apprentice, who did not belong to the Orphan House, but whom an unseen Power had guided hither. He afterward related that, on his way to the meeting, he felt all the time impelled to run. When the teachers could not attend to all the prayer-meeting calls, those children already converted prayed with the awakened, and often so fervently that the angels in heaven must have rejoiced."

One remarkable feature throughout is the wonderful demand for prayer and the prayer-meeting. Indeed, the greater the felt necessity, the greater the desire for prayer. Still, little prayer-meetings are continued among the boys and girls, and if any find opportunity to hear, unperceived, the child-like, fervent, powerful prayers, worked by the living, mighty power of the Spirit, they can but give thanks to the Lord, who, out of the mouths of babes and sucklings, has prepared for Himself praise.

Remarkable incident of a backslider.—In the Townsend Street Church, Belfast, during the late revival, the following case occurred: The subject of this brief reference was a young man of prepossessing appearance, excellent character, reflecting habits, and religious profession. He was well educated in the Scriptures, and much liked. He was a successful Sabbath school teacher, and a regular communicant in the church. After some time he was appointed superintendent of a Sabbath school, and all went on well under his management. By-and-by a striking change passed over him. He became dissatisfied with everything, and gave up the charge of the school—fell away from the communion of the church, and finally ceased to attend the house of God. The secret of all was, he had begun to read infidel books, by which his faith was overthrown, and he was unfortunately drawn into the darkness of Deism, and openly avowed his contempt of Christianity. In this state of mind he continued for several months. When the Spirit of God visited our town and congregation, the manifestations of His power were treated by him with utter incredulity, and the whole movement was regarded as woman's weakness and nervous sympathy. The work of grace was denied; and when, on one occasion, the conversation turned on the power of prayer, that power was defied—"Let any six men try and pray me down." One humble fellow workman—himself awakened at a *prayer-meeting*, and a *reclaimed backslider*, and at that very time anxiously alive about his own soul—secretly accepted the challenge. His was a heart which loved that erring brother through and through. As a friend he had rejoiced in his rise, and now grieved over his fall; and, since the day he heard it, did not cease to pray for him, and to desire that he might be "filled with the knowledge of His will in all wisdom and spiritual understanding." Whilst the prayers were being offered, the case which we have detailed was presented. This loving companion reported the fact to him. The earnest tone of that working man, himself a monument of mercy, went to the heart of his erring friend. He went home that day in silent anxiety, and retired at once to his closet. He took down his neglected Bible, and, opening it at random, his eye fell on the 51st Psalm, and as he read it, he wondered. He closed it, and, opening it again, his attention was drawn to the 39th Psalm, with all its solemn warnings. Melted down, he fell on his knees, and casting himself on God in Christ, for forgiveness and acceptance, all his difficulties vanished, he could not tell how, and there was no objection urged by Tom Paine to which he could not have given a sufficient answer.

Here, the power of concerted prayer—like Jacob's wrestlings—prevailed with God, and brought the wandering backslider from his infidelity. And what a testimony to the fitness of the Psalms for true revival exercises, and the pre-eminent fitness of the 51st Psalm to deepen conviction and encourage conversion in an awakened soul!

A REMARKABLE PRAYER-MEETING CONVERSION.

The commencement of the revival at Dundrod, Ireland, is reported by its pastor, Rev. William Magill. He gives the following statements:

"I had been at Belfast. I came home filled with strange thoughts, cherishing high hopes, and breathing earnest prayers that the Lord would come over the mountains and visit my people. On the morning of the day after, I rose from my bed with the thought that something strange and unaccountable was about to happen at Dundrod. I cannot account for the feeling; but I had a strong presentiment, not of evil, but of coming good. I expected something, and I was not disappointed. When dressing, I observed a man approaching the manse, and the thought at once arose in my mind, This man is, perhaps, coming for me—the work is begun. It was even so. I was soon on the way to his house. He told me, as we went, that one of his daughters, after returning home from the prayer-meeting, had fallen ill, strangely ill—that she was up all night, and had raised the whole family to engage in prayer with her and for her—that she had never ceased praying and reading the whole night, and when he left her she was worse than ever, and he feared she was 'going wrong in her mind.'

"Before reaching the house, I heard her voice in loud, earnest, and continuous prayer. When I opened the door and looked in, I saw her mother and two sisters, all on their knees and in tears. In the centre of the group, was the 'stricken one,' the picture of woe, with eyes upturned to heaven, and face covered and seamed with tears. Her arms were now extended to their utmost length, as if to grasp some distant and coveted object, and then brought together with violence, as she clasped her hands, as if in mortal agony, whilst from her lips there burst forth words of fire, as living streams from a burning mountain.—Then, as her eye rested on me, as I stood riveted to the spot, witnessing, in silence, this exciting and wonderful scene—for I never had heard such prayers before—she exclaimed, without rising from her kneeling posture, 'O, here is my minister! I knew I would have no peace till he came. O, come;—come, pray for my guilty soul!' I knelt beside her and prayed, her voice accompanying mine all the time, while her expressions, at intervals, were so rich, so varied, and so Scriptural, that I had often to pause, and then to follow, instead of lead, as text after text from Old and New Testament, prophet and psalmist, Christ and apostle, were changed into beautiful and impassioned prayer. Such asking, seeking, striving to enter the kingdom, I never saw before. It was, indeed, Mercy knocking her loudest knocks at the door of the heavenly mansion, so that the

Lord himself, startled by the peals which roused up all the inmates, comes quickly, and, with a smile, opens the door, and takes her by the hand, and brings her in.

"The struggle is over. She rises up, and begins the song of triumph! What a change—a perfect transformation! The cloud is passed away, and God, like the sun in his glory, is lifting upon her the light of his countenance. Her eye, as she sings, is lighted up with strange and unearthly fire. Her voice is no longer tremulous and plaintive, but now rings like a trumpet; while her whole face is covered with a smile, such as we might suppose an angel to wear.

"'Let us sing,' said she, 'the 51st Psalm. O, I bless God for that Psalm, and for all the Psalms I learned in the Sabbath school and Bible class!' I may here remark, that the Psalms have been, with all the converts here, sources of great joy. 'What would we have done without the Psalms!' was an exclamation often made. 'Sir,' said a servant girl to her master, after hearing the 51st, 130th, and 116th Psalms, 'surely some persons long ago must have felt as I feel, for those Psalms seem to have been written for their use and comfort.'

"Ah, how these rude chants of our ancestors go to the heart at such times! The Psalms are our epic, but an epic more deep and real than ever was written or sung by any people; an interminable poem, of which each one of us becomes in his turn the author; a sacred treasure of personal and individual remembrances, joys, sorrows, desires, heaped up with national associations; not a verse, not a strophe, but is quite a history or a poem. This was sung by a mother beside the cradle of her first-born; this other, one of our martyrs sung on his way to death; this is the song of the Vaudois returning in arms to their country; this, that of the Camisards marching to battle;

this verse is one that the balls of our enemy interrupted; that other is one of which a father, when expiring, murmured the half, and went to finish it with the angels. O, our psalms! our psalms! who could ever express in human words what your language is to us in our solitudes, on that soil red with our blood, and under the vault of that heaven from whence they look down upon us who have prayed, and wept, and sung before us!"—*Bungener's France Before the Revolution*, vol. I., p. 110.

In the above narrative we have some topics of interest presented worthy of our very grave reflection. 1. Revivals of religion begin in the hearts of the godly, by arresting the mind to some object of interest; or the desires are quickened for revival; sins are felt pressing the soul, and standing in the way of divine manifestations; hopes and expectations are excited; some unrest is felt, though its causes and character may not be well understood. So, the narrator in regard to himself: "I cannot account for the feeling; but I had a strong presentiment, not of evil, but of coming good. I came home filled with strange thoughts, cherishing high hopes, breathing earnest prayers."

2. The awakening began in the prayer-meeting; there the hidden implantations of the Spirit were brought to the surface; on the way home, the outward manifestation makes its appearance. The deepened impressions of the prayer-meeting are carried home; the first visible subject of the revival calls around her the other members of the family, and they spend the night in concerted prayer.

3. The psalms are the sword of the Spirit here to slay the enmity of the heart; the balm to heal the wounded soul; the song put into the mouth to express the feelings inspired by grace. Ah! these had been memorized in Sabbath school and Bible class, and grace revived praises God for these privileges of childhood.

A NARRATIVE OF INTEREST, TAKEN FROM "WORK IN THE WYNDS," BY REV. D. MACCALL, D. D., PP. 157, 158.

"*The Revival in the Wynds* made no revolution on our methods of work. Our weekly meeting for prayer became nightly; a second meeting was required when the first was closed; soon a third, and often a fourth. Instead of three brethren being asked to pray, every one on whom a tongue of fire had fallen was required more than once in the course of an evening. We did not need new truth. What texts we had preached from in four or five years, we preached from again, with added thought and more power, in five months. We did not need new songs. What Psalms we had read, and studied, and sung in five years, having nearly finished the Psalter when the revival commenced, we found best fitted for all kinds of singing during these wondrous nights. Before every prayer we had a few verses, suited for confession, or faith, or hope, or thanksgiving, read and briefly explained, and the prayer naturally rooted itself in them, and gave branches for many bird-like petitions to find rest and food ere they took wing heavenward. Our most useful addresses to the anxious were from the Psalms. We led them there into green pastures, and they lay down by still waters. Once or twice in these early days we tried a hymn, but found it would not stand exposition. It did not seem to have the deep soil of the psalms, which could be turned over and over again, and be all the richer for the digging. We had not quite finished the psalter when the revival began. We were about to begin the closing hallelujah Psalms, and the revival helped us easily into them. Hymns were used elsewhere by those who attended our meetings, and hymns have been, to some extent, used since; but much of the stability and rooted strength of the work I attribute, among other subordinate causes, to the continuous and intelligent use of the Psalms through all the exciting work of the first years. I remember when one of my elders proposed in the session, two years after the work commenced, that we should introduce hymns for the sake of those of weaker capacity. No, said another, let us bring them up to the Psalms.

CARNMONY REVIVAL AND PRAYER-MEETINGS, NEAR BELFAST, REPORTED BY REV. BARKLIE, PASTOR.

"When the Lord is about to visit a neighborhood in mercy, he usually puts it into the hearts of his people to pray for it. It was so here; for, having heard what the Lord has done in other places, a deep anxiety pervaded every bosom that we should not be passed by; and, although there were no formal concerts for prayer, there was many a praying Jacob, in the family and in the closet, wrestling for a blessing. One lady in particular, months before its appearance, said to a friend, 'We shall shortly have the revival with us.' And on being asked why she said so, 'Because,' she replied, 'the Lord has put it into my heart to pray for it.' Others, I am aware, were anticipating and praying for it likewise. The answer was not long delayed; but it came in a way none of us had anticipated. A few weeks after the commencement of the awakening, a communion was held, on which occasion upwards of one hundred were added to the church."

Some time after the writer adds:

"The work is still progressing steadily, though in a more silent and imperceptible manner than heretofore. Rarely a week passes that I do not hear of one or more conversions, and I am confident I do not exaggerate when I say that, within the bounds of this congregation alone, not fewer than from three to four hundred souls profess to have found peace during the past six or eight months. It is a cause of much thankfulness to be enabled further to state that, almost without an exception, their 'conversation is such as becometh the gospel of Christ.' A marked and marvellous change is now visible over the entire district. *Twenty prayer-meetings are held weekly, where not one was in existence before.* Mere factory lads and girls are holding their concerts for prayer. A short time ago one of the little fellows came to me, saying, 'See, sir, this is my comrade in the mill; I have *prayed him out,* and he is now rejoicing with *me.*' Those who have found Christ themselves are most anxious to bring others to him; and hence, whilst teachers for our Sabbath schools could not be had some time ago, there is no lack of them at present."

PRAYER-MEETING INCIDENT AT BALLINAHINCH.

"The ministers here waited long, as they imagined, before they witnessed any decided indications of a gracious work in their own bounds. In the calm of a summer evening, however, whilst one of them was addressing a number of persons in the open air, and recommending an organization of prayer-meetings in the district, the audience were all at once arrested by a piercing cry, which invested the scene with a new interest; and though many months have since elapsed, the influence of that meeting is distinctly felt by many to this hour. It is unnecessary to enter into details. Enough to say, that every testimony of the divine presence, elsewhere vouchsafed, was experienced at Ballinahinch. Prayer-meetings sprang into existence, and helpers were raised up on every side. The work was full of labor, but it was likewise full of joy."

MAGHERA PRAYER-MEETING INCIDENTS.

Here, 'no means that could be supposed useful in fostering the revival were left untried. Prayer in the family and in the public congregation was offered without ceasing for the outpouring of the Divine Spirit. The instructions of the Sabbath bore, more or less, on the subject. A weekly congregational prayer-meeting was started. Large public meetings were called and addressed by young converts, as they were usually designated. Conversions were numerous, but not confined to the public meetings. Often they occurred at home, and while engaged in the ordinary avocations of life. Sometimes in the fields, by the way, in bed during the night seasons, and in private meditations. Some of the most intelligent of the young people, persons regarded as the flower of the flock, became seriously impressed in regard to their spiritual condition, and, after passing through a season of darkness, and doubt, and temptations, were enabled to give themselves to the Lord, and to rejoice in the hope of the gospel.

"So soon as a sufficient number of young men had been awakened and converted, they immediately showed an inclination to be active and useful. Prayer-meetings were established in town and country; Sabbath schools which had been suspended were revived; and, at the various meetings held in the town and country, the young men attended, and either led in prayer or delivered addresses, as their capacities enabled them. One of these meetings has been held *every morning* for the last six months, and is conducted by the young men of the town; another, attended exclusively by females, is held every Friday evening, at which some twelve or thirteen of the young ladies of the congregation officiate, each in her turn. Every country district, also, has its prayer-meeting. In general, they e all well attended, and have done much good.

"The result, so far, has been very beneficial. It is true, indeed, that the awe with which the general community was inspired at first, and which held vice in check for a season, is wearing gradually away; but the movement has left behind it memorials that give fair promise of their ability to stand the test of time."

Some serious reflections force themselves upon the mind in reading and analyzing the above historical extracts. Here, as in all other cases of revival, universally the prayer-meeting is the resort as the essential instrumentality in awakening, conducting, and fostering revival. Without the prayer-meeting nothing—nothing is begun, nothing carried forward, nothing accomplished, nothing secured. Then why the general, if not universal, " wearing gradually away, the awe with which the general community was at first inspired, and which held vice in check for a season?" May not all this almost universal decline, following revival, be, to a great extent, accounted for from the loose views and practice of Christians and the churches in regard to the prayer-meeting? If all other ordinances of religious worship were subjected to the same spasmodic influences, would not the decline be still more remarkable? If secret prayer, family worship, public Sabbath worship were allowed to fall off and be neglected as the prayer-meeting too often is, would not the revival decline be more sudden and far greater? Then, if the observance of the worship of the prayer-meeting would take hold of the judgment, heart, and conscience, and if it were perseveringly maintained, would not revival fruits be far more lasting? If a revival increase the prayer-meeting force ten-fold, or one hundred fold, why, after the revival, cannot that effective force be kept in the field, and, by it, the prayer-meeting be carried into every district and every corner of the congregation, and every corner of the country where vice had been once checked by the revival. How is it that religion, after revival, has never been able to retain its vantage ground? Must it always be so from the nature of things? Will millennial revival be no less evanescent?

PRAYER-MEETING INCIDENTS IN BALLYKELLY.

Rev. Killen, the pastor, thus describes:

"For some time at first, some of those who had been converted during the revival addressed the meetings, relating their own experience—how they had been awakened to a sense of their guilt and danger, and led to see the uselessness of those refuges of lies in which they had hitherto trusted, and how the Spirit of God had revealed Christ to their souls, as the only Saviour for guilty sinners. Always at the close of their statements they prayed; and if absorbing fervency and child-like confidence, and deep self-abasement and powerful pleading, constitute the very essence of prayer, then I have, indeed, listened during the past summer to some of the most genuine specimens of true prayer it has ever been my lot to hear. Very few of the converts were willing to address our congregational meeting after the first statement of their experience. Many of them, however, are still ready to lead in prayer, and take their part in conducting district meetings.

"Besides the prayer-meetings now in operation, which are conducted by adults, a number of the children of one of our daily schools remain by themselves twice a week after school hours for mutual prayer. This meeting was commenced of the free motion of the children, and without the knowledge of the teacher. One evening, as his own children did not follow him home as usual, he became anxious about them, and, after waiting some time, returned toward the school house to ascertain the cause of the delay. On approaching it, he was met by the children in tears, and found that they had already met for prayer in this way for several days, and that on this day, while they prayed, one of the boys had been stricken, which produced a deep impression on the rest.

"Another children's prayer-meeting was held for several months in the barn of one of our elders, with an attendance of about twenty of the lambs of the flock. It had met several times before he was aware of its existence, but has lately been discontinued, as the children could not attend in the dark evenings. 'Mamma,' said a little boy of eight years, who had been left at home one Sabbath to watch the cows, to his mother, on her return from public worship, 'we had a fine day to-day.' 'What were you doing, dear?' asked the mother, expecting to hear of some childish plays. 'O,' replied the child, 'so-and-so came,' mentioning some of his young companions, 'and we had a prayer-meeting on the road-side.' "

PRAYER-MEETING INCIDENTS CONNECTED WITH THE HISTORY OF ORANGEMEN AND IRISH CATHOLICS.

Since the battle of the Boyne, and the victory of William, Prince of Orange, which secured constitutional liberty on the ruins of Papal despotism, in the north of Ireland, an unreasoning hostility toward Irish Catholics has long existed. Too often has the anniversary Twelfth of July closed in scenes of hate and blood-shed. To the vulgar gaze there was, no doubt, something imposing in the parade of the processions of those festal days as they returned. The congregated masses, as they marched along in holiday attire, each man decked with some distinctive badge, a sash, or a cockade of the cherished color, while the superior officers flaunted in their flowing robes of scarlet, the entire array marshalled in semi-military "rank and file," while the drums were beating, fifes discoursing shrill music, and banners fluttering in the breeze, presented no mean embodiment of all those elements that command the admiration of the multitude.

"For several years there was a certain quarter in the town of Belfast which had attained an unenviable notoriety. As the Twelfth of July drew near, it had been customary to re-enforce the military and police, that they might keep the peace, if possible, between the turbulent inhabitants of Sandy Row and the nest of Ribbinmen who occupied a neighboring district. Not only had the ordinary street missiles been flung in plentiful profusion on the scene of conflict, but deadly collisions had taken place; shots had been fired, and blood had run upon the streets. For weeks the magistrates and military were nightly on patrol. The strong arm of the executive had at length to interfere by martial law, and by a disarming of the parties who had shown that they were wholly unfit to be entrusted with arms. Although a marked change had taken place in the feelings of the Orangemen towards their Roman Catholic neighbors, the mode in which the anniversary of the Boyne would pass off was a subject of much anxious speculation. 'Wait till the Twelfth of July,' said our good Bishop to an English gentleman who was conversing with him in the end of June, respecting the effect of the revival on party spirit, 'Wait till the Twelfth; that will test all!'

"How the Twelfth came and passed, let the following statement with respect to the noted district referred to above, testify:

"'In compliance with your request, I hasten to give you my experience of the revival, more especially with reference to its influence in quelling party spirit on the Twelfth of July last. When that gracious movement reached Belfast, I joined an organization that had come to the help of the Lord, and the field assigned to me was that very famous district called Sandy Row, and its adjuncts, where the people had been taught to catch the Papist birds by throwing stones at them. Yes, the essence of Protestantism and the conversion of the Romans in that region, consisted in the abundant use of brickbats and bludgeons; but the old war-cries were now hushed by a mightier voice, and in few parts of our beloved land was that short sermon oftener preached, *Believe in the Lord Jesus Christ, and thou shalt be saved*, than in this very district. The cases of awakening were very numerous—at the mill, in the factory, at their own firesides, in the neighboring houses, in the public street, the prayer-meeting, and, in fact, in every place of human resort.'

"When the revival was at its height, Sandy Row was visited by persons from all parts of the country—indeed of the kingdom. Clergymen and pious laymen were constantly holding open air meetings; and often at these and other exercises, in the hours of release from labor, in 'the gleaming,' or under the starlit roof, did many a sweet hymn ascend far above the stars. It was on the evening of the Twelfth that I first took part in one of those meetings. I had been assisting at a temperance meeting elsewhere, and my direct road was through some of the most intensely Popish and Orange districts in Belfast. On the evening of any similar anniversary, I would have performed no ordinary feat to have passed through those districts; but I had no fear now. There were no breaking of lamps and constables' heads—no flinging of 'Macadam' missiles, nor of the paving stones. The streets were crowded with the young of both sexes, but good humor and enjoyment were the distinguishing features of the scene. I marked the improvement. I knew the cause. The sun will shine even through a wet blanket. But things improved as I advanced. I heard the songs of Zion chanted by hundreds of voices amid our rocks and dells, in our green meadows; but I never heard with anything like the same emotion as

I did on that occasion, the soul-inspiring strains float on the still, calm air of that sweet July evening. There, where one of the principal thoroughfares joins the street, were assembled a large number of young females, and these surrounded by men, women and children. As I approached, the 23d Psalm was falling in sweet cadence on the gale; and I do believe that there were not a few in that assemblage who got a foretaste of the time when the redeemed shall sing the song of Moses and the Lamb.

"Throughout the day, none of the usual emblems of the Twelfth appeared—no orange garlands nor arches flung over the streets. The only regret I heard expressed was, that the past had been so unlike the present. There was no military or semi-military parade this evening.

"Seven months have passed away since then. Time, that great tester, and a winter, one of the most unpropitious we ever saw, have not seen the revival work arrested. In-door has taken the place of out-door worship. In a district where formerly some four or five prayer-meetings could with difficulty be maintained, there are now, I believe, twenty-five; and if to this be added the week evening services, well attended in the six different churches, which, like a chain of fortifications, surround the district, a tolerably fair conclusion may be arrived at that the good work has stood the trial."

In another statement, says the Rev. W. Magill, of Dundee:

"From the commencement of the revival, some of the Orangemen had attended our prayer-meetings, and had seen and heard the strange things which occurred in and around the first house where the Lord began his work of grace. The chiefs of the party lived in the adjoining one. One member of their family, especially, from the first, was deeply, and, I believe, savingly impressed. His case was a singular and most interesting one. He is almost deaf, yet gifted with a wonderful talent for understanding what is said to him, engaging in all the services of religion, praise, prayer, and reading the Scriptures, with the greatest delight, and confessing himself strengthened by thus waiting upon God. It was partly through his influence that his brothers and other members of the Orange Society kept the Twelfth of July here as it was never kept before.

"In revenge for the supposed injury of purchasing and pulling down a public house, an Orange hall was erected in the immediate neighborhood of the church and manse, as a rallying-point for the brethren who, night after night, met with fife and drum, and noisy clamor, to annoy the quiet dwellers in their homes in the neighborhood, and especially myself. But the Lord did not pass over them; and they too, as well as others, underwent a great change, and we hope a permanent one.

"Before the Twelfth came, I was asked by these men, whom I had looked upon as bitter enemies to me, and to the cause of religion and morality, if I would meet them on the evening of that day, and hold a prayer-meeting in their hall. I at once consented to do so, on being assured that there would, during the day, be no party display, and no intoxicating drink used. The morning was ushered in with no firing of guns, no beating of drums, and no display of party banners. All was still and calm as a Sabbath. It was a holiday among the people, all labor being suspended; and, early in the forenoon, men and women in holiday attire, were seen in groups, here and there, marching along, not with Orange Lillies, but with Bibles in their hands, as if going on a Sabbath morning to the house of God. A deputation, including the master of the Lodge, waited on me in the manse, and requested me to go over to the hall and pray with them, before proceeding to a field at some distance, where they were to meet others, and engage in religious exercises.

"With Bibles in their hands, and peace and good will in their hearts, with no music playing, no flags flying, and with no jar of whiskey to refresh them on the march, they walked soberly and decently, and in good order, to the field, where many hundreds met them, and joined them in praise and prayer, and other religious exercises."

"The month before the revival in this neighborhood," says the Rev. J. Geddes, (County Tyrone) "was a ferment—nightly maulings, law proceedings, etc. Since the movement began, not a drum has been struck in the bounds, and the leading Orangemen meet and pray for the Romanists, whom a little ago they hated."

"There is an Orange Lodge in this neighborhood," says the Rev. J. Elliott, Clarkesbridge, (County Monaghan) "which is composed of some forty young men. They meet monthly, and each contributed a fixed sum at every meeting for the purpose of procuring refreshments, which consisted almost entirely of whiskey. So much as £13 has been expended in one year in this way. They now meet principally for religious exercises—singing, prayer, or reading God's word. They continue their monthly contributions, and twice since July have asked me to expend a very considerable sum for the purchase of books for a library which they have established, and which is likely very soon to contain a large and valuable collection of books. Now they never have any intoxicating drinks in their meetings.

"If such a powerful and united body as Orangemen now yield to religious conviction, and the spirit of the gospel of peace turn their lodges and gatherings into *prayer-meetings*, and their collections for feasting into library and missionary contributions, as I have heard of being done, may we not say that the Spirit of the Lord has gone forth among the Protestants of Ulster?"

From Newtonards the following statement is given:

"In passing through districts where the noisy laughter of the fool, or the impure language of the profane was wont to be heard, the voice of Psalms caught the ear in all directions. The Twelfth of July, the anniversary of Satan as well as of the Orangemen, came and went, and left no trace behind. 'Not a drum was heard,' not an arch was erected, not a shot was fired. *The prayer-meetings took place as usual—were thronged as usual.*"

From Broughshane the following is given:

"On the Twelfth of July, the Orangemen of the district asked me to preach them a sermon. About four thousand assembled in the open air, without beat of drum, or any insignia of their order, and, after engaging in religious exercises, returned peaceably to their homes; no drink and no disorder appearing among them. On the Broughshane June Fair day, a band of strolling players, as usual, made their appearance; a *prayer-meeting* was immediately convened opposite their showy platform. The players had but two visitors, in the persons of two Roman Catholic policemen. The business of the fair was summed up by a prayer-meeting of not less than five thousand people."

"Not less than twenty Roman Catholics came under the power of the truth, and were made to acknowledge the errors of the church of Rome. Three of these were rebaptized, at their own urgent request, and afterwards admitted to the Lord's Supper. The others still attend the prayer-meetings, and, now and again, the public worship of the sanctuary."

Ladies' prayer-meetings in Broughshane.—"In one district of country, almost all the matrons within an area of more than two miles were graciously visited and converted in the most satisfactory and conclusive manner, if we can speak about another's conversion at all. These women have exercised a mighty influence on their families and neighborhood; and if one wishes to see the religion of the cross in her loveliest features, in the simplicity, beauty, and power of primitive times, he has but to pay this district a visit, and see and hear for himself. I have no doubt he will return, saying, as the Queen of the South, the half had not been told him.

"The gift of prayer bestowed on these matrons is beyond conception, and certainly is not left to rust. They have a prayer-meeting of their own—none but females being admitted—the exercises of which are praise, prayer, and reading the Scriptures, without note or comment. This meeting has tended greatly to fan the flame of love in their own hearts, and kindle it in others who come. We have many such female prayer-meetings, and I am satisfied of their utility.

"The Holy Spirit, we rejoice to say, has not been as a wayfaring man with us. His gracious operations have not as yet ceased. From time to time we have been constrained to note unmistakable signs of his power and presence. Seldom does a week elapse without some groping, hoping, praying soul finding Christ, and pardon, and peace, in a way more or less marked and visible. Frequently our prayer-meetings have experienced a sudden, mysterious, and overpowering impulse, swaying the whole assembly as one man, and leaving all weeping, praying, rejoicing. Men have felt as if the Lord had breathed on them.

"The thirst of the young for Sabbath school instruction is intense and insatiable. Not less than fourteen hundred children attend, every Sabbath morning, desiring the sincere milk of the word, while my own class averages some eighty young men and women. We are reading the 'Confession of Faith,' and have circulated, through the congregation, some two hundred and fifty copies of it, with about an equal number of 'Patterson's Shorter Catechism.' Social meetings for prayer, reading the Scriptures, and exhortation, are held throughout the parish, *each district having its own prayer-meeting*, and each prayer-meeting its own staff of conductors. No person is allowed to engage in the services unless approved of by this bench of managers. These meetings are attended, with very few exceptions, by the whole population—young and old, rich and poor, Episcopalians and Roman Catholics, taking pleasure in listening to the simple prayers and earnest exhortations of their Presbyterian neighbors. The interest in them is still well sustained; and in the darkest, fiercest nights of winter, and now, in the busiest days of seed-time, the number of those who meet together to thank and praise the Lord has not diminished. The Bible is the book of constant study. Many carry it about with them, and read it by the wayside, or at intervals in their labor, and refer to it for the settlement of every disputed point. Two of our National school houses have been enlarged, in order to make them capable of accommodating the *prayer-meetings*."

CHAPTER XIII.

PRAYER-MEETING INCIDENTS AND NARRATIVES, CONTINUED.

Incidents among Quarrymen, Ireland—Among Quarrymen, Wales—Remarkable Prayer-meetings on a Mountain—Incidents illustrating the Importance of Concerted Prayer—"Work among the Wynds"—How Revival came to the Wynds of Glasgow—Reflections upon the Principles exhibited and illustrated by these extracts.

Prayer-meetings among Quarrymen. Reported by Rev. Killen, of Comber, Ireland.

ABOUT two miles from this, near the outskirts of the parish, there is a quarry, which was formerly notorious for the wickedness of those who wrought in it. It was, in fact, an emporium for all sorts of vice; but when our revival commenced in Comber, it was such a strange and unheard of thing amongst those quarrymen, that they resolved, through curiosity, to come and see how it was that people were so mysteriously knocked down. They, accordingly, attended the nightly prayer-meetings in our congregation. Gradually a change crept over them. Drinking was diminished, swearing was given up, seriousness and anxiety prevailed. I was requested, as I could not go in the evening, to go and preach to them during the working hours in the middle of the day. I did so. Immediately, on my appearance, all work was suspended; and, at the very busiest time, master and men attended for upwards of two hours. Whilst under the open sky, in a sort of large amphitheatre, formed by the excavation of the quarry, and surrounded by the mountain's rocky walls, I proclaimed to them the glorious gospel of the blessed God. Much good, I understand, was that day effected. *Prayer-meetings* amongst the men were immediately established. The occupier of the quarry, and head of the whole establishment, soon announced to his men that he himself was entirely changed, and declared that he had resolved to live henceforth only to Christ."

Among the Quarrymen of Wales. Reported by Rev. D. Edwards.—"Five Years of Prayer," p. 326.

"About three weeks ago (2d Nov., 1859), a few young men from Bettros-y-coed came to work in the Festinaig slate quarries. They were in deep concern about the state of their souls. They came on Monday morning, and their deep distress was observed by several of the quarrymen. They followed their work in this state, occasionally weeping on account of their lost condition as guilty sinners before God. After dinner, the following day, they were observed by some working people making their way to the top of the hill. Immediately they were followed by all the workmen in that quarry, being about five hundred in number. They halted on the summit of the mountain, and on that spot, under the broad canopy of heaven, they held a *prayer-meeting.* While they prayed, the Holy Spirit was poured out upon them most abundantly. Nearly all present wept and sobbed aloud. On the same evening they met at their respective places of worship to hold a *prayer-meeting.* On the following day they met again on the mountain, leaving their work unheeded, for by this time the people were in a state of great religious excitement. They met every night during the week at their several places of worship, to offer up prayer to Almighty God. The rocks seemed to re-echo the voice of prayer and praise. On the following Saturday, those who lived at a distance went to their homes, carrying with them the newly-kindled revival fire, and on the morrow the surrounding churches and chapels were in a blaze. Our people met at Maentwrog to hold a Saturday evening prayer-meeting. I attended it, and witnessing the effects already produced upon those who were present, it was announced that another prayer-meeting would be held next morning, at eight o'clock. Such a prayer-meeting I never, never attended. The most ungodly persons present were overwhelmed. We prayed and wept, and wept and prayed, until nature was exhausted. Instead of the Sabbath school, as usual, in the afternoon, we met to pray again; but in the interval, at noon, all the congregations, church and chapel, met on the brow of a hill above the village, *to pray.* It was a glorious meeting while it lasted, which was about one hour and a half, when the rain came down in torrents and dispersed us."

A Welsh paper has the following account of a very remarkable prayer-meeting on a mountain:

"A prayer-meeting was held on the 12th of July, 1859, on a mountain called Frongoch, near the mine-works of Frongoch, about two miles from Ysbytly Ystwyth, in the County of Cardigan. It was held in the open air, on a high mountain. The masters of the mine-works gave orders that, on account of the meeting, no work should be done on that day, and they themselves attended. It was the most wonderful prayer-meeting that I ever witnessed. There were some of every denomination present, and two languages were used. The number of those assembled was more than three thousand. At the meeting at two o'clock, nine prayed, and short addresses were given at intervals. Three prayed in succession, two Welshmen and one Englishman between them, and then a verse of a hymn was sung. The vast assembly all knelt at prayer, and I saw two or three on their knees who, I feel assured, had never been seen before on their knees in prayer; but they knelt down on that day. Heaven poured down its blessings in a powerful and irresistible manner, so that scores were praying, and hundreds were weeping and crying out, 'Praised be God.' At two o'clock, thirteen prayed, and short addresses were delivered between the prayers; the whole was finished in two hours, and all returned home. At seven, all went to their separate chapels in the neighborhood, and the holy fire was carried home in their bosoms by many."

INCIDENTS ILLUSTRATING THE IMPORTANCE OF CONCERTED PRAYER.

It is not so much our design here to collect and spread out, over a few pages, incidents simply; but to condense, in *historic form,* the argument enforcing the great importance of concerted prayer, as a Christian duty, and as an important part of the great and important subject—*social prayer.* We have already noticed the *principle,* but briefly. Nor can we here find space for voluminous collections of incidents, which might be gathered from scores of treatises on prayer, on revivals, and on kindred subjects. The numerous histories of the Fulton Street, New York, daily noon-day prayer-meeting, of the Sansom Street, Philadelphia, prayer-meeting, and many others of kindred character, furnish the history of a series of daily prayers for specific objects, read out in the meetings, with statement of cases, names, places, persons, and characters, called for and agreed upon as the subject matter of the united prayers of the assembled hundreds in attendance for that very specific purpose. And so for years, while those meetings lasted, and retained their power, day after day, prayer after prayer, each day concentrated upon an object stated and agreed upon. *This was the rule.* Any other kind of prayer, promiscuous and undetermined, its object unknown to all, was the exception. The known and united object of the prayers being *the rule, here* lay the secret of the wonderful power of those meetings, which sent out over the world, on the seas and on every continent, their electric shock, starting into life revivals of religion everywhere. No form of prayer so powerful, as a heaven-ordained instrumentality, in accomplishing Divine purposes—no power can compensate for the loss of this, as an instrumentality, in the revival of religion.

Christ states the principle in that precious promise recorded in Matt. xviii. 19: "Again I say unto you, that if two of you shall agree on earth as touching anything they shall ask, it shall be done for them of my Father which is in heaven." Here we have the social prayer-meeting—two or three met together for prayer. Here we have concerted prayer—agreement as touching anything they shall ask. Here we have warrant for a special object of social prayer. Here, too, we have a warrant for the previous covenant, or agreement, in regard to the special object of the united prayer. Concerted prayer is the subject of the text, and of the Saviour's promise. Concerted prayer has here a divine warrant, as an ordinance of religious worship, forming an important part of the exercises of the prayer-meeting. Our object here is a historical illustration of this ordinance, an enforcement of the duty of its observance, as also the advantages of this high privilege.

In a very interesting book, bearing the title, "WORK AMONG THE WYNDS," by Rev. Maccoll, Glasgow, Scotland, 1867, p. 102, we have an interesting statement of this subject in a sermon, by the author, preached to the poor people of the Wynds of Glasgow, among whom he labored as a missionary. He says:

"But the prayers that, in these words, I desire of you,

is not simply individual. 'I beseech you, brethren, that ye STRIVE TOGETHER with me to God in *your prayers for me.*' Promises are given to individual prayer; but there are large, and special, and prompt blessings to united prayer. The latter, indeed, includes the former. Each strives, while we strive together. Jesus teaches us to come together around Him, and join our prayers with His, saying, 'Our Father.' If you, who are already gathered here, shall find it good to be here, it will be in some proportion to our union in love, in faith, in prayer. I beseech you, therefore, not to stand apart, praying, like the Pharisee, each by himself. Be ye all of one mind, having compassion one of another; love as brethren, be pitiful, be courteous, not rendering evil for evil, or railing for railing, but, contrariwise, blessing, knowing that ye are thereunto called that ye should inherit a blessing. I beseech you, therefore, to *strive together for me*, husband, and wife, and child, around your table, when you give thanks for the past, and ask grace for the present and the future; and around your hearth, when you are gathering up the fire for the night, and asking the Lord to keep you, ask Him also to keep me. Remember me when, two or three together, you meet in His name. I beseech you, strive together, members of this church, who, whether as hand or foot, are professedly ready to act here as one body, that when I speak, it may be as one mouth glorifying God, that even when I am silent I may feel the electric thrill of the same pulse of prayer and blessing between you and me and God.

"But I do not ask you to any work, or any warfare, in which I shall not accompany you, in which I am not prepared, by God's grace, to lead you; for, I beseech you, brethren, that you strive together with me. My work is yours, and yours mine. You know not how often, in looking at the work here, and then at the worker, I may be ready to turn back in despair. Your prayers may come upon me like a soft, cool wind, amid the heat and burden of the day. Your prayers may come upon the hot sky as a cloud laden with showers, when the seed has just been sown. As I enter your houses, my tongue shall grow eloquent if I feel assured you have been asking God to enable me to speak as I ought to speak. As I sit in my study, gathering up some thoughts for you, day and night, the thought of your earnest prayers for blessing will help me to sift the seed, and cast away what might glitter in some lights like gold, but would not taste to your hungry souls as bread. And as I enter this place, on the Sabbath morning, I shall need no thunders of the organ, quivering amid these beams, to stir or still my spirit, or play the voluntary for our after service, if my soul has already heard the music of your earnest hearts greeting my steps and quickening my approach; for, the beating of hearts, loving and beloved, makes magic music to keep us moving, the only monotonous music of which we never weary. Only when it is still, when the silver chords are broken, or harshly struck, do we know the full power their low whispers possess. I shall need no incense to perfume this place, and cling in fragrant fragments about these walls, if your prayers ascend from lips touched with a live coal from the altar of God. If we have been thus earnestly striving together during the week, we shall not spend the Sabbath in listlessness and sloth; we shall rest, indeed, but our rest shall renew our strength."

Again, p. 209, the author of "Work in the Wynds" goes on to say:

"But, above all, our central Weekly Prayer-meeting became crowded, and a spirit of earnest prayer seemed to be poured out. The prayer-meeting had, from the first, been the centre of our work. Here our motive power was largely generated. Every wheel in our machinery was attached to some part of the gearing that was moved here. The great driving belt, however far it travelled, always passed back again here. We had always two or three *special prayers*, led by some office-bearer, or gifted member, called up at my request. We prayed for *places*, and *persons*, and *churches*, and *stations* that thus interested us. But about this time we were specially interested, first, for the successive months in the Revival in America, in 1858, and then in Ireland, in 1859. The desire became intense to share in such wide-spread blessing. So much was this the case, that one of my elders and most devoted helpers from the first, came, at the suggestion of others, to ask me to pay a brief visit to America, that I might both see the work and perhaps carry home something of the fire. We talked of this for a little, but soon agreed that there was a shorter route than across the ocean, and so we agreed to go together to the Lord. Half a dozen of us began then to meet for half an hour, immediately before the congregational meeting. Three of us took part, giving out a verse or two of a Psalm, and then briefly spreading out our petitions. The very first night we felt 'How dreadful is this place'! We sometimes could hardly speak for emotion. We were like men looking out for rain, and, lifting up our faces in the dark, we suddenly felt the first drops on our cheeks. The same deep sense of an invisible presence, and of new power, accompanied our Sabbath service. We were in the banqueting house."

Thus came Revival to the Wynds of Glasgow.

The above extracts illustrate the *principle* of concerted prayer—what we mean by it—as furnishing example of its power and importance. A Scripture example or two here may aid in giving force to other historic examples which might be multiplied indefinitely to a volume itself.

The author of *Work in the Wynds* seems to have taken lessons from some of these when, instead of crossing the Atlantic, he, with his friends, went directly, on the direct route, by concerted prayer, to the Mercy-seat, and there took counsel of the Lord, and caught the heavenly fire from the altar at once.

Ezra, heading a column of returning captives, in perplexity in regard to the way, called together the bewildered travellers, and at the banks of the river observes a fast, and holds a concerted prayer-meeting, for the expressed and single purpose of seeking direction in their journey back to the city of their fathers. (Ezra viii. 21–23): "Then I proclaimed a fast there, at the river of Ahava, that we might afflict ourselves before our God, to seek of him a right way for us, and for our little ones, and for all our substance. For I was ashamed to require of the king a band of soldiers and horsemen to help us against the enemy in the way: because we had spoken unto the king, saying, The hand of our God is upon all them for good that seek him; but his power and his wrath is against all them that forsake him. So we fasted, and besought our God for this: and he was entreated of us."

In this Ezra and the captives were not disappointed. The Lord was entreated of them, and answered them: "Then we departed from the river of Ahava, on the twelfth day of the first month, to go to Jerusalem; and the hand of our God was upon us, and he delivered us from the hand of the enemy, and of such as lay in wait by the way. And we came to Jerusalem."

Esther, Mordecai, and the Jews were in straits from the malicious machinations of Haman, the Jews' enemy. All were in mourning, and fasting, and weeping, and wailing, lying in sack-cloth and ashes. A special prayer-meeting is called, with fasting as the ostensible form of the call; but prayer is inseparable from fasting; and the call, in this case, for fasting without prayer, would have been unmeaning. Its spirit was to plead with God for deliverance from the sweeping ruin prepared for them. This presented a special and pressing case: all would understand and feel the object of the call, and enter earnestly into its spirit. "Then Esther bade them return Mordecai this answer, Go gather together all the Jews that are present in Shushan, and fast ye for me, and neither eat nor drink three days, night nor day. I also and my maidens will fast likewise; and so will I go in unto the king, which is not according to the law: and if I perish, I perish. So Mordecai went his way, and did according to all that Esther had commanded." What heart, among all the Jews, in all the realm, was not in concert with this call and its object? In answer to this remarkable concerted prayer, remarkable deliverance came.

After the fall of Judas Iscariot, the eleven apostles were called to the very responsible work of filling the vacancy. For this duty they felt themselves utterly unequal. They at once, by previous agreement, go to God together in prayer—hold a special, concerted prayer-meeting. "And they prayed, and said, Thou, Lord, which knowest the hearts of all men, show whether of these two thou hast chosen, that he may take part of this ministry and apostleship, from which Judas, by transgression, fell." Their prayer was answered. They had faith in the promise of their Master, who had so recently said in their hearing, and to them, "If two of you shall agree on earth as touching anything that they shall ask, it shall be done for them of my Father which is in heaven."

When Herod, with outstretched, persecuting hand, vexing the church, cast Peter into prison, a very special case of deep concern presented itself to the trembling disciples and Christians. They meet in their various and respective places of prayer-meeting—all for the concerted purpose of praying for Peter. "Peter, therefore, was kept in prison; but prayer was made without ceasing of the church unto God for him." "And when he had considered the thing, he came to the house of Mary the mother of John, whose surname was Mark, where many were gathered together praying." For they had all been praying for Peter, and their prayers were answered.

These historic references, with many others in the inspired word, give ample encouragement to concerted prayer as a special and very precious means of grace, and of securing promised blessings from God. That this is so little practised in the church now, must be owing to the fact that the state of religion is so lamentably low—Christians notice so few things of interest calling their attention and enlisting their prayers; concerted prayer seldom occurs to their minds; seldom any matter of prayer presses upon the heart, and, consequently, they are seldom shut up to earnest, agonizing, concerted prayer. Were the Spirit of God poured out upon us—would God give us a spirit of grace and supplication, how many objects of pressing interest would spring up in visible form around us, and bring live Christians together in Christian conference, out of which would grow argument for prayer for specific objects, drawing together in groups for concerted prayer! And how different then, would our prayers be! How unlike our cold and pointless prayers in our prayer-meetings now! We too often come together without an object or an errand, and so coming together we pray without an object, and return without our errand.

Out of a hundred instances that might be selected, and

in addition to the examples already given in other connections, permit us to detain the patient reader with two or three striking instances of recent occurrence, illustrating the power of concerted prayer:

In one of the Noon-day Fulton Street Prayer-meetings, where concerted prayer was a matter of daily routine occurrence, a clergyman from the interior of the State of New York, related the following case of conversion, which was followed by a revival and the conversion of many others. He said:

"I have been, for thirty years, connected with the people of my charge. I have seen many deep and powerful revivals of religion. I have witnessed the triumphs of the grace of God in the conversion of a multitude of souls. But I think I saw, last Monday morning, the happiest man I ever saw in all my life. I think I never witnessed such a marked and wonderful triumph of grace. It was the conversion of a lawyer, a man of marked ability and high standing. It occurred in a parish where there was no minister and no stated means of grace. It was in this wise: *Three pious ladies, acting on a hint thrown out in this meeting, of the importance of united prayer for some specific object, agreed to pray for the conversion of this lawyer. They entered into solemn covenant with each other to make his speedy conversion the subject of daily prayer,* and many times a day; and beginning as they agreed, they soon became deeply burdened with anxious desire, so much so that they could not rest, and they could not be satisfied with simply praying. They went to the lawyer and told him what they were doing—that they were unitedly and daily praying for his conversion. They asked him if he would not pray for himself. He told them he would, without any distinct impression of the responsibility which he was taking upon himself. He was a man of strict probity and honor. As night approached this lawyer began to meditate upon the promise he had made. He at first thought he would not keep his engagement; then again he said to himself, 'I am in the habit of keeping my promises to my fellow-men, why shall I not keep it with these ladies? Why not? But I do not know how to make a prayer. I have not prayed, or tried to make a prayer, for years. I *cannot pray*. It is a mockery for me to attempt it. I ought not to have promised.' 'But you *have* promised, and you must keep your promise,' the voice within him seemed to say. 'You *must* pray.' He put it over to a later hour, postponing it as long as he could.

"At last a late hour of the night was come. His mind was in a tumult. O, what shall I pray for? Let me think what most I need. I have got to look up to God and ask for something. What shall it be? Then he began to think of his posture for prayer. 'Am I to go down on my knees? I have not bent a knee for ever so long.' And when on his knees before God, he said, 'What shall I ask for? What shall I acknowledge?' It was a terrible conflict. Before this he had not the least idea what his promise involved. To pray was not a mere matter of form. It was something that must be honestly done. So he bethought himself, 'I can ask God to bow this stubborn heart; for he already began to feel how stubborn it was. I can ask God to show me how such a wretch as I can be forgiven; for already he began to feel that he was a wretch undone. He knelt down, and such an overwhelming sense of sin and shame came over him that he was filled with agony. What he had promised to do in a light and thoughtless frame of mind, he was now trying to do in great heaviness of heart. But he determined to be honest and earnest. Who shall describe what followed? Who shall say what passed in that solitary chamber? Suffice it to say that last Monday morning my eyes beheld the happiest man they ever have rested upon in all my religious observation and experience.

"As soon as I heard of these facts in my neighborhood, I left my own charge to visit throughout this rural country place, having no minister. I visited fifteen families in one day, and prayed in every house; and in every one of these fifteen families I found awakened persons. They had all heard of the conversion of the lawyer with much surprise. That lawyer had visited many of them, and I doubt not that now—yes, at this very moment, when I am speaking—you may see him, if you see so far, in that neighborhood, in Dutchess County, with a few tracts in his hand, going from house to house, persuading sinners to come to Christ, telling them what a dear Saviour he has found."—*Five Years of Prayer*, pp. 51–54.

The author of "Work in the Wynds," after narrating numerous instances of the kind, gives the following:

"Not long after, a little note, in the same hand, was read in the meeting: 'Some time since I desired your prayers and the prayers of this meeting. I now desire to give thanks, having received the blessing then asked, and I will crave still more.' This asking of prayer became, almost from the first, a great feature in the meeting. We had gradually a large list of places, in every one of which some measure of awakening, I believe, was experienced. As in all such meetings, many requests came in for friends. One evening, a woman of a sad countenance came to me and said: You are often praying for friends. Would you ask for my husband? He was a good, kind husband, but one day, in drink, he listed, and is now in the East Indies. I have four children to provide for; but he's my great burden. O, ask his conversion! By the first mail she had a letter from him, written about the time we began to pray, saying, O, Mary! I am a new man. The Lord has been with me, and drawn me to Himself. O, that I was back to you! I would be a different husband and father. She brought me the letter to read. O, she said, her pale face growing paler, do you think we might ask another request? May we ask the Lord to send him home? That night, and for many nights, we asked. After awhile another letter came. O, Mary, I am ordered home! I have been in the hospital, and my passage is taken by the first ship. And he came home, and has been for several years an active agent in our mission work."—P. 285.

CHAPTER XIV.

PRAYER-MEETING IN CONNECTION WITH MISSIONS—FOREIGN, HOME, CITY—AND COLPORTAGE OPERATIONS.

Mission Work in the Wynds of Glasgow—The Prayer-meeting the First step—Report of Missions in Egypt. By Rev. B. F. Pinkerton—The *Christian Instructor*, Phila.—A Model Church—Reflections—American Tract Society on Home Evangelization—That Society friendly to Revival and the Prayer-meeting—Thrilling Narrative of the wonderful labors of a German Colporteur.

IN that remarkable Treatise, to which we have made frequent reference, "Work in the Wynds" of Glasgow, Scotland, an important principle, bearing upon all successful mission work, is clearly stated. In speaking of the City Mission, he says:

"It is interesting to notice, in the history of the Mission, the development from a prayer-meeting to the outline of a church. This is not so much from the force of external appliances as from the internal effort of the Christian life to work itself into the ecclesiastical form. The City Mission, doubtless, did a good work, which the churches had long neglected, but it was a work too narrow and defective to be more than temporary and transitional. It aimed at a prayer-meeting, rather than a church, thus influenced a more limited circle, and lost much of the good of its own labors in sending off to neighboring churches those who might have been otherwise retained and trained for service, and who, in such churches, could often get no assignable place and no sufficient superintendence."

That is, to say: In City Missionary operations, the first step toward organic life is to bring into form the prayer-meeting just so soon as material can be prepared for it, but, from the beginning, with the idea that this material is not to be sent off to be incorporated with congregations already organized, but retained and held together as the material for a new congregation; and so exemplify the true Mission history of development from the incipiency of a prayer-meeting, passing on from outline to full ecclesiastical form—an organized church, with pastor, elders, and deacons, as was, at length, the Church of "The Wynds." For the author proceeds to say:

"Mission work in our large cities and towns has made a history within the last half century. In the earlier part of that period, the form the work assumed was that of visitation from house to house, by volunteers from some neighboring church. We have still this form perpetuated in the Christian Instruction Associations and District Visitation Societies connected with various congregations."

The regular Mission in the "Wynds" changed this state of things. The missionary was sent to gather together new material, and prepare it for a new church organization. At first, when he entered the field, "the service provided was generally on a fragment of the Lord's day, usually in the evening, and it consisted only of preaching and the prayer-meeting, without breaking of bread and fellowship of saints. Something more like the glorious gospel of the blessed God, had, in connection with the new movement in Glasgow, been brought nigh. If the churches were not yet ready to bring the poor to their own sacred houses, or if the poor were not yet ready to come in, the churches were providing decent houses in which the poor might be feasted by themselves."

Speaking farther of the new City Mission operation, after entering the new Mission Church, he says:

"In those early days we had few young people in

church. Our attendance was principally composed of very old and middle-aged people. We started a Sabbath morning school for those who were getting up in years, besides the usual Sabbath evening classes. We had always, from the beginning, an admirable prayer-meeting, on the Sabbath morning, for young men."

In referring to an advanced state of the Mission, the author says:

"But the Elders, though all busy men through the day, did a noble and large service in this way. Our frequent meetings gave opportunity for seeing and speaking to hundreds during the year; and our fellowship-meetings tended to interweave one with many, so that the members visiting, or only speaking to one another, exercised a great help in bearing one another's burdens. As the Wynd Church increased, we were able to subdivide our common territory for household visitation; and as the younger churches gradually secured a large portion of the crowd that for some years almost overwhelmed us, we were able to pay closer attention to the members and households belonging to us. Elders and deacons vigorously visited their respective congregational districts. Prayer-meetings were opened in various parts of the city, and new efforts were made to give efficacy to our mission work round the church."

In the Thirteenth Annual Report of the Ladies' Association for Promoting the Christian Education of Jewish Females in Alexandria, Egypt, we find the following, from which we extract a paragraph:

"Abbey Close, United Presbyterian Hall,
"*Paisley*, 14*th Jan.*, 1869.

"Report.—*Weekly Meetings.*

"There is a semi-weekly meeting for prayer, held in the house of one of the members. It has been well attended by both members and adherents. And it may be regarded as next to the Sabbath services in its effects on the spiritual life of the congregation. All the male members who attend it, lead in prayer, and most of them have given gratifying evidence of spiritual growth. The order of exercises is similar to that observed in prayer-meetings at home. The missionary presides; the members present are called in turn to lead in prayer. A portion of Scripture is read, and a few explanatory and practical remarks made. The above exercises are interspersed with the singing of Psalms, in which all heartily join, and seem to take great delight. Frequently the neighbors have been attracted by the singing, and some have come to see and hear what is going on. The good effects of these meetings have not been confined to the personal edification of the members; the unification of the congregation has also been greatly promoted by them; brotherly love has been increased. There is evidently a desire for an organization, and there is now no doubt that there are some good and tried men among them, who are qualified for the office of Eldership and Deaconite. It might be well for the Presbytery now to consider the propriety of granting this congregation an organization.

(Signed) "B. F. PINKERTON."

In the *Christian Instructor*, Philadelphia, Sept. 11th, 1869, we find the following:

"A MODEL CHURCH."

"In conversation, a few days since, with a devoted laborer in one of the churches under the care of our Home Mission Board in the far West, we learned a remarkable fact, which, it has occurred to us, may be mentioned, with good results, to the church at large. It was this: that *every member of the church regularly attends the weekly prayer-meeting*, and that in these meetings *every male member takes an active part in the exercises*, either leading in prayer or making remarks. As might be expected, under such circumstances, the meetings have life and spirit in them, and the members of the church, coming thus regularly together in such meetings, and engaging thus with one another in the exercises, steadily keep up their interest in the church, are more and more closely drawn together, are ever ready to make efforts and sacrifices for the cause, and finding it good for themselves thus to draw nigh to God, are often moved to say to others, 'Come ye with us, and we will do you good.'

"Is this state of things common in the United Presbyterian Church? Would that we had good reason to believe it was! What means would there be in steady use for all to be growing in grace, and in the saving experimental knowledge of Christ! What a powerful influence would there be exerted for having brotherly love continue, for encouraging and strengthening all to be active, earnest, useful workers for Christ and his cause, and for holding fast their profession! Happy the pastor that has the support of the prayers and the co-operation of such a people! Happy the community that has such a church and people in its midst! Reader, is your church like this? Are *you always, regularly, and earnestly*, at the prayer-meeting, and willing and ready to take part in it?"

No church of this kind will long remain a charge on the hands of the Home Mission Board. No other kind should be permitted long to live upon the Treasury of the Home Board. And more: no congregation, or mission station, without a prayer-meeting, should ever be permitted to draw upon the Board for support. The funds of the church can never galvanize life into a dead society or mission station.

We have before us, a little work of the American Tract Society, written by one of its Secretaries, bearing the title, "Home Evangelization," in which the importance of the colportage work is presented to the public. In a Report of one of the Society's Colporteurs, we find the following:

"Of the 38,864 families visited in the mountains of Virginia, within the space of four years, 7,612, or more than one-sixth, were destitute of all religious books, and 4,348 were destitute of the Bible; of the latter, 3,731 have been supplied. More than 75,000 volumes have been sold, for $18,000; and 19,600 volumes distributed gratuitously—making a total circulation of 94,600 volumes, or more than 20,000 each year. Besides personal conversation with 25,467 families, 2,456 *prayer-meetings*, or public meetings, have been held." P. 94.

From this, we see that the American Tract Society, an institution rich in Christian benevolence, does not overlook the prayer-meeting in its operations, and through its agencies, the Society has done much in the cause of Revival, and, in this connection, necessarily has favored the prayer-meeting. One of its Agents, reporting on the subject of "Revivals of Religion," says:

"Last winter a revival occurred, and forty or fifty hopeful conversions ensued; but there had been no regular dispensation of the word. In one case, a tract, incidentally dropped, was loaned from hand to hand; the people assembled to hear it, and talk it over; *a prayer-meeting* was then established, a church formed of thirty-two members, and a house of worship built. No preacher has yet been found for them."

Some things are worthy of notice here. The revival, the conversions, and the prayer-meeting moved hand in hand, as one and inseparable. The church organization began with the prayer-meeting. The new converts laid it down as the foundation, and on it they built up into a congregation. True converts would be friends of the prayer-meeting. And loving friends of the prayer-meeting must love one another. Those who love one another, love Christ. These are the stones with which to build a durable church. So the Tract Society evidently understands this matter.

Again, noticing some of the blessed fruits of the labors of the Colporteur, the Agent adds:

"Habits of reading have superseded the idle gossip of this neighborhood; and in that, the *prayer-meeting* and religious conference have supplanted the gaming-table and the noisy revel. The foul-mouthed infidel has become, through grace, a praying Christian."

We think we are warranted to say, the Tract Society, through its colportage, is an effective agency, indirectly, perhaps, in the cause of the prayer-meeting. This we may learn from the approved course of its agents in the field, who are doing a good work in this department of practical and vital godliness. In an Appendix to the work before us, the Society gives an example of the operations of its colporteurs. It says:

"It would be easy to furnish a volume of illustrations of this topic, drawn from the various classes of laborers engaged in the service of the Tract Society. Again and again, when the field has been opened and the means provided, God has provided the man adapted to the special work, as subsequent results have shown.

"The only illustration we present here, is drawn from the interesting band of *German* laborers. Perhaps it may give interest and variety, to insert the narrative in the broken English of the colporteur himself, as the simple story was told in the hearing of the Faculty and students of Lane Seminary, and reported *verbatim et literatim* by one of the number. To *translate* it into pure English would weaken its impressiveness."

Though the "impressiveness" may be weakened, we shall endeavor to give the substance only, in making a few extracts bearing upon the prayer-meeting. The converted German Catholic commenced his labors in the city of Cincinnati, where he resided. He began among his neighbors, the German Catholics, after much earnest prayer for the outpouring of the Holy Spirit. His first step was to gather together, in his own house, a little meeting, in which he read the Scriptures and had prayers with his friends. The Bible-reading increased and the prayer-meeting enlarged. Soon opposition rose, and the prayer-meeting was opposed by Catholic argument in the form of brickbats and stones entering the meeting through the windows. Still the prayer-meetings were held, and the work went on. Some time after, the colporteur removed from the city to a village in the vicinity, where a large *German* Catholic population resided. There, among the Catholics, he opened a prayer-meeting, and engaged in Bible-reading, as he had done before in the city, and with similar success. Many Catholics were converted, and became ardent Bible-students and praying Christians. In the course of time he returned to the city, and there devoted his whole time to the work. Every day he circulated tracts and copies of the Scriptures, and *every night*, as he stated, he held *prayer-meeting*. Thus, by tract and Bible distribution, with the nightly prayer-meetings, a great work was done, and many converts made. From the city he was again sent to the country, to labor in a locality which, with his labors and his success there, we will permit him to describe in his own way:

"Den me go out of de city vare de big steal (distillery,) stand right in de middle of de beoble; doo or dree hundred beobles leafe (live) here. And me begin to dalk mid em, and dell em aboud Chris, and me give em Bible, and me *dalk* und *dalk;* and den me hold metin. After dis da call me *schwamer* (translated by Prof. Stowe, fanatic), but do come do de metin all de time, and de Sperit of Got come down mit power, and dey mos all stop drink em visky. And ven me go dare fus, dey all drink visky. *De vomen shus like de men*, all drink em. Me stay here five mont. And ven me go vay from dis blace, de beoble mos all not sware, nor drink visky, and hundred and sixty convert." P. 162.

CHAPTER XV.

REVIVAL PRAYER-MEETINGS AND UNION CONVENTIONS.

The Church Memorial"—Resolutions of Union Conventions, 1838—Circular calling the Xenia Convention—Ten important topics for discussion in the Convention—The Xenia Convention—Communication from Philadelphia—Similar from New York—Remarks made in Convention on Social Prayer—R. A. Brown, D. D., James Rodgers, D. D., J. Clokey, D. D.—Report of Special Committee—Recommends the establishing of Prayer-meetings—The Allegheny Convention—Recent expressions of opinion in regard to the Prayer-meeting—*Christian Instructor* and Social Prayer—Reflections on important points—United Presbyterian and Noon-day Prayer-meetings—Installation charge by Rev. Joseph Thompson, deceased—Letter from a ministerial brother in regard to Revival and the Prayer-meeting—Its practical importance.

THE year eighteen hundred and fifty-eight, with many of its precious incidents and associations, justly claims a place in the soul-stirring recollections of many who were actors in its thrilling events; and the record of its times will long command the interest of all true United Presbyterians who drink into the same spirit that moved the fathers in the churches, so happily brought together in one, at that eventful time. That was the year of prayer-meetings not soon to pass away from memory. On those precious seasons, affections still linger. Because we now have in view, principally, events connected with the United Presbyterian Church, and belonging to the period of the Union, we shall, therefore, draw largely from *The Church Memorial*, a work to which the prayer-meetings of these times, and the consummation of the Union gave existence. In his "Introduction," the author says:

"We have also inserted the proceedings of the two religious conventions recently held in Xenia and Allegheny, deeming them worthy of preservation. The recollection of these happy meetings, where brethren of different denominations *met and sung, and prayed and wept together*, until their hearts were warmed with heavenly influences, and knit together in holy love, will not soon be forgotten by those who were present. Such scenes are not often witnessed on earth. They have already yielded fruit to the glory of God. They are worthy to be had in everlasting remembrance."

In 1838, a Convention of Reformed churches met and conferred on the subject of ecclesiastical union. The deliberations resulted in the passage of the following resolution:

"*Resolved*, As the judgment of this Convention, that the ministers of the churches here represented may interchange pulpits; and it is recommended to both ministers and people to unite as often as opportunity offers in *meetings for prayer* and other religious exercises."

Subsequent conventions were held till the year 1846, when the convention met for the eighth time, in which discouragement seemed to prevail; no progress was made, and after adopting the following resolution, the convention adjourned *sine die:*

"*Resolved*, That this Convention finds nothing more that it can do at present in furtherance of the object of its appointment."

When this was made known, such was the effect upon the public mind, that a meeting of the people of the three churches represented was called for *prayer and conference,* when the following resolution was adopted:

"*Resolved,* That we will not relinquish our *prayers* and our efforts in behalf of the unity of the church, hoping our beloved pastors will lead and encourage us in the work, and that the Chief Shepherd will approve and bless."

"Various communications passed between the Supreme Judicatories of these churches, and at different times meetings were held for *conference and devotional exercises.* The result was, the two bodies became better acquainted with each other, their hearts were drawn more closely together, and the desire for union, both among the ministry and the people, became stronger and stronger.

"As the time approached when the long-desired union was to be consummated, the anxiety of those who had long labored and prayed for that consummation became more and more intense. It was not only our heart's desire to see the union effected, but to see it accomplished in such a way as to secure harmony and unanimity among brethren. Deeply impressed with the conviction that without the blessing and concurrence of heaven, all our efforts must be in vain, a convention was called to assemble in Xenia, Ohio, for the purpose of seeking, *by united prayer,* the outpouring of the Holy Spirit, that the churches might be prepared to come together in the bonds of fraternal love."

Here permit us to insert the call, in full, to assemble in Xenia for prayer and conference. We received a copy of this call eleven years and a half ago, which we have carefully kept on file till this day. Feeling that it breathes so much of the true revival and union prayer-meeting spirit, we deem it worthy a record and transmission to the generations of our children succeeding:

"CIRCULAR TO THE MINISTERS, ELDERS, AND MEMBERS OF THE ASSOCIATE, ASSOCIATE REFORMED, AND REFORMED PRESBYTERIAN CHURCHES."

"DEAR BRETHREN:—We wish you grace, mercy and peace, from God our Father, and the Lord Jesus Christ.

"There is a matter very near to our hearts, in regard to which we seek your prayers, your countenance, and your co-operation. Believing that God will put honor on the means of his appointing, and having faith in the power of united, persevering prayer, we have concluded to invite, and do hereby invite, you earnestly to meet with us in convention in Xenia, on Wednesday, March 24th, at 7 o'clock, P. M., for the purpose of joint prayer to Heaven, for its promised blessings; and of advising with each other in regard to the interests of religion; and this we do with a view of securing an actual and general revival of practical godliness in our several churches.

"It is a matter of lamentation, dear brethren, that the standard of piety is so low at present in the redeemed Church of the Lord Jesus Christ. What dwarfs we are in holiness! How far from the elevation we should be standing on! How slow our progress! How confused our views! How unequal to the tasks with which we should be busy! We go halting on the Lord's errandry, instead of moving on in the strength of his might. It is to be feared that, owing to the prevalence of a worldly spirit, and to the imperious demands of even our lawful avocations, as well as to other causes which we need not name, the fire burns low on the altar of our hearts, and God gets but a moderate degree of glory from us. And as the result of this, the world around us is yet in all the woe and all the wickedness of its fallen state. We see its perishing multitudes pushing past us day by day, not simply to the house of silence, but to the chambers of death, and we are powerless, comparatively, to arrest them.

"Now, dear brethren, the only corrective of this lamented state of things is, for the church to gird herself anew with the might which is divine, to 'receive' afresh 'the Holy Spirit.' All is death in that howling wilderness that borders on the garden of the Lord. The influences that are to quicken and save are resident in the church. The life is here, though sadly dormant, and what we ask is, that you will come and entreat the Lord with us for its revival. Among these appointed means we find specially recognized prayer and mutual conference. After summing up the most precious blessings to be bestowed on Israel, God says: 'For all these things will I be inquired of by the house of Israel to do it for them.' And the Saviour says: 'If two of you shall agree on earth as touching anything that they shall ask, it shall be done for them of my Father which is in heaven;' and the special regard of God for such prayer and conference was manifested in the time of Malachi, a time not unlike, in many of its prominent features, to our own day. 'They that feared the Lord spake often one to another, and the Lord hearkened and heard.' In the days of primitive Christianity, it was in the social circle for prayer that Christ appeared to his disciples. It was when they were thus assembled together that they received the first baptism of the Holy Spirit, from whence such wonder came on the day of Pentecost. If we expect the church to exert on a sin-cursed world a Pentecostal power, she must have a Pentecostal baptism of the Spirit of God. If she will enjoy that, she must not neglect the honored means of the spirit. We would not overlook the consideration that our brethren of other and larger bodies of Christians have led off in this work much to their own encouragement, and, as they tell us, to the gladdening of their Zion; and surely, if God has heard their prayers, and poured out his Spirit with reviving power upon them, may not we be partakers of the same blessed influence? The smallness of our number, the scattered condition of our charges, and the limited state of our finances, need be no hindrance. These will but add sweetness to the offering, if our hearts are set on the work.

"We invite you, then, brethren, of all the various branches of Christ's church, ministers and elders, and other members whose hearts the Lord may move in this great work, to meet us in conference, and talk with one another, until our hearts are warmed in love, and wrestle with the Almighty until, in fulfilment of his promise, he pours out his Spirit as rain upon the mown grass, as showers that water the earth, until the barren waste be turned into a fruitful field, and judgment dwell in the wilderness, and righteousness remain in the fruitful field.

"Surely, dear brethren, we have many precious encouragements to the work. God has said, 'I will pour water upon the thirsty, and floods upon the dry ground; I will pour my spirit upon thy seed, and my blessing upon thy offspring, and they shall spring up as among the grass, and as willows by the water-courses.' 'Come and let us return unto the Lord, for he hath torn, and he will heal; he hath smitten, and he will bind us up; after two days will he revive us; and the third will he raise us up, and we shall live in his sight.' Reason might teach us to expect good from the mutual prayers and counsels of brethren from many and distant portions of the heritage of God; but we have a higher guarantee for it than the uncertain voice of human reason. God himself hath said, 'It shall come to pass that there shall come people, and the inhabitants of many cities; and the inhabitants of one city shall go to another and say, Let us go speedily to pray before the Lord, and to seek the Lord of hosts. I will go also.'

"That our meeting may be for edification and profit to ourselves and others, permit us, brethren, to suggest a few topics to which your minds may be directed as appropriate subjects of consideration on an occasion of this kind:

"I. The true nature of a revival.

"II. Indications of the need of a revival.

"III. Encouragements to hope for a revival.

"IV. Causes of the present deadness of the Church.

"V. Sins of the day as impeding the progress of religion.

"VI. Means of promoting revival.

"VII. Necessity of the influences of the Holy Spirit.

"VIII. Evidences of a true revival.

"IX. Revival of religion essential to the success of missions.

"X. Aspects of Divine Providence toward the church and the world.

"On these and kindred topics, such as the convention may adopt, we ask your prayerful study and your conscientious deliverances. Let prayers for the convention itself be daily offered to God. Let it be like the gathering of the princes of the people, even the people of the God of Israel. Let this call be read in every pulpit, that the people may hear and join their hearts and voices with ours in fervent prayer for the revival of God's work among us. Let all obstacles and hindrances be removed out of the way, that ministers and elders may attend without distraction. Let those who are blessed with abundance say to their ministers, We wish you to join the counsels of the church; here are the means; go, and may the blessing of God go with you. Fathers and mothers in Israel, you who have but few days to labor in the vineyard on earth, but who sigh with deep anxiety for your children, whom you must soon leave behind you, let us have your prayers and your sympathy at the Throne of Grace. Young men, on whom the burden of the work of God must soon rest, enter our list, and by the united work of all in this matter, under the blessing of Zion's King, this convention may be the brightest spot in the history of our day; the dawning of a new epoch in the church of God; the fulfilment of that blessed promise, when the 'Lord will create upon every dwelling-place of Mount Zion, and upon all her assemblies, a cloud and smoke by day, and the shining of a flaming fire by night, for upon all the glory shall be a defence. Behold, I create Jerusalem a rejoicing, and her people a joy.'"

THE XENIA CONVENTION.

"Here brethren met and united most pleasantly in prayer and supplication, in singing the songs of Zion, and in conferring together with reference to the revival of true godliness in our souls. The effect of this convention was most happy. God was manifestly present, and the hearts of brethren were drawn closely together in the bonds of fraternal love, that from that time forth it was manifest that no human power could prevent the Union."

The convention opened with indications—not of a business meeting merely—but of a deeply solemn and earnest prayer-meeting. Rev. R. A. Brown, D. D., said, "this was not a business convention. These preliminary matters, were, perhaps, well enough; but he had come to attend a *prayer-meeting* for a revival, and he hoped the convention would proceed to that business now—to-night. We had come together not only to talk about revivals, but to have a revival. He wanted a *prayer-meeting* to-night."

Similar remarks were made by others, and it was concluded to fix the hour of meeting at 8 o'clock in the morning. This was an unusually early hour for deliberative bodies or conventions to meet; but men were in earnest; a spirit of devotion and of prayer pervaded the whole assembly, and, indeed, almost the entire mass of the people at that time, and in that locality.

A communication from Philadelphia was received, sent by an association of ministers and elders, and other members of the Associate, Associate Reformed, and Reformed Presbyterian Churches, holding continuous daily prayer-meetings at the same time with the convention at Xenia. The following are extracts:

"DEAR BRETHREN:—The association composed of the ministers and elders of the above-named churches in this city, have appointed us a committee to address you a letter in response to a circular sent by you to the brethren of these churches, and to express their sympathies with you in the objects of your meeting, which we accordingly do with great pleasure.

"Our hearts, dear brethren, have been greatly refreshed by the intelligence received through your circular, that you have called a convention of the ministers, elders, and members of these churches, from different parts of the country, with the view of deliberating concerning the interests of religion, and of pouring out your hearts in united and earnest persevering prayer, for a revival of practical godliness in our several churches.

"In this circular you have kindly invited us to meet with you on this interesting and solemn occasion. It has been, with some of us, a matter of serious consideration whether we should not, for the time being, forget any other claim upon our time and attention, and joyfully accept your invitation to meet with you. There are considerations, however, which, we think, will prevent us from yielding to these first promptings of our hearts. Among these we may mention the fact, that the present time is, in this city, marked by events of the most extraordinary character. A mighty influence is at work in this section of our land. Never, in the history of our country, has there been such an awakening among all classes of the community to the interests of religion. In different parts of our great city assemblies are being held every day, in which persons are drawn together by thousands, filling, to their utmost capacity, the largest halls and churches in our city. Merchants are leaving their stores, professional men their offices, and mechanics their shops, in the business hours of the day, that they may hear and proclaim the word of salvation by Jesus Christ, and pour out their hearts in prayer to Almighty God for his blessing. But we need not tell you of these things. Doubtless, you have heard of them, and, doubtless, they have awakened your deepest concern.

"With thankful hearts we recognize in this great movement the finger of God, pointing to a better state of things in the land; and in it, too, we hear the voice of our great Captain calling upon us to arouse ourselves to a more vigorous conflict with the powers of darkness. This conclusion, dear brethren, has been not a little strengthened by the reception of your circular, breathing a spirit so much in unison with the signs of the times, and the feelings they awaken in our hearts.

"It will, doubtless, rejoice your hearts to know, as you urge us to united prayer, that in some of our churches we have been meeting daily through the past week, or more, for this special purpose, and we have reason to hope, thus far, that our meeting has been attended with good results.

While thankful for any manifestation of the Lord's goodness, in this respect, we would, at the same time, desire to be found watching, lest the great adversary of souls, through our sinfulness, may get an advantage over us. We ask you, dear brethren, to help us by your prayers."

A similar communication, from New York, signed by twenty-five brethren of the same churches, was received by the Convention. The following are extracts:

"DEAR BRETHREN IN JESUS CHRIST: We have received your Circular. We approve your proposal, and we hail you in the name of Christ while you gather round the Throne of Grace, to seek a new baptism of His Holy Spirit from above.

"There is a great power in prayer. Power to avert evil, to command the blessing, and to 'move the hand that moves the world,' that it may be opened to dispense revival to the church, and salvation to sinners ready to perish around her. Let this power be used, dear brethren, by you. God has promised to give His Holy Spirit to them that ask Him; and, laying hold of this by faith, you may confidently expect that the blessing, for which you may agree to ask, will be dispensed.

"An awakening of the public mind to the importance of religion, is now existing in our city and its vicinity. It pervades all classes. It leads men to *social prayer*, to the hearing of the gospel, and to inquiry for salvation through Jesus Christ. Let us request you, dear brethren, that when you gather in your holy convocation, you will remember, before God, the large cities of our land, where Satan's seat is, and where it is our lot to labor for our common Lord and Master.

"We trust that some of our brethren will be able to meet you in convention, and from such you will receive more extended information on these subjects. We will therefore, conclude by saying that we have read your Circular in our churches; we have made your meeting a subject of special prayer, and it is highly probable that at the same hour on which you meet, assemblies among ourselves, which have been advised of yours, will be joining with you in supplication at the Throne of God. That you may enjoy the presence of the Master of Assemblies, and be made joyful in His house of prayer, is, respected and dear brethren, the prayer of yours, in the gospel of our common Lord and Master."

The second day of the Convention, the following telegraphic dispatch was received from Philadelphia:

"Large meeting last evening—three bodies for united prayer in concert with Convention. Three meetings this evening—Wylie's, Cooper's, Sterret's. Send immediately full dispatch about Convention. Work reviving all around."

REMARKS MADE IN CONVENTION.

Rev. Blair said: "A want of faith lies at the root of a defective application of the gospel. God had brought together the bodies here represented; and this shows they ought to be one. We have not prayed together—such meetings are new. For forty years such meetings have not been witnessed. They mean that we have been in error heretofore, and teach us that we should be united in future."

Rev. R. A. Browne, D. D., said: "There are three millions of human beings in bondage in this land, to whom the word of God cannot be preached. Our fearful complicity in this giant wrong is one great reason why God has made the heaven as iron and the earth as brass. This system claimed not toleration merely, but was a ruling power in the land. A dram of whiskey might procure the passage of a law which nullifies the law of God. We should utter our protest against this crime, *and pray* against it *wherever two or three of us are together.* The eyes of many are on us to-day, looking up from every corner of the land, to see whether Presbyterianism can rear its standard in behalf of the poor bondmen."

Dr. Rodgers said: "When God's ministers and people become dissatisfied with the present state of things, and feel their need of a revival, it is a sign of a better day coming. It is an indication of the Most High. Our meeting together is an evidence of this. *A prayer-meeting to which brethren have come from so great a distance!* There is a feeling of dissatisfaction with self, and one object should be to deepen this feeling. I shall then call your attention to this point: the indications that we need a revival." And, as an evidence of need of revival, farther said: "Another matter. How difficult a thing it is to keep up meetings for prayer! Is religion prospering among us when we cannot *meet, and pray, and talk* over the interests of our souls?"

Oh, these words come up like a voice from the dead, speaking living truth in regard to the outstanding evidences of a low state of religion now in our churches, and our need of revival! *The times* of the Xenia Convention, it is much to be feared, are gone by.

Dr. Clokey remarked: "We should get up our *prayer-meetings* in the lanes and alleys, wherever we can get a chance." Words few, but fitly set.

Dr. Wylie, in a very elaborate speech, said: "From the very signs of the times, we have reason to believe that it is not long, it may not be more than ten years, until the Millennium will come. There will be a conflict with the powers of darkness before that time comes. The hosts will be arrayed. The Spirit is gathering his own elect from all the corners of the world. *Such meetings as this one* are encouragements that the day of their redemption draweth nigh. That day will be to the redeemed as Noah's Ark in the flood. All who are not in that Ark will be destroyed. I need not refer to the workings of Providence. Here are Christians assembled from different parts of the land to *pray together*. We have one faith, one hope, etc., etc. For years we have been resolving, now we seem to be ready to declare, we are one—so much unity of heart, of sentiment, of faith."

Report of Special Committee, from which the following are extracts:

"*Resolved*, That it is the duty of this Convention to give an expression to our churches in regard to the *specific* measures which should be adopted by our Sessions and members, so that a proper direction may be given to the present awakening on the subject of religion.

"While we have no new measures to recommend, it may be proper for us to set about the use of God's measures and means with new life and vigor; these are the faithful, direct preaching of the word, earnest prayer to God in the closet, in the family, *and in the social meeting*—opening our churches for prayer through the week, where the circumstances of our people, and the need of the community, render such a measure expedient. Establishing *meetings for prayer and conference in as many localities as possible*—urging on our members and elders the duty of taking an active part in these meetings."

Well would it be for the church did she heed these recommendations, and earnestly endeavor to carry them out faithfully and practically. This is certainly just what is now needed—*prayer-meetings* established *in as many localities as possible.*

"The Convention, after spending a few days in most delightful Christian fellowship, adjourned to meet in the City of Allegheny, immediately previous to the time appointed for the assembling of our respective Synods. A large number of the brethren of both churches accordingly met, and spent several days in conference and in devotional exercises. After anxious solicitude, and fervent prayers, and earnest efforts, persevered in for more than twenty years, the hearts of those who love the peace of Zion were made glad by seeing brethren who were substantially one in the faith, but who had long been ecclesiastically separated, brought together in the bonds of Christian love, under one banner, and dwelling together in unity."

THE ALLEGHENY CONVENTION.

In some respects this Convention presents a contrast with the one held in Xenia. Among all the speeches and remarks, during the conferences in the Allegheny meeting, scarcely an allusion was made to the *prayer-meeting*, or to *social prayer*, while at Xenia this seemed to be the burden of many speeches, documents, and resolutions. In the Allegheny Convention, any reference to the subject seems to have been merely incidental, and thrown in upon the meeting from without. We give all in the following extracts:

On Wednesday, the third day of the convention, "before proceeding to prayer, Dr. Pressly announced that he had received a dispatch from the Reformed churches in Cincinnati, requesting an interest in the prayers of the convention, and stating that they met daily for prayer and conference." Shortly after, "Dr. Pressly stated that he had received through the post-office a letter from a lady about sixty miles distant from the city, desiring an interest in the prayers of the convention, in behalf of her unhappy family. She is the mother of seven small children, and the wife of an intemperate husband. She adds: Our pastor is laboring hard in the pulpit and in the *prayer-meeting* for our good, but he never visits the down-trodden and the oppressed." Nearer the close of the convention, the following remarks were made:

"It may seem presumption in me to venture a suggestion in the midst of so much assembled age and wisdom, but if you are sincerely engaged in these services you will cheerfully accept the suggestion of the humblest disciple of Jesus. All seem disappointed here. The exercises have not met the expectations of many. I confess that the conference has not come up to my own feelings as to what it should be. What is the reason? What is it that arrests, so often, the growing interest? What is it that dampens so often the rising fervor of devotion? It is the inordinate concern about an event anticipated in the future."

RECENT EXPRESSIONS OF OPINION IN REGARD TO THE PRAYER-MEETING.

The following is taken from an article in the *Christian Instructor*, Philadelphia, Sept. 4th, 1869:

"SOCIAL PRAYER."

"It has been often remarked, that the best thermometer to indicate the spiritual warmth of a congregation, is the attendance of its members upon social prayer-meetings. That man who neglects the social prayer-meeting, no matter how long and loud he talks about 'contending for the faith once delivered to the saints,' has, at best, but a frozen orthodoxy. That faith that don't work by love, and don't produce good fruits, is very likely a spurious faith. Ordinarily, faith manifests its life and developments as conspicuously in a prayer-meeting as anywhere else. The attendance at the sanctuary on the Sabbath, is not so good a test of genuine religion as the attendance upon the prayer-meeting is.

"With many the Sabbath is a day of leisure. They cannot pursue their secular labor during its sacred hours, conscious that it does not comport with the Christian profession to make it a day of amusement or social visitation; its time hangs heavily on their hands. To sleep away its quiet hours would be, to one accustomed to active life, irksome. At the house of God, even those whose tastes are such as not to relish the exercises of the sanctuary, often meet such society as their social nature demands, and by such meetings they feel they are compensated for any outlay of effort they may have made to be present. Conscience, too, not altogether dead, is somewhat quieted by such attendance; hence they have their reward.

"At the sanctuary the curious can find something to feed their curiosity, the devotees of fashion have an opportunity to exhibit their finery, and find something to administer to their pride; sometimes the refined and literary can find that which is pleasing, and the admirers of eloquence and learning, that which satisfies them.

"Ordinarily, they do not look for these in the social prayer-meetings. These are usually held on week-days and nights, and those who are devoted to this world rarely find time to attend them; sacrifices of time, ease, and worldly comfort are required, and the formal professor is not willing to make such sacrifices. The attractions that draw many out on the Sabbath are not there. The gay and fashionable, and the admirers of learning and eloquence do not expect to find what they seek at a prayer-meeting. Prayers may be offered up by the illiterate and unlearned, and exhortations offered by the same class of persons. Praise may not be so well performed as on the

Sabbath, in the sanctuary. It is the saints who generally frequent the prayer-meetings; and as there is more of the fear of God, and less of human parade, there, these meetings are more made up of God's own children, and fewer worldlings, than ordinary Sabbath services are. In these meetings of the saints, God is feared, and those who meet speak often one to another; they tell what God has done for their souls, and it is no wonder that these revelations of Christian experience should be insipid and uninteresting to those who have not tasted that God is good. When we consider who it is that ordinarily attends these meetings for social prayer, we need not wonder at the marvellous results that have been effected by them; that these exercises, everywhere, and at all times, have been so crowned with success, and so owned of God for the conversion of sinners and for the edification of the church. These results exemplify the power of fervid, united, humble prayer. When many attend these meetings habitually, we readily recognize the fact that spiritual life is there, and hence we look for manifestations of divine power. When God's own children travail in believing, importunate prayer, souls are born unto God, and new life comes down upon cold and languishing congregations. God will be inquired of to bless his church, and 'where but two agree as touching anything they shall ask, it shall be done for them.'

"One of the saddest aspects of the present time, is the fewness of Christian professors that attend social prayer-meetings, and the little interest taken in them, sometimes, even by those from whom we would expect better things. In many places, ruling elders seem to have lost their relish for social prayer-meetings. It is in these meetings especially that elders should 'take heed to themselves and the flock over which the Holy Spirit has made them overseers, to feed the church of God which he hath purchased with his blood.' After all, it may be, the ministry is somewhat at fault in not properly encouraging and countenancing these meetings for social prayer. It is with no wish to bring a railing accusation against the ministry of his own or any other church, that the writer says the ministry is at fault in not properly encouraging and countenancing meetings for social prayer. Sometimes the inquiry is started, Do they recognize social prayer as an ordinance of God? If so, why not honor it as such?"

There are some points in this article important as way-marks in tracing the history of the prayer-meeting, and important as an application of tests by which the state of religion may be determined:

1. This article is very seasonable; there is pressing need that the attention of the church should be thoroughly waked up to the subject. There is danger of forgetting this blessed and precious institution, and so falling off from its observance. 2. The writer, very justly, holds this ordinance to be "the spiritual thermometer," by which the state of the spiritual health of the church, and of the professed Christian, is to be determined. Because, to secure punctual observance of the prayer-meeting, there must be piety—not dormant, but wakeful—constraining love to Christ, to his children, and to his ordinances. 3. And it is to be feared that the apprehension is too well founded of a very general neglect, on the part of so many professors, of this ordinance of worship. 4. The suggestion that sin lies at the door of the ministry, may be entitled to very grave consideration. Let the ministry be waked up to their duties and responsibilities here, and this article will be found to be not in vain. 5. The article presses upon us the important inquiry, Is the prayer-meeting an ordinance of religious worship? And if it be, why not honor

it as such? We might add, just here, another inquiry: If the prayer-meeting be an ordinance of Christ's appointment, how should it be honored?

The following article may be seen in the *United Presbyterian*, Pittsburgh, Sept. 18, 1869:

"NOON-DAY PRAYER-MEETING."

"We would remind our readers that the meetings for prayer, at noon of every day, are continued at No. 23 Fifth Avenue. These prayer-meetings are intended for business men and others, whose engagements will allow a half hour's attendance at this time of day. In past times these meetings were largely attended, and were the means of much good. Latterly they have been much neglected, and an effort is made to revive the interest in them. They should have an interest for all denominations."

This notice is cheering. May we receive it as a token for coming good? May we hope for an outpouring of the Spirit in the revival of religion, and entertain this as some of its first fruits? Then shall we feel encouraged to hope that our feeble attempt to do something, in this cause, at this time, is not in vain, and will not, by the blessing of God, be in vain.

The following extract is taken from a volume of sermons, published by Rev. James Thompson, New York City:

"A CHARGE, DELIVERED TO THE CONGREGATION OF VENICE, AT THE ORDINATION AND INSTALLATION OF REV. A. R. ANDERSON. BY REV. JOSEPH THOMPSON, DECEASED."

"It is also your duty to co-operate with him in organizing praying societies in the congregation. I have heard of professing Christians who entertained doubts about the propriety of such societies. I hope, however, there are none of this class in this congregation. It is very discouraging for a minister to travel perhaps several miles, to attend a prayer-meeting, and find, when he goes, that some of his congregation, who perhaps live in sight, are absent. It is the duty of all who can to attend such meetigs; and it is especially the duty of heads of families, and others, who are capable of taking a part in the exerceises, to attend. This will greatly strengthen the hands and encourage the heart of your pastor, and promote your growth in grace. These are some of the ways in which you are bound to co-operate with your pastor."

This "Charge" is important, not only as the expression of the opinion of a beloved brother, deceased, and here speaking from the dead, but also, because it speaks the view of the Standards of the Church. Praying *societies* should be organized in the congregation—not one only; whether monthly or weekly, but as many as circumstances may require, so as to secure the attendance of all the membership of the congregation.

The following is from a letter received from a beloved brother in the ministry, whose congregation enjoyed a precious revival in the year ——:

"The work to which you refer appeared to have its commencement in a greater interest than usual manifested throughout the congregation. There was, for some time previous, evidence, I think, of greater concern and sincerity than had been. This resulted in the Session's appointing a day for conference and prayer, in view of the welfare of the congregation, and the good of the cause. We held this conference as a Session. We consulted freely in relation to duty, and the best course to be pursued; frequently, in our deliberations, approaching the throne of grace, and asking for light and direction. In this way we spent as much of the day as could be conve-

30*

niently spent—all the members being present. The result was, that it was concluded to hold a series of meetings about the time of the week of prayer; and, as it was thought to suit better, in a country place, to have the meetings during moonlight, the time was put a little beyond the week of prayer. It was also understood that the members of Session, in their families, should specially remember the object in view, in their devotions; and the congregation, as such, was requested to have the matter in view, particularly in their prayers, as individuals and families. During the period of our meetings, the pastor gave very frequent opportunities to persons to meet with him for conversation. The Session often met to converse with and receive applicants.

"We had prayer-meetings in the congregation. But there was no special arrangement to this end beyond what I have mentioned. I have every reason, however, to believe that the people were very much engaged in prayer. The interest manifested could not have been separated from this. And I do believe that there can be no true revival where prayer is not most prominently associated with it. And I believe, also, that no congregation will unitedly engage in sincerely seeking the outpouring of the Spirit, where there shall not be evidences of his power, which shall make their hearts rejoice.

"I think that, during that season, much, under the blessing of the Divine Spirit, was done through prudent individual effort. Members of Session, and private members of the congregation, and the pastor, sought every opportunity of conversing with individuals, of learning their feelings and views, and of urging upon them their duty. I think that these efforts were specially blessed, as I think such efforts made in the proper spirit always will be. One hundred and eight persons made a profession of religion.

and were received into the church. Eighteen adults were baptized. Of this number, only three, of whom I have heard from, were unfaithful; and in their case there was something peculiar.

"I think we have reason to believe that a true revival begins in the hearts of the people of God. When they themselves, through prayer, and careful observance of all the means of grace, are refreshed by the influences of the Spirit, they necessarily are prepared to exert an influence, which, through the blessing of God, must have its effect. With them a revival commences; through them it is carried on; and by them the instrumentalities are employed which the power of God makes efficient."

This letter is of practical importance to every congregation, and worthy of earnest attention:

1. To enjoy a revival of religion, the pastor, elders, and leading members must take a *leading interest* in revival, and in the employment of the instrumentalities divinely appointed to secure it. 2. They must make it a subject of earnest conversation. This is Christ's way of making disciples' cold hearts burn with renewed love. 3. They must make it a matter of earnest, united prayer. Then will God's Spirit come down with a blessing and revive.

CHAPTER XVI.

CHURCH CREEDS AND THE PRAYER-MEETING.

Discipline of the Methodist Episcopal Church—Testimony of the Reformed Presbyterian Church—Directory for Worship of the United Presbyterian Church—Reflections.

THE deliverances of all the churches upon this subject, whether in the form of organic law, or occasional declaratory acts, would form an interesting chapter here; but we have neither space, time, nor the means for it in this connection. We give a brief specimen only.

In the doctrines and discipline of the "Methodist Episcopal Church," we find the following:

"In the latter end of the year 1739, eight or ten persons came to Mr. Wesley, in London, who appeared to be deeply convinced of sin, and earnestly groaning for redemption. They desired (as did two or three more the next day) that he would spend some time with them in prayer, and advise them how to flee from the wrath to come; which they saw continually hanging over their heads. That he might have more time for this great work, he appointed a day when they might all come together; which, from thence forward, they did every week, namely, on *Thursday*, in the evening. To these, and as many more as desired to join with them (for their number increased daily), he gave those advices, from time to time, which he judged most needful for them; and they always concluded their meeting with prayer suited to their several necessities.

"This was the rise of the UNITED SOCIETY, first in

Europe, and then in *America*. Such a society is no other than 'a company of men having the form and seeking the power of godliness, united in order to pray together, to receive the word of exhortation, and to watch over one another in love, that they may help each other to work out their salvation.'

"That it may the more easily be discerned whether they are, indeed, working out their own salvation, each society is divided into smaller companies, called classes, according to their respective places of abode. There are about twelve persons in a class; one of whom is styled *the leader*."

"OF THE BAND SOCIETIES."

"Two, three, or four, true believers, who have confidence in each other, form a band. Only, it is to be observed, that in one of these bands all must be men, or all women; and all married, or all unmarried."

"RULES FOR THE BAND SOCIETIES, DRAWN UP DEC. 25, 1738."

"The design of our meeting is to obey that command of God, 'Confess your faults one to another, and pray for one another, that ye may be healed.' James v. 16. To this end we agree: 1. To meet once a week, at least. 2. To come punctually at the hour appointed, without some extraordinary reason prevents. 3. To begin exactly at the hour, with singing, or prayer. 4. To speak, each of us in order, freely and plainly, the true state of our souls, with the faults we have committed in tempers, words, or actions, and the temptations we have felt, since our last meeting. 5. To end every meeting with prayer suited to the state of each person present."—Discipline, edition 1852. Pp. 25–6, 81–2.

TESTIMONY OF THE REFORMED PRESBYTERIAN CHURCH.

"Christians should frequently meet, at stated times, for acts of private social worship, in order to strengthen each other in piety and zeal, and maintain sincere friendship upon evangelical principles." Chapter xxiv., Section 5, "Of Christian Worship." P. 231.

DIRECTORY FOR WORSHIP OF THE UNITED PRESBYTERIAN CHURCH.

"*Prayer-Meetings:* 1. Meetings for prayer should be held in every congregation. Matt. iii. 16, etc.; Acts ii. 42, etc. When a minister is present, he should preside and give direction to the exercises. In his absence, an elder, or member of approved piety, should conduct the meeting.

"2. The exercises should consist of reading the Scriptures, the singing of Psalms, the offering of suitable prayers, and remarks founded on some passage of Scripture, or interesting event of Providence. The whole should conduce to brotherly love, personal piety, and the general interests of religion.

"3. Meetings for prayer may be held at one or more times, and in one or more places, in the congregation during the week. But they should never be allowed to interfere with, or to take the place of, important religious duties in the family.

"4. Church Sessions should hold a Sessional prayer-meeting at least once a month, at which they may consult about the condition and interests of the flock, and implore divine guidance in all that to which they are called.

"5. When a congregation has no pastor, or when he is absent, it may be profitable to spend a part of the Sabbath in social prayer; and if none are present capable of making appropriate remarks, let some one read an evangelical and instructive sermon.

"Church officers should exhort the people to a faithful attendance on prayer-meetings, and none should excuse themselves from attending, without good reason."

CONCLUDING REFLECTIONS.

These deliverances of the churches have not only an advisory character, but the force of organic rule, to which members of the church are expected to conform. If they are salutary rules, the spiritual health of individuals and churches will be affected both by their observance and their neglect. Like all other means of grace having an institution in God's word, and like that word itself, the prayer-meeting will be to the church member a savor of life unto life, or a savor of death unto death. And here, as in the case of all church creeds, rules, and deliverances of church judicatories, whether organic or merely occasional, there should be a faithful observance of the rules, or they should be rescinded altogether. Better have creeds with less detail, rules too few, and Directories defective, than to have more extensive ones a dead letter in the book. Whatever we may have, whether organic law, or rule in other form, let us observe it while it remains in force, especially when we believe it to be founded in the Divine authority in the word. Faithfulness here is important to unity among brethren, and harmony and efficiency in ecclesiastical operations, enterprises, and labors in Christ's cause.

Church Directories for Worship form an important part of the voluntary church covenant into which every member enters, with the whole brotherhood of membership, in entering the communion of the church. We are then all bound by our brotherly covenant to observe the prayer-meeting. And here let us reflect how dangerous it is to trifle with vows! It damages the spiritual interests of the soul, offends God, and grieves the Holy Spirit, wounds brethren, and harms the cause of Christ. Creeds, confessions, testimonies, are worthless, if they have no counterpart in the conversation and lives of those pledged to them. *This* is the effective epistle known and read of all men. As it has been well remarked by a very judicious observer and writer, so let us remember, "The prayer-meeting is the Thermometer of the church, by which the state of religion is distinctly indicated."

Friends of Christ: In now parting with you, after travelling together the pathway of the earnest followers of Jesus, from Enos down along through the successive cycles of the centuries, may we not ask you, Have you not seen, and are you not persuaded, that the followers of the Lamb have ever been found—in prosperity and in adversity—walking in the way of prayer—in the way of the prayer meeting, with Him who so often met with his disciples and the women, in the upper rooms, for private social prayer? And are you not satisfied that if we shall, in the future, ever see and enjoy a day of Revival, it must be in the way in which God has, in times of past refreshings, so remarkably sent down the fiery baptisms of pentecostal times?

O, may the time soon come, when all who love Jesus, who love the godly bearing his image, who love prayer and the sweet communion of saints, shall speak one to another, and shall agree to ask together that God will fulfil his promises of revival! "And I will pour upon the house of David, and upon the inhabitants of Jerusalem, the Spirit of grace and supplications: For I will pour water upon him that is thirsty, and floods upon the dry ground; and I will pour my Spirit upon thy seed, and my blessing upon thine offspring: And they shall spring up as among the grass, as willows by the water courses. Thy watchmen shall lift up the voice; with the voice together shall they sing: for they shall see eye to eye, when the Lord shall bring again Zion. Thus saith the Lord God: I will yet for this be inquired of by the house of Israel, to do it for them."

www.ingramcontent.com/pod-product-compliance
Lightning Source LLC
LaVergne TN
LVHW010155110826
845151LV00002B/529

* 9 7 8 1 4 2 5 5 3 6 4 6 6 *